CONSAFE GROUP NORGE
Vakåsveien 9, N-1364 Hvalstad
Telefon 6685844,.Fax 6687059

THIS IS NORWAY

THIS IS NORWAY

Edited by Arne Bonde, Picture editor: Jan Greve

J·M· Stenersens Forlag A·S

Edited by: Arne Bonde
Picture editor: Jan Greve
Eight pictures (oil on paper) by Jakob Weidemann
Translated by: Julian Garner. Captions by Erik J. Eidem
Jacket and design: Enzo Finger Design
Printed in 10/13 point Times
by Centraltrykkeriet Grafisk Service AS, Bærum, Norway
Paper: 135 gr. HannoArt matt-coated, Hannover Papier AG
Repro by Lito Print, Oslo
Binding by Norbok as, Gjøvik
Editing completed: 15. august 1992

ISBN 82-7201-184-0

Contents

This book presents a small country, situated on the outskirts of Europe, where since time immemorial a sparse population has been fighting a hostile nature, a rough climate and a meagre soil. It takes you across the centuries, outlining our history from the golden days of the High Middle Ages through four hundred years of Danish rule, then through the cultural revival of independent Norway during the last century and the recent evolution towards a modern welfare society.

However meagre its soil, the country is rich. Throughout our entire history, people have been exploiting to their advantage our extended coastline. The sea offered enough fish to feed not only themselves, but large parts of southern Europe as well. From the early Middle Ages they built ships capable of carrying them to the farthest shores, thus inaugurating the world-wide shipping activities which have become so important to our economy. Even on dry land we found exploitable natural resources, and, having had the luck of discovering oil on our part of the Continental Shelf, we are today one of the world's richer nations.

As individuals, also, Norwegian women and men have shown outstanding qualities, for instance in the field of sports. Since the first Winter Olympics, Norway has won a fair share of the medals.

In the cultural and artistic fields, Norway has engendered works known all over the world. According to the Olympic Charter, the Games are supposed to stress the cultural aspect along with that of athletic performance. Norway is planning to fulfil these intentions in 1994 by offering an extensive presentation of our music, our literature and our pictorial arts within a unified architectural framework.

Behind the XVII Winter Olympics in Lillehammer, you will find a united nation. I sincerely hope that the numerous participants and supporters gathering there from all over the world will feel at home in this country, and that the combination of noble contest and cultural inspiration will promote a feeling of brotherhood and mutual understanding between the peoples.

Sonja

weidemann 92.

Norway – Poverty to Prosperity

Helge Seip:

NTB

Helge Seip (b. 1919) has been at the centre of Norwegian politics throughout the post-war period. He was a member of the Norwegian Storting for 16 years. He was the Minister of Local Government in the Per Borten government, from 1965 – 70. He has also been the party secretary for Venstre and for Det Nye Folkeparti. He has worked as an editor for the daily Dagbladet, and later for Norges Handel- og Sjøfartstidende (Dagens Næringsliv). When the Data Inspectorate was set up, Seip was appointed its first director. For years, he has been very active in public debates.

As an independent nation-state, Norway is a child of the 20th century. The Declaration of Independence of 1905, which released Norway from the union with Sweden, was however the consequence of economic, social and cultural developments with components way back in history. In this context, we must not forget the Norwegian Constitution of 1814, which today remains the second oldest working constitution in the world, after that of the United States of America. The content, and much of the form, of the Norwegian Constitution is anchored in concepts of liberty and independence which made such a strong imprint on the close of the 16th century, both in Europe and North America.

Picture, opposite: Nusfjorden in Nordland.

HUSMO-FOTO

A winter night at the Mysuseter, a mountain farm in Hardanger, on a horsecart, past the untamed Briksdal waterfalls.

HUSMO-FOTO

KNUDSENS FOTOSENTER

«Brudeferden i Hardanger» is among the most widely known paintings, made in 1848 by Adolph Tidemand and Hans Gude. On exhibition at the National Gallery in Oslo.

Through generations, Sikkilsdalen has been an equestrian centre. Today, town dwellers are being taught how to ride on a horseback.

SAMFOTO/Pål Hermansen

NATIONALGALLERIET/Jaques Lathion

JOHAN BRUN

Large parts of Norway are covered by forests, though all forests aren't as well kept as the one seen here.

Well into this century, one could still see the old Nordland vessels along the coast. They were solid cargo sail-ships.

SCAN-FOTO/Arkiv

Fishing on the piers in Kristiania was a popular pastime, many attentively looking for the chance of buying a reasonably prized dinner. . . .

SCAN-FOTO/Arkiv

Not all could afford proper timber for the building of their houses. Some settled for the remains of a ten-oar. Also, food was scarce, the soup bowl only occasionally more than half-filled.

SCAN-FOTO/Arkiv

NORSK FOLKEMUSEUM

The compromise which led to Norway keeping the major part of her remarkably libertarian and progressive constitution of 17th May 1814, eventually became something of a model for parallel constitutional reform in neighbouring Sweden and Denmark. The changes connected with Norway becoming a state in union with Sweden, instead of a kingdom under the Danish crown, gave new momentum to growth and independence in the country. Most important to economic developement was the establishment of the Norwegian Bank, in 1816. On the cultural front, one can see the founding of the Royal Frederik's University in Christiania in 1811 as a cornerstone for broader developments in society.

It is also natural to emphasise the momentous developments in the 19th century of commerce and settlement, which resulted in a well-spring of energy leading in turn to developments within production, transportation, the credit system, and the economy generally. These changes gradually brought about a completely different set of conditions for the Norwegian people.

In the course of the past two hundred years, Norway has developed from being a poor country with the vast majority of its population involved in agriculture and fishing, to a society in which a high degree of affluence is evenly distributed – perhaps more evenly than in any other country – but we must not forget that the foundation for this development was laid, at least partially, much earlier. Natural forestry and fishing resources, traditions of global seafaring, hydro-energy sources which were to prove so vital to so much of Norwegian industrial development – all these factors were in place long ago. Whilst only small areas of Norway are suitable for arable farming, relative to other European countries, she has always had considerable deposits of both iron-ore and minerals.

The Dawning of Industrial Development

One of the first major steps forward in Norwegian industrial development came with the introduction of the water-powered saw, during the 16th century. The 17th century saw the growth of various mining concerns, including silver-works in Kongsberg and copper mines in Røros. The production of bog-iron became a common industry in many districts, and many towns began to expand rapidly led by the Hansiatic port of Bergen, the base for much of Norway's international trade, where various craft and productive enterprises developed the characteristics of small industries in their own right.

Already in the 1690s, Bergen was experimenting with a system of paper money instigated by the prominent merchant, Jørgen Thor Møhlen, known for his trading connections with the Danish African colony of the Gold Coast, among other economic activities. The experiment was eventually abandoned owing to the difficulty of creating confidence in the value of the notes. The first Danish national bank based on paper money was not established in Copenhagen until 1736, though it did have a certain relevance for Norway.

JARLE KJETIL ROLFSETH

The old water powered saws were a great relief to those who had previously sawed wood by hand.

In 1801, well over 90 % of the Norwegian population lived in the rural districts, the vast majority of them engaged in farming. Various towns and villages grew up around mining communities, and in the middle of the 18th century Kongsberg was the second largest town in the country, considerably larger than Christiania. It was only after the turn of the the century that the capital overtook Kongsberg in size, and in the following decades it outstripped Bergen, also.

Norway's small, sparcely distributed population mitigated against the raising of many large buildings or other monuments to the greatness and glory of previous times. «Cabin and house, but castles, no», as the poet has written, with more than a little justification. Of course, Norway has seen class division and social variations in living standards through the ages, but there has never been a large aristocracy or land-owning class to talk of. Land and resource-ownership was far less concentrated and, socially speaking, the gap between rich and poor considerably less than was the tendency further south in Europe.

In a country with Norway's geography and natural resources, there was bound to be a close relationship between development potential and access to import and export markets. Even

KNUDSENS FOTOSENTER

The petroglyphy at Alta constitute valuable parts of the Norwegian cultural heritage – and are also protected by the UNESCO.

Even though agriculture was to provide a living for most of the population until well into the 19th century, increasingly growth-potential lay in industry, mining, shipping and trade.

The introduction of the potato into Norwegian agriculture from the middle of the 16th century did much to secure food supplies for the majority of the population. This South American plant contributed literally to the survival of many Norwegians, with a particular breakthrough in its use during the crisis years of 1807–1814.

The Sea: the Most Important Trade Artery

For centuries, the sea provided Norway with its most important trade artery, rendering possible the task of holding together a long and impractical country, and opening up lines of communication and trade with the outside world. Norway acquired roads only at a very late stage. Transportation by land was usually as expensive as it was hazardous. As late as 1850, a politician from the midland county of Trøndelag wrote home from Christiania announcing that, as parliament was to reconvene after only a six week break, he would unfortunately not be able to return home for the summer holiday! The journey over the mountains of Dovre was long, exhausting and very expensive. The coast offered an easier route along the 2 000 kilometers from the border with Sweden, at Bohus in the south, to the eastern extreme of Finnmark, where Norway met the Russian border in the north. The growth of towns in south and central Norway prove that both Norwegians and non-Norwegians understood the importance of the coastal route. In Finnmark, at Talvik in Alta, the Alten Copper Works were established with British capital. During the first half of the 19th century, this firm developed into the largest industrial enterprise on the entire Scandinavian Peninsula. Over a thousand people were employed in the export-based company, resulting in the development of a centre of surprising cultural breadth and importance. During the 1850s, the English-born director of the company was even voted into the Storting (national parliament), though in the event he left Alta and Norway before the Storting assembled for the new session. The immigration of specialised professionals during the 16th and 17th centuries in Norway played an important role in the development of new businesses and industries. In addition, we recieved large number of immigrant Finns and, to a lesser extent, Swedes in the north, especially when the harvests failed in these neighbouring countries, lured by the chance of earning a living in the the fishing industry along the northern Norwegian coast.

OLA RØE

The express shuttles, «hurtigrutene», running between Bergen and Kirkenes, have through generations forged bonds along the country's coastline.

There were also a number of population shifts within Norway, sometimes the result of action by the authorities, which ought to be mentioned. A good example is the emigration of people from Østerdal and Gudbrandsdal, in the central south of Norway, to Målselv, Bardu and Øverbygd in the northern county of Troms, in the 1790s.

Despite the lack of any substantial land-owning or aristocratic class in Norway, the notions of rank and class-differentiation were not unknown in our rural society in previous centuries. A sharp increase in the number of peasents, both with and without their own land, contributed to the differentiation between social groups.

The gradual growth of industry, and the lure of easy emigration to America, soon led to structural changes within Norwegian patterns of settlement and business structures. The opportunity offered by emigration was grasped, especially by the poor – peasant farmers, servants, coastal fishermen and the urban working class and emigration, at its height, caused the virtual de-population of hundreds of villages and hamlets. The southern coastal communities and the valley communities of central Norway were strongest hit by this movement of people out of the country.

For long periods between 1850 and 1910, emigration reached between 10,000 and 20, 000, yet this did not inhibit a steady population growth in the country beginning in the crisis period prior to 1815 and continuing into our own era.

A quick study of the geographic distribution of population loss through emigration shows a distinct correlation with certain regional changes that occurred from the 1850s through to the First World War. The steady reduction of the percentage of the population residing in the southerly Sørlandet region, over a period of almost a hundred years right up until recent decades, was due not only to the relative poverty of agricultural resources in the district, and the abandonment of farms and small-holdings operating close to minimum-subsistence levels. Changes within the shipping industry, especially the change-over from wooden construction to steel, reduced levels of employment in, for example, Agder, whilst other areas drew advantage from the same changes.

It is symptomatic of the scale of de-population in Sørlandet that it took Aust-Agder nearly three-quarters of a century to regain its 1895 population level, during a period from the 1890s until deep into the 20th century, during which the Norwegian population as a whole grew from 2 to 4 million.

The industrialisation of Norway occurred in stages, based almost entirely upon the availability of natural resources, and often involving relatively primitive processing technologies. Forestry gave rise to timber exports. Fish were processed by such methods as drying, curing and salting. Mining led to the export of ore in addition to some domestically-smelted product, also produced for the overseas market.

Eventually, production of consumer items for the home market increased, including textiles and limited manufactured goods, though on the whole clothing continued to be produced within the home environment. Dairies and cheese-factories were established in each region.

KNUDSENS FOTOSENTER

A large flow of emigrants crossed the seas. The memorial in Bergen is in commemoration of the two first ships leaving for the Great Lakes and Chicago. They were the brigschooner «Sleipner» and the shaft «Skjøldmoen», departing respectively in 1862 and 1863.

Production of tobacco and tobacco-related products, writing paper, matches, shoes and other consumer items was eventually industrialised, as was the production of beer, spirits and non-perishable foodstuffs. During the huge expansion experienced by the Norwegian shipping industry in the 19th century, shipbuilding flourished along large sections of the coast.

This expansion is perhaps best illustrated by the fact that Norwegian tonnage increased more than fivefold between 1850 and 1890. In 1880, Norway, with its 1,510,000 tons, had the third largest fleet in the world after the USA and Great Britain. Although, it should be added that the Norwegian fleet contained a very high percentage of wooden sailing-clippers, which found it increasingly hard to compete in the developing market.

Already in 1826, Norway acquired its first two steam ships, purchased by the Norwegian State to link the coastal services from Southern Norway to the distant north of the country. Whilst it's true that neither 'The Constitution' nor the 'Prince Carl' offered their passangers much in the way of creature comforts, they did ensure weekly calls at the various small northern ports, as far as Kirkenes and the Russian border. It is interesting to note that marine steam-power was introduced to Norway as a result of public initiative, by the then Minister of Finance, thus illustrating the pragmatism shown by Norwegian politicians over the role of the state in social development. The same willingness by the state to participate in trade development is illustrated by the practice of the central bank – Norges Bank – of granting favourable loans to business from its regional branches throughout the country. Not least, the establishment of the first credit-bank for agriculture, *Kongeriget Norges Hypothekbank,* occurred remarkably early. This institution, today known as *Landbruksbanken* (The Agricultural Bank) began trading in 1851, giving rise to credit-banks for other industries during the 1900s.

There was a clear correlation between Norway's developing trade, shipping and industrial sectors and the increasing need for a national credit-system. As the country only gained its first savings-banks in the 1820s, and had to wait further decades before the first share-holder bank saw the light of day, we can see that government participation in the credit market was vital to the country's capacity to exploit the potential within various industrial sectors, arising from both domestic industrialisation and the general liberalisation of international trade.

The first phase of this industrialisation process saw the establishment of industries in the towns and villages, and Christiania – Oslo as it was to become – finally developed into the country's principal centre. Between the turn of the century to 1830, the population of the capital leapt from 8,000 inhabitants to almost 30,000; by 1860 this figure had become 78,000.

In 1875, Norwegian industrial and mining concerns could boast approximately 100,000 employees, or around 14 % of the workforce. Of these, some 30,000 were women, who recieved far less pay than their male colleagues. The first industrial strike was carried out by female workers in the match-making industry, in 1889. The Matchmaker's Strike was, in its way, a pioneering contribution to both the campaign for trade unionism and the movement for women's emancipation, coming as it did just as the first trade unions were beginning to emerge and concerning itself principally with the low pay of working women. At a time when the issue of women's emancipation was beginning to produce its pioneers amongst the upper classes, the Matchmakers' Strike was a sharp reminder that the matter was of no less importance at the bottom of the social scale.

Agriculture was still the dominant industry in Norway as the 19th century entered its last quarter. Farming, forestry and hunting employed almost 50 % of the working population. Almost a quarter of these, mostly women, were classified, euphemistically, as being engaged in «personal services», meaning in effect that they were engaged in house-work or work in the home.

Taking into consideration that 7 % of the workforce were employed at sea, and 5 % in the fishing industry, we get quite a clear picture of the structure of business-life in Norway at that time. Once the programme of public works – road and railway construction, the raising of public and government buildings, etc – had got under way, the building and construction sector would account for another 5 % of the workforce.

Changes in the structure of business and employment, with the resulting adjustments in patterns of settlement and accommodation, led, of course, to considerable social upheaval. Despite the fact that most people left the countryside for the towns due to the increasing difficulty of supporting themselves on their small-holdings or as farmworkers, conditions in the urban industries were also very hard. Although they were gradually reduced, child-mortality rates remained extremely high. Epidemics and sickness were rampant. Early in the 19th century, cholera epidemics in the poor areas of Christiania claimed hundreds of lives. Hansen's Disease, or leprosy, was still quite common, even after the Norwegian doctor, Gerhard H. Armauer Hansen, discovered the leprosy bacillus in 1873, thereby laying the foundation for the fight against this insidious illness. At this point, there were 2-to-3,000 registered sufferers from Hansen's Disease in Norway. Tuberculosis was another illness which took many lives, both in the towns and the countryside.

The rural postmen not only carried mail, but were also a source of information about what was happening in the neighbouring areas.

SCAN-FOTO/Arkiv

Transportation over Land and Sea

The 19th century experienced a development of transport and communication facilities which was to radically alter the nature of both business and social conditions in general. At sea, this change manifested itself in a massive expansion of the ship-building industry. Between 1850 and 1880, Norwegian shipyards completed more than 200 ships per year.

Both coastal traffic and long-haul shipping expanded aggressively. In the mid-1850s, the coastal steamer companies were founded, with a permanent coastal carrying service operating in Northern Norway, and along large sections of the coast.

In the middle of the last century, the railways began to offer a service in some parts of the country. The network of lines in use up to the turn of the century had a combined length of over 2,000 kilometres. In other words, within forty six years of the opening of the first railway between Christiania and Eidsvold, Norway had developed a length of track equal to half its entire railway network today, though the quality and dimension of much of this track was considerably inferior to our modern railways. Again, much of the railway building was organised and financed by the State. The first major link in the north was the line between Røros and Trondheim. Otherwise, this early network included the Drammen Line, the Kongsvinger Line and the Smålens Line.

Even more important for the country than the railway, however, was the network of roads which grew up all over Norway. Yet again, the State was the prime mover behind the major arteries, whilst the councils, parishes and other interested parties took responsibility for local roads.

A huge improvement in the postal service had a considerable effect on the general state of communications throughout the nation. When the first postage stamps appeared on the market, in 1855, marking an important step towards a modern postal service, Norway had somewhere in the region of 350 post offices. By the turn of the century this had increased to almost 2,500. Also towards the end of the century, the first telephone companies went into operation, and the arrival of the telegraph-service opened up completely new possibilities for long distance communication. Not least, this had its effect on a rapidly-expanding press, and, again by the turn of the century, Norwegians were reading, between them, a total of 172 different newspapers!

Money and the Credit System

Despite the initial lack of financial and credit infrastructure in the New Norway emerging after 1814, the growth in economic activity and new forms of business venture laid the ground for new new initiatives here, also. The founding of the Norwegian Bank, in 1866, marked the beginning. The majority of the Norwegian people had contributed to the enterprise through the so-called 'silver treasure', when many families literally gave away the family silver in order to provide a credible foundation for the new national bank.

The first savings banks came in the course of the 1820s. In 1850 they numbered ninety, and 50 years later this figure had risen to over four hundred. *Christiania Bank og Kreditkasse* opened a chain of joint-stock banks in 1848, with *Den Norske Creditbank* providing competition barely a decade later. Before the end of 1900 more than eighty joint-stock banks were in operation.

As the State bank, *Hypotekbanken* has built up a large customer-base in the agricultural sector during the period of development and readjustment in Norwegian agriculture of the second half of the last century. A liberal economic policy placed heavy demands also on those traditional trades and industries wishing to keep pace with new developments.

The first fire-insurance companies were established within the existing insurance industry in the mid-18th century, with the founding of the Norwegian Fire Insurance Company as an official, mutual insurance company as early as 1767. Insurance with this company was obligatory for householders in towns other than Christiania, until 1845. Companies specialising in shipping insurance began to develop from 1838 with Langesunfjords Assurance Company and Arendal Assurance Company leading the field. With the rapid development towards a money economy, and new towns and villages springing up, as well as an increasing volume of foreign trade, the insurance industry steadily acquired a more important role in a society needing to insure its principal services.

Another important point was the confidence in the Norwegian *daler*. To begin with, the Norwegian Bank experienced some difficulties honouring its own bank notes with payments of silver, but eventually, as the national economy strengthened, confidence in the currency increased and the *daler* acquired more stability. The great currency reforms of 1871, when the Scandinavian countries changed over from the *daler*, or dollar, to the crown, or *krone*, simultaneously embraced Scandiavian monetary union, allowing the mutual use of Norwegian, Swedish and Danish paper money across national borders.

Scandinavian monetary union represented the most comprehensive attempt at practical Scandinavian cooperation during the 19th century, coming to an end as late as 1924. In 1875, the union members changed from the Silver Standard to the Gold Standard as a basis for their currencies.

SCAN-FOTO/Rune Baashus

SCAN-FOTO/Rune Baashus

Among the first bank-notes, the 20-speciedaler, from 1816, and, bottom, private money, launched by the tradesman Thor Møhlen in Bergen, in 1695.

Education, Health and Hygiene

The new development programme included investment in an education system. The 1827 Law establishing the system of board-schools, or compulsory basic education, relieved the rural district authorities of their responsibilities embodied in a decree of 1739 and a bill of 1741. The

Board-school Law represented a considerable step forward from the long-standing commitment of the education system to the provision of basic literacy and religious education. Regulations were established concerning compulsory school attendance. Each parish was charged with maintaining at least one permanent school, with back-up peripatetic teachers moving between schools during the course of the term.

Various initiatives for more technically orientated education and training, within agriculture, construction work, etc, gradually developed, parallel to this basic education system. When the university was established in Christiania in 1813, it represented a particularly valuable investment in academic subjects and more research-orientated disciplines. One ought to mention the voluntary Royal Society for the Benefit of Norway, for their pioneering training work in agriculture and land-use. The first teacher's-training seminary was established in 1826. That this was located in Trondheim, in the middle of the country, provides an interesting insight into the macro-national perspective Norway was adopting even then, underlining the political importance of the North of Norway, despite its limited and sparcely distributed population.

There was a strong focus on schools and the educational system generally throughout the development phases of the 19th century. Numerous reforms and a considerable channeling of government financial resources, encouraged the development of an educational system to measure favourably against those in the rest of turn-of-the-century Europe. A characteristic example of the progress of the system is the increase of pupils sitting their A-levels, from an average of sixteen per annum between 1813–15, to over four hundred by the end of the century.

The central belief in the importance of general education in the development of economic and human resources, the work towards cultural development and in social reform, and the task of building up a democratic society, was characteristic of 19th century Norway. «Knowledge shall govern both country and nation», was a motto deeply relevant for many of those engaged in the efforts to create a strong society.

The systems of primary schools and public libraries, offering ready access to knowledge and qualifications, in turn released a flood of human resources. Universal basic, all-round education helped increase the quality and effectiveness of workers and professionals in all areas of employment. It is also undeniable that our relatively advanced education system also provided later generations of emigrants with the skills required for success in their new lives.

The population-increase over the past two hundred years is clearly related to the establishment of a health service and social services for the care of the poor and under-privileged. Nonetheless, infant mortality rates remained for a long time stubbornly high. As recently as 1875, two hundred and twenty five boys and two hundred girls per thousend died before reaching their fifth birthday. The corresponding figures for the end of the 1980s were twelve boys and nine girls per thousand. Even after the establishment of better hygiene and an improved medical service, illness continued to represent a serious threat to many sectors of the population. Tuberculosis was rife amongst the young and affected many families, and cost the lives of 290,000 Norwegians between 1910 and the present day. Children's diseases which are today easy enough to control claimed thousands of young lives due to the lack of vaccines or appropriate medicines.

The public health system, built up during the 19th century, did much to improve conditions and fight disease. Many aspects of the 1860 Health Act were still in operation until very recently, and a few points still prevail at the beginning of the 1990s.

Countering epidemics was the main priority of the new health service, with an emphasis on information on cleanliness and hygiene. Both the health authorities, schools and private organisations became involved in health-promotion projects. The development of medical research and access to new medicines meant more effective treatment of disease. Norwegian doctors have, down the years, distinguished themselves in a number of medical areas, so contributing to the reduction of suffering and raising of life-expectency both in Norway and other countries.

It is said that a people's culture is reflected in the way it treats its poor and helpless. In Norway, certain aspects of what we today term health and social care are rooted in the practices of Mediaeval farming communities and guild associations, when it was the tradition for families to care for those of their relatives unable to fend for themselves. Others of the 'deserving poor' were provided with help according to various regulations, although there were certainly many in the 19th century who fell outside the system.

A series of laws and the organisation of remedial measures led to considerable improvement, such that by the turn of the century one can safely assume that minimum degrees of support were available to all who needed it. At the same time, the ancient system of parish charity, in which the old and sick had to travel from farm to farm in order to secure themselves food and the barest existential minimum, was discontinued.

Rules governing the security of children were also gradually introduced and acted upon. The Factory Inspections Act of 1892 went a long way to insuring the limitation, and eventually the phasing out altogether, of child labour.

In 1894, the first steps were taken towards the establishment of a comprehensive national insurance system, with the adoption of a law requiring accident insurance for industrial workers. Various forms of aid funds had been operating for many years, not least by the craft guilds, contributing to a solidarity ethic amongst groups of workers.

Political and Cultural Conflict

The 19th century was characterised by great political and cultural conflict within Norwegian society. The forced union with Sweden was a contentious issue, despite the fact that the Constitution of 1814 ensured Norway considerable freedoms, not least the possibility of introducing reforms in many instances far more radical than anything applying in Sweden. The struggle between the farming community and the civil service resulted in laws pertaining to local councils and the establishment of local self-government from 1837. The final breakthrough for parliamentarianism, in 1884, placed control of the state apparatus with the Storting (National Parliament). The demands for voting rights, the freedom to organise and equal rights for women were proclaimed from the rooftops.

Otherwise, the revolutionary currents in the rest of Europe were barely registered in Norway. An exception was during the Year of Revolution, 1848, and its immediate aftermath, when the Thrannite Movement rose up and tabled demands remarkably similar to those of subsequent socialist organisations.

New social relationships and the potential for cultural development greatly influenced Norwegian society in the 19th century. The mobilisation of national feeling connected with the struggle for independence from Sweden, played an important role in the development of a cultural identity amongst the broad mass of the Norwegian people. In addition, this coincided with Norway's adoption of an extremely liberal economic policy, whilst Sweden chose a more protectionist path. From 1897, tolls were introduced on goods passing between the so-called «twin nations», following the Swedes' 1888 abandonment of the 1815 Customs and Excise Exemption Act. The fact that increased economic resources and new material conditions should result in such a strong and comprehensive mobilisation for cultural identity is in itself interesting, providing, as it does, an important explanation for the process of social and political liberation we notice occurring later in the century.

One social development increasingly prevalent in the period following the year 1900, was the growth of voluntary organisations. Modern Norway is remarkable for its myriad organisations, a tendency with roots in developements and experiences of the 19th century.

Religious groups formed their various associations prior to this period, though there was little enough margin for religious freedom in the 1814 Constitution, or in laws dating from that time. The Religious Assembly Law's ban of lay preaching was enforced with a strictness that created a martyr to the system of a preacher like Hans Nielsen Hauge, condemned to years of imprisonment. Not only did the Constitution prohibit the entry of Jews or Jesuits into the kingdom, it would also be half a century before the first Roman Catholic congregation was allowed to establish itself. Eventually, the Christian lay-organisations became an important force in the country's struggle for political and cultural freedom.

ARBEIDERBEVEGELSENS ARKIV

SCAN-FOTO/Arkiv

Two of our famous personalities of the last century. Marcus Thrane (1817–1890) built a strong popular movement based on the socialist currents in Europe. Hans Nielsen Hauge (1771–1824), on the picture below, was a lay preacher, and the founder of a strong Low Church movement.

Meanwhile, the Liquor Law of 1814 was, according to one Norwegian historian, «ridiculously liberal», opening the way for alchohol use and misuse which soon created its own backlash. Eventually, the law was replaced, by which time a number of groups had formed with the aim of eradicating the «evil of drink» completely. The first teetotal-association was founded in Stavanger in 1836, with Asbjørn Kloster the undisputed pioneer of the Norwegian temperance movement.

In the rural areas, various groups, clubs and organisations began to appear. Søren Jaabæk's *Bondevennforening* (Farmers Association), which flourished from the 1860s and onward, was one of the more party-political of these. The political parties *Venstre* (Liberals) and *Høyre* (Conservatives) appeared in 1884 as national organisations, with *Arbeiderpartiet* (the Labour Party) following in 1887.

The growth of trade unions in industry is one development which has made a deep impression on our society. The trade and professional organisations have developed a strong power base. From being opposition and pressure groups, they are now an officially recognised part of the semi-corporate model of government which presides over 1990's Norway. The first Norwegian trade union was founded in 1872 by print workers, and was later joined by various other groups, until in 1899, the Norwegian Trade Union Organisation was established as the umbrella organisation for all specialist trade associations. The signal was thus given for the start of an entirely new social development characterised by confrontation, collectivism, class struggle and the solidarity ethos, which would fundamentally influence the new century. The employers' organisation followed already the year after. These two forces have become decisive power-bases in our society, articulating impulses and views leading to a social model underpinned by the consensus principle. The Norwegian people that took the step from the 19th to the 20th centuries, was strongly focused on the conflicts arising from the union with Sweden. The Swedes' abandonment of the free trade arrangement between the two countries was interpreted as a sign of Swedish perceptions of Norwegian economic advantage in the relationship. Simultaneously, the period around the turn of the century was one of great and fundamental reforms, both in business and social life.

Universal franchise for men came into force in 1898, with the first female councillors assuming their positions in 1902. The university, which has closed its doors to female students for the best part of a hundred years, finally opened them to young female students, who, surprisingly, opted for science subjects in the early days.

A hundred years of growth and maturation had provided the Norwegian people with a foundation from which to enter the new century, and from which it could develop. At the same time, the harnessing of hydro-electric power from waterfalls opened the way for industrial and economic developments that few had imagined possible.

The new society was not unaffected by the fact that the number of retail and wholesale outlets in the country had doubled in the course of the 19th century. The capital had finally secured its position as the country's centre and largest city, with all the social challenges and problems such growth implies. It is also relevant that uncertainty and wanderlust led to mass-emigration. In the fifteen year period from 1900–1914, over 16,000 Norwegians left the country every year, mostly for America. This is nearly three times as many as in the last fifteen years of the last century.

HUSMO-FOTO

The ocean is a source of income. Codfishing brings in large catches. They are small, however, in comparison to the catches of herring obtained through purse-fishing, where the nets are bursting with the silvery fish.

HUSMO-FOTO

KNUDSENS FOTOSENTER

Today, vessels are modern, but used to be ten-oars and sails. Picture: the ten-oars alongside the characteristic boathouses in Lofoten.

Today, most agricultural activities are mechanised, and great combine-harvesters do the work of ten (right).

It used to be different (below). It took a lot of hard labour and many sore backs to harvest the potatoes.

HUSMO-FOTO

KNUDSENS FOTOSENTER

In the cities, times were hard. Wherever the «soup stations» were set up, large queues followed.

Diseases flourished, and the poor in particular were hit by epidemics. Edvard Munch found many of his motives in the hospitals. Picture: «The Sick Child», from 1885.

SCAN-FOTO/Arkiv

KNUDSENS FOTOSENTER

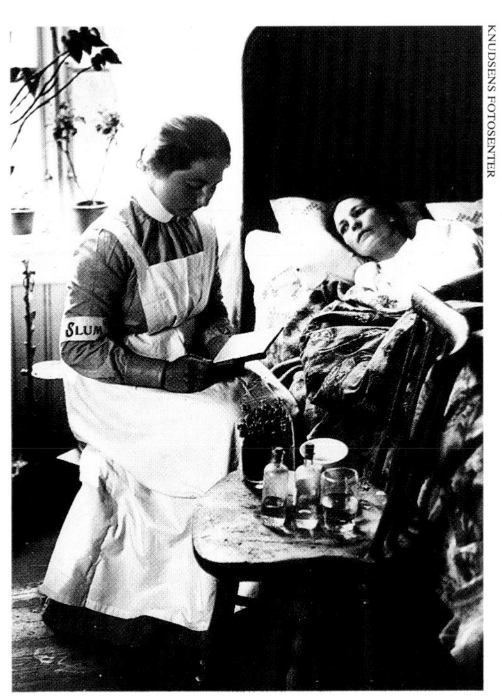

KNUDSENS FOTOSENTER

The kind sisters working in the slums were among the most self-sacrificing in the community. Tirelessly, they would go from house to house, helping and comforting the sick. Also, they taught people the importance of proper hygiene.

Today, the transportation of timber is done by trucks with heavy-duty cranes. The wood is then transported to the factories or to modern sawmills for further processing. As seen on the picture below, it didn't used to be that way. Manual labour was used to work the wood, and horsepower was needed for transporting the timber to the village or to the rivers.

JARLE KJETIL ROLSETH

SCAN-FOTO

SCANFOTO/Johan Brun

Raftsmanship required speed, an athletic stature, and strength.

The waterways were a natural choice both for the transportation of people and timber. Picture, right: The passengerboat Victoria, on the one hundred-year-old Bandak-Nordsjø canal, in Telemark.

Large wood-processing sites have been built around the country. Pulp, paper products and cardboard are the end products of forestry. Picture, right: Saugbrugsforeningen, literally, the «association of sawmills», in Halden, Østfold.

SAMFOTO/J. B. Olsen/R. Sørensen

SAMFOTO/Ragnar Frislid

HUSMO-FOTO

The forest can be beautiful, especially when dressed in its winter clothes.

HUSMO-FOTO

The opening of airports with shorter landing-fields around the country gave a boost to communication, especially in the northern parts of the country. Picture: A Widerøe-plane has just landed in Honningsvåg. Picture, right: Horsedrawn post-carriages were a common feature of townlife up until the First World War.

Few can the imagine the hard labour it has taken to build roads and railways in a country like Norway, with its abundance of mountains, rivers and fjords. Along the steep hills the labourers would need to hold on to ropes and otherwise with their spades and pickaxes. But they were tough men, these railway labourers. Picture: The construction of the railway to Bergen, Bergensbanen.

SCAN-FOTO/Aktiv

Today, the country is bound together by an elaborate railway network, and the electrically powered trains defy both the snow and the storms of the hostile mountain crossings.

SCAN-FOTO/Aktiv

KNUDSENS FOTOSENTER

SAMFOTO/Helge Sunde

In the old days, what pupils feared the most were the protocols and corporal punishment, or the cane. The buildings weren't large (picture, right), but much knowledge was passed on to pupils through the years.

At school, one should sit straight up and listen attentively to the words of wisdom from the teachers. The teachers demanded respect, not only in the classroom, but in society at large.

SAMFOTO/Pål Hermansen

The University of Oslo is the oldest in the country. But Bergen, Trondheim, and Tromsø also have their own universities, and polytechnics are widespread throughout the country. The monument is by Arnold Haukeland.

SAMFOTO

KNUDSENS FOTOSENTER

SCAN-FOTO/Arkiv

These railroad workers, left, have an air of carelessness and joy, that the men and women in the large telegraph offices lack.

Strict supervisers make sure the transmissions, reception and transcription of telegrams were properly done.

SCAN-FOTO/Arkiv

SCAN-FOTO/Arkiv

HUSMO-FOTO

Mostly women worked at the telephone exchanges. It used to be one of few female professions of a certain status. Today, things have changed, and women have penetrated all professions, e.g. the jobs in engineering on oil platforms.

'The New Working Day'

At the start of the 20th century, Norway's population was two and half times larger than it had been around 1814. The economy was much improved, business life more varied, and social and health conditions considerably advanced. Nonetheless, as a nation, Norway was still one of the poorer in the world, though a relatively high level of general education was a great asset to it.

Whilst the last decades of the 19th century were characterised by vigorous political struggle, both in terms of internal issues and the question of the union with Sweden, by 1905 the nation was united in its demand for a dissolution of the union. Political divisions were buried, at least for the time being, and Christian Michelsen, heading a broad-based coalition government, was able to present the Norwegian people with the so-called Karlstad Reconciliation, in September 1905.

Around the time of the dissolution of the Union with Sweden, there were many who wished for the continuation of this form of broad consensus government, but the political realities of the time proved incompatible with such an idea, and it found little support from the electorate. With the exception of the Occupation period, government of the country has alternated between the parties, and/or different coalition alliances, but always with a strong opposition serving as a political corrective in parliament.

ARBEIDERBEVEGELSENS ARKIV

Anna Rogstad was the first woman to enter the Norwegian Storting, as a deputy member from 1911 to 1913, when women gained the right of vote.

The so-called New Working Day, from 1905, was influenced by the desire for political reform and by commercial and cultural optimism. There was much conflict over the laws of concession, which were to safeguard ownership rights of Norwegian natural resources. The social security system was developed further to include health benefits which applied to all employees earning below a certain income. The Castberg children's laws provided security and protected the rights also of children born out of wedlock. Universal franchise was introduced in 1913.

Industrialisation continued apace, basing itself not least on Norway's extensive hydroelectric sources. Initially, foreign capital played a decisive role in a series of important projects, but the domestic capital markets soon came up to strength. A new element in business life was the cooperative ethic. Consumer-cooperation arrived in the form of The Norwegian Cooperative Association, in 1907. A modest twenty eight cooperative societies initiated this developement, but this number rapidly increased. Producer and purchasing cooperatives in agriculture and fisheries would later become important links in the development and securing of staple-industries.

Relatively liberal economic policy had strengthened Norwegian ability to compete overseas, though our export markets continued to be dominated by traditional raw-material products. Shipping continued to be a key industry, despite the intensive capital investment required by the development of first steam and later turbine ships.

Access to electricity supplies created great potential for the electro-chemical and electro-metallurgic industries, which also provided openings for Norwegian technical creativeness and a productive drive from world-class companies, such as Norsk Hydro.

At the same time, Norwegian pay levels, and costs generally, were comparatively reasonable, seen in an international context. With a relatively well informed and educated workforce, Norway had considerable advantages over its competitors, which was maintained for the duration of the first half of the century and well into the second. At the same time, low incomes were mirrored by considerable social problems and domestic poverty.

Communications Changed Everything

The extensive development of the communications network was also extremely important for the Norwegian economy and the standard of living in the country from the beginning of the century. The introduction of the telephone and the subsequent developments within tele-communications had a huge effect on the business community, the public authorities, and the private individual. The railways continued to be developed, whilst Norwegian roads could boast a total of *two* cars in 1899! Two or three short decades later, the car had already become an important link in the transport network.

During the 1914–18 War, the Norwegian merchant fleet assumed an important role, not only for domestic supply, but also in the context of international transportation, though this advancement was not without problems, placing great stresses and strains on both ships and their crews and relatives.

The war and the resulting shortages placed huge strains on large groups of the populations, especially in the towns and industrial areas. Food supplies were limited, and towards the end of the war the government found it necessary to introduce rationing of certain foodstuffs. Coupled with steeply rising prices, the result was that many families and elderly individuals went without.

When, in addition, the boom period led to small groups of people being able to achieve high earnings and a life of luxury, the stage was set for social and industrial conflict, as Norwegian society noted the revolutionary spirit abroad in the rest of Europe.

The Norwegian Labour Party drew much support from the industrial workforce and those engaged in the construction and building sectors. Conflict intensified. The state authorities' attempts to solve wage disputes through compulsory arbitration met resistence from both sides. There was a clear correlation between the radicalisation of the Labour Party and the increase in professional and economic conflict in the workplace. The introduction by the authorities of economic policy aimed at raising the value of the *krone* to its pre-war level, led to economic retrenchment which was to prove disastrous for the whole of Norwegian society. Mass unemployment and bankruptcy, large sections of the population living on, or below, the bread line – these conditions made their mark on the inter-war period. Public assistence and food-coupons, meant to ensure the supply of the most basic requirements, became part of everyday life for many people.

In the middle of this difficult period, however, forward-looking initiatives and reforms were being set in motion, which would play a central role in the development of a society able to achieve durable solutions to its problems, to secure acceptable standards of living for all its members, and encourage comprehensive mutual understanding. Pioneering work was undertaken, for example, in labour legislation. The Labour Disputes Act of 1927, with subsequent refinements, has been of great importance for the development of the system of peaceful negotiation that now operates in Norway. The Industrial Tribunal, manned by representatives from both sides of industry, was a judicial initiative which, over the years, has achieved excellent results.

Though the great industrial conflicts at the beginning on the 1930s led to violent confrontations, general strikes and unrest of various kinds, relations in society did eventually improve. Certainly, Norway managed to avoid the most dramatic confrontations occurring in other parts of Europe at the time. Although the Norwegian Labour Movement was on the advance, its banners were of a more social democratic than overtly communist complexion. When the Labour Party, with Johan Nygaardsvold as Prime Minister, took over government in 1935, the foundations were laid for a new political model in Norway, though the party distribution in the Storting was not to alter to any great extent until after the Second World War.

The fact that no party espousing national socialist views ever managed to win representation in parliament during the 1930s, contributed to a large measure of peace of mind in the country at large, although the collaborator Vidkun Quisling's Nasjonal Samling was to play a special role during the Occupation.

The great, fundamental social reform of the 1930s was the introduction of a pension system in 1936, representing the culmination of a discussion that had dragged on for decades, and forming the central pillar of the wider social security system. The notion of a system of unemployment benefit underwritten by the state, as a supplement to the trade union's own unemployment benefit structure, also took root during this period, and would eventually contribute to the development of a broader welfare-concept in Norwegian society.

When the Second World War finally enmeshed Norway, in 1940, unemployment was considerably reduced and the economic and social infrastructure of the country was much strengthened. (It falls beyond the brief of this article to examine the weakness of our *military* infrastructure!)

The German Occupation in the Spring of 1940, placed heavy burden on the whole of Norwegian society, both in terms of the economy and resources. Despite the infringements and destruction, however, in retrospect we must admit that levels of actual suffering in Norway were limited. Most people managed to get by, somehow. Unemployment was eradicated completely thanks to increased levels of self-sufficiency and German requisitioning. Conditions of health were bearable, with a complete absence of those diseases related to overconsumption which have since established themselves so strongly. Rationing of consumer articles was tough, but even though malnutrition affected small numbers of people, the vast majority emerged from the war without any lasting diet-related health problems. Towards the end of the war a limited system of child benefits was even introduced, for families with two or more children.

The economic costs for the period 1940–45 eventually manifested themselves in the need for reconstruction, reparations after five years of stresses and strain, and efforts to recover investments. The special problems in the northern counties of Finnmark and Troms, where the German's scorched-earth policy during their retreat from the Russians had lead to the forced evacuation of most of the population, of course took priority.

The Welfare State and the Affluent Society

The transformation from a war economy to a period of national reconstruction was achieved with a surprising lack of conflict. No unemployment was incurred and virtually everyone experienced a steady improvement in their standard of living. True, there was some conflict over regulations policy and encroachment by the state, but the solidarity engendered by the war, which was reflected in the Joint Programme of 1945, was to characterise development for many years to come.

With a relatively even and virtually unbroken increase in productivity, employment and standard of living throughout successive decades, culminating in the «golden sixties», Norwegian society experienced a sence of progress and confidence in the future. The development of hydro-electric power and new communication networks, not least within air travel and the expanding national road-network, provided the basis for rapid growth in industry and the business sector, also in the regions.

The redistribution of wealth which strengthened the position of low and medium income groups, also paved the way for comprehensive income increases. There were attempts to reduce the pressure on the outlying districts of the country through various government initiatives, and the social benefits system was further developed, with the introduction of National Insurance in 1967 completing the monumental edifice. A major investment in new housing was already under way soon after the end of the War, with among other things the establishment of the Norwegian State Housing Bank. Changes in family structures and housing aspirations have led to a huge increase in the number of units of accommodation, the vast majority of which have been built during the post-war period, with all that implies in terms of technical specifications and design.

The expansion of schools and educational institutions have led to the doubling of the average number of years Norwegians spend in education, since 1930. Educational opportunities, which had previously been open to comparatively few, have become accessible for the majority in a position to take advantage of them. The State Loan Fund for Education has played an essential role in this development. The expansion of secondary schools, establishment of universities in Bergen, Trondheim and Tromsø, and a network of district high schools offering university-level education in more exclusive subjects, amount to a huge investment in both the acquisition and application of knowledge and skills.

Health and Life

It is not easy to measure to what extent a people's standard of living and quality of life are determined by social factors. Some statistics can provide a few clues, however, e.g in relation to health and physical development. For example, the average conscript today is ten centimetres taller than his great grandfather who reported for his initial medical examination in 1900. In those days, every sixth recruit was under 165 cms. Nowdays, it is only one in a hundred. In 1900, less than 1 % of recruits were taller than 185cm; today it's more than 23 %. It is tempting to see a connection between these figures and the fact that the Norwegian Sports Association is the largest voluntary organisation in the country, involving more than 40 % of the country's population.

Another measure of the improvement in the health of the country is the increase of life-expectancy by twenty to twenty five years from the last decade of the 19th century to the beginning of the 1990s, a figure which speaks not only of more effective obstetrics, but also the successful combatting of infectious and other diseases on all fronts, through systematic vaccination, etc. Though we perhaps should not ignore the fact that increased affluence has not only had positive effects. So called «lifestyle diseases» have begun to make themselves apparent, with a rise in the rates of premature death, especially amongst men.

Oil and Gas as Economic Resources

From around 1970 the Norwegian economy and social development entered a new era with the initiation of large scale oil and gas production on the North Sea Continental Shelf. This subject is covered in more depth elsewhere in this book. The offshore oil industry has meant increased income and resources for the country as a whole, though this new wealth has also brought certain problems in its wake. There has been relatively little growth in on-shore business activity, and productivity levels have been noticeably lower than in neighbouring countries. Average profit-yields from business investments have been modest, at best.

In terms of the country's balanace of payments and overseas economy, however, the oil and gas industry has enormous implications. It has been possible for us to maintain a high level of imports, and increase levels of consumption, which in the short term has helped create a sense of affluence. The large numbers of Norwegians travelling abroad on package tours is a clear symptom of a high and evenly distributed standard of living. Recently, there has been an increasing feeling that the oil money should be used more carefully. It is, after all, a resource which can only be exploited once.

There are still large areas on the Norwegian Continental Shelf which have not been subject to exploration, not least further north and in the Barents Sea. Exploitation of oil and gas resources must be planned and executed in the context of the needs of future generations; these resources are neither unlimited nor renewable.

One of the most important questions for the Norwegian business community, therefore, is how it can create new areas of enterprise, and secure a more balanced development of productivity and jobs. Our country has, for decades, been involved in an international restructuring process, based on the liberalisation of markets and agreements allowing for the freer exchange of goods and services. A country depending on the sale of over 50 % of its products overseas, and which is equally reliant on imports in many areas, must reckon on tough competition and continuous pressure to readjust. The relatively high unemployment figures of more recent years, are a direct result of our inability to readjust adequately.

Long Term Perspectives – a Summary

Norway began the 19th century as a caste society. It was characterised by a government and business structure based on a caste system, with relatively clear delineations between social groups.

As the century unfolded, the country developed into a class society, based more on economic and social criteria. The introduction of a money economy and increasing degress of democracy paved the way for increased standards of living for large groups of the population. The growth of interest-groups and organisations began to have an important effect on people's perception of their own power.

In the course of the 20th century we have moved towards a social model without any clear class differences, or inequalities. Extreme poverty has disappeared. The class mentality has little relevance for the up-coming generations, with people feeling a greater degree of equality and freedom to use their skills as they themselves see fit. Specialisation and sectorisation has become more acceptable. This is illustrated for example by the fact that we now have three nation-wide trade organisations, where previously the Trade Union Congress had something of a monopoly.

Two main perspectives give evidence, respectively, of the extent of readjustment in the business and professional communities, and of the stability in population patterns in different parts of the country.

We may recall the domination of agriculture at the beginning of the 19th century, the towns were still small and the majority of the population lived in the rural areas. The following table defines the development of different industries over the past 100 years:

Working Population 1890–1990, divided into main areas

Industry	*1890* %	*1930* %	*1960* %	*1990* %
Primary industries (agriculture, forestry, fish.)	60	36	20	7
Secondary industries (mech. industry, etc)	27	26	36	24
Tertiary industries (services, etc)	13	38	44	69
	100	100	100	100

These figures show the dramatic changes in occupation and work conditions which have occurred in the course of the past hundred years. The move towards an affluent society is mirrored, above all, in the changing nature of work and working practices, particularly in the reduction of physical strain put on workers.

This development also includes a large reduction in the percentage of self-employed people in society, and a corresponding increase in various groups of salaried workers. The development has also included the gradual reduction of the average working day. In 1918, the 8-hour day/48-hour week was introduced by parliament, and the reduction continued after the Second World War, first to 45 hours, then 42.5, 40 until the current level of 37.5 hours per week.

Norway's Population Distribution by Region

In the period from 1769 to 1991, the Norwegian population has grown by a factor of six, from 724,000 to 4,249,000.

Despite the fundamental changes in work structures and conditions in various occupations, the population distribution between the different regions has remained remarkably stable. The table below shows relatively small fluctuations, with the exception of Agder, which was particularly effected by the waves of emigration, especially around the turn of the century.

Norwegian population dealt into regions (%)

Region	*1769*	*1865*	*1970*	*1990*
South East Norway	46	46	49	48.7
Agder	9	8	5	5.6
Western Norway	26	26	25	15.7
Trøndelag	11	11	9	8.9
Northern Norway	8	9	12	10.9

North of the Dovre Mountains, in central Norway, there has been a certain displacement, but taken as a whole the northern counties have had about 1/5th of the population throughout the period covered by the table, with 19 % in 1769, a peak of 21 % in 1970, and a shade under 20 % today.

The Future

A characteristic tendency in post-war Norway has been the increasing reliance on overseas contacts and international cooperation, in which we have participated on many levels. In recent decades we have experienced our previous tendency to lose people through emigration turning into a net increase, through immigration, partly from other continents. This has a certain effect on our society as it approaches the millenium, though the numbers of foreigners living in Norway add up to barely 3 % of the population, of which 1 % hail from Asia, Africa and Australia, and another 1 % from neighbouring Scandinavian countries. Compared to other European and American countries, Norway's «immigrant-problem» is extremely modest, at the same time as the presence of people from other nations and cultures can have an enriching effect on a homogeneous and somewhat peripheral society.

The great current danger is the threat to the environment, and there are numerous demands now being made on society to harmonise itself more with nature, involving a reduction of the pressures we put upon the environment and unrenewable natural resources, and an eradication of social problems inherent in our affluent society.

It is paradoxical that modern society, in eradicating the poverty of previous eras, and with access to resources unrivalled by any earlier generation, should create so many other social and human problems. We experience far more violence than previously. Drug abuse and addiction is a common problem which leaves many scars in families and communities. Affluence-related crime is a problem for the police, the judiciary and society as a whole. Isolation and loneliness are problems partly created by our modern living and family conditions.

Those who have worked and been responsible for the development of Norwegian society ty during recent generations, have invested greatly in the infrastructure of the country and ensured that most people can enjoy one of the highest standards of living in the world. The coming generations will have to learn to be far more careful in their use of natural resources, and find a more humane way of running our affluent society, such that there is less cost in terms of human loneliness and failure, and the social network is richer and better developed.

The war descended on Norway in 1940, during the night of 9. April. The cruiser Blücher, carrying large parts of the German administrative personnel, came face to face with its destiny in the Oslo fjord. The cruiser was set on fire and sunk with the help of some of our oldest cannon, fired from Oscarsborg.

SAMFOTO

SAMFOTO

In most towns the occupying forces met little resistance. The peaceful Norwegian people had expected they could stay out of the war, as during WWI. In some places the Germans were met by heroic resistance, but in the larger cities, like in Trondheim, they could march in and parade on the central square, Torget, beneath the Olav Trygvason statue.

During the War, Vidkun Quisling, here seen during a meeting with Adolf Hitler, led a so-called national Government answerable to the German occupying power. The government of Nygårdsvold continued their legitimate work in London, where the King and Crown Prince also resided.

KNUDSENS FOTOSENTER

SCAN-FOTO/Pressens Bild

SCAN-FOTO/Arkiv

In Finnmark the Germans carried out the scorched earth policy. Huge parts of the population were evacuated before their homes were burnt to the ground. Space in the evacuation camps was scarce.

SAMFOTO

During the War one had to be self-sufficient. The planting of potatoes and vegetables took place in almost every green spot. Below: The ploughing of the Royal Park, by the Royal Palace, for the seeding of potatoes.

SAMFOTO/Pål Hermansen

KNUDSENS FOTOSENTER

SCAN-FOTO/Arkiv

KNUDSENS FOTOSENTER

Many critical voices were raised in 1952 when Norway hosted the Olympic Winter Games. The reconstruction of the nation was not completed, the economy wasn't still very strong, in Oslo or elsewehere. But the games turned out to be stimulating for the entire population, and when we obtained a fair share of the medals, criticism was silenced.

FJELLANGER/WIDERØE

JARLE WÆHLER

The power industry was an important part of the reconstruction works. Norsk Hydro's Vemork installation was rehabilitated, new power stations were built and solid power cables stretched across the country. The heavy industries, such as the aluminium industry, entered a flourishing period of great growth.

The construction of housing only came about slowly, due to the shortage of materials and capital. The state stimulated growth through the setting up of a mortgage bank, Husbanken, and small individual houses, apartment blocks, and terrace houses were soon built all around the country.

KNUDSENS FOTOSENTER

KNUDSENS FOTOSENTER

But education remained a priority. The University of Oslo could no longer cope with the increasing number of applicants for higher education, and new universities and polytechnics were set up around the country. A high level of education is a necessity in a country wanting to maintain its level of prosperity.

KNUDSENS FOTOSENTER

Norway as an Industrial Nation

Finn Lied:

NTB

Finn Lied (b. 1916), a trained engineer, was an officer with the Norwegian Army in London during the war, but soon became a researcher. Lied was appointed the chief researcher at the army's research institute, Forsvarets Forskninginstitutt, and was its director from 1957 to 1983. In 1971–72 he was appointed Minister of Industry in the Trygve Bratteli cabinet. He has for many years been very active in promoting wider debates on in particular public research- and industrial policies. Acting as the director of the board of the state petroleum company, Statoil, has been one of his many public commissions.

Relative to its population, Norway is the most energy-rich country in the world. We have hydropower, natural gas and oil. These resources led first to a strong investment in energy-intensive electrochemical and electro-metallurgy industries.
The country became one of the leading producers of aluminium, magnesium and ferro-alloys. Since the beginning of the 'oil-adventure', the country has also developed an advanced oil industry and associated maritime technologies. Developments in advanced technology offers challenges in many new areas.

KNUDSENS FOTOSENTER

HUSMO-FOTO

Today, Norwegian fishing vessels are among the most advanced of their kind. Picture left: The ocean-going trawler Randen, from Ålesund

SCANFOTO/Svein E. Furulund

Electricity is brought from the power stations to the consumers. For the installation of the heavy power cables, great strength and courage is required.

Man cannot live off nature's beauty alone, but the mountain water has been made use of. It created wealth in an otherwise poor country. Large picture: Aurlandsfjorden, a favorite spot for visitors to the western fjords.

HUSMO-FOTO

OLA RØE

Many of the waterfalls have been tamed, led into pipelines or tunnels, bringing the water to the power station. Mollisfossen remains in its natural state.

The technologically advanced oil platforms in the North Sea are showpieces of Norwegian engineering. The dimensions above the sea level are impressive, as are the massive concrete foundations which carry weights of up to 50,000 tons. Picture: One of Statoil's platforms in the Gullfaks A-section of the North Sea.

STATOIL

KNUDSENS FOTOSENTER

Agricultural production is still of importance, in the midst of technological advances. But the agricultural sector is under constant pressure of structural change.

The construction of ships is a deeply rooted tradition in Norway and all types of ships are built at Norwegian shipyards, bar the largest supertankers. Kværner/Kleven, in Florø, is among the most modern along the coast.

HUSMO-FOTO

Norwegian expertise in shipbuilding is internationally acclaimed. Some of the most advanced propellers are developed in Norway, and are used by a great number of ships worldwide.

KNUDSENS FOTOSENTER

Norway is a young nation, in every sense. The ice slowly loosened the land from its grip a mere 10,000 years ago, and even the industrial revolution came later to Norway than to the countries of central Europe. As long as history has been recorded, however, we find evidence of fine craftsmanship in the country; particularly in boatbuilding, architecture and metalwork. Influence from oversees was certainly important, but the products acquired their own national character. The craftsmen, not least the smiths responsible for the manufacture of weapons, were highly valued members of the community. A master of his trade was considered a great artist, one who had received his gifts from another world. Occasionally, traces of these masters have been found in burial mounds, in the form of tools and implements.

Foreign influences have repeatedly made their mark on the country, not least in technology. The influx of technology was particularly widespread during the period around 1600, when Norway was governed by Christian IV of Denmark. This energetic monarch ensured the spread of German mining technology into Norway, a fact which still influences the old mining communities, and the terminology for everything connected with mining practice.

The industrial revolution, with steam-ships, railways, electricity and all that followed in their wake, finally came to Norway in the last half of the 19th century. Its foundation was laid by the sense of purpose and energy released by the country's achievement of statehood in 1814. The combination of international engineering, foreign capital and Norwegian initiative and natural resources resulted in an explosive developement in the period following independence, from 1905 to the First World War. In Norwegian history, we talk about «the new working day», but the development of Norwegian industry only reached full momentum after the Second World War, when shipping, fishing, and metal, timber and pulp production were supplemented by shipbuilding, mechanised industry, chemicals and medicine, all on a considerable scale.

In 1970, came the discovery of gas and oil – with all the potential and problems this implied – causing the economic structure of the country to shudder at the seams.

Today, Norway is a modern industrialised nation, particularly rich in raw materials and energy, but also boasting new developments in manufacturing industry and advanced technology which point to an exiting future.

HUSMO-FOTO

Red-fish – a very popular fish with large numbers of the coastal population. It can be served fresh, smoked, or salted.

The Sea and the Coast

The Gulf Stream, which brings warm water from the south up along the Norwegian coast, has created and maintained the basis for what we may term our coastal culture. The temperate waters provide favourable climatic conditions, with a rich supply of plankton thriving along an ice-free coast. The importance of this is put into context when we consider that the southernmost tip of Norway lies on the same latitude as that of Greenland. Three quarters of the Norwegian people live on or near the coast.

The oldest archealogical discoveries from coastal areas evidence the important role of the sea in terms of transport and trade. Fishing has always been the main industry, and, throughout hundreds of years, fish, whether dried, salted or, more recently, frozen, has been as vital to the country's self-sufficiency as for its export market. Of the world's total annual catch of around 70 million tons, Norway has consistently been resposible for 2.5 million tons, notwithstanding normal margins of fluctuation. Recent years have also seen the growth of fish-farming, principally of salmon and trout, but with other types of fish gradually being introduced. Annual production now stands at around 150,000 tons and growing, with exports of fresh, frozen or processed fish going to Europe, the U.S.A and, increasingly, Japan.

Apart from being nature's larder, the sea has also served as the most important highway and communications route. To begin with this highway ran the length of the Norwegian coast, with its deep fjords, but later it extended to include a network of routes throughout the oceans of the world. The sea represented not a barrier but an opening. The early conquering of the sea by the vikings, their long ships equipped both for trade and war, belong to the most exiting, and largely inexplicable, periods of Norway's early history. The many voyages to Iceland bear witness to impressive innovations such as sailing against the wind, and highly accurate maritime navigation. The extraordinarily elegant, open viking ships were the beginning of a tradition which over hundreds of years developed sailing ships for exporting fish and logs, and later a modern 'steel and steam' fleet. The original shipping industry, based on local needs and conditions, gradually developed into an international concern, controlled from Norway, but operating in all the world's oceans. The modern fleet covers the whole spectrum of shipping, from specialised vessels of various sizes, oil tankers up to 500,000 tons, to the floating luxury liners, most of which have hardly been near the Norwegian coast. The Norwegian fleet is today the third largest in the world, with approximately 55 million tons deadweight, divided between approx. 1,500 vessels, of which almost 1,100 sail under the Norwegian flag.

KNUDSENS FOTOSENTER

Shipping still plays a major part in the Norwegian economy. Apart from the income from freight, the shipping firms place considerable orders with Norwegian companies generally. The workforce both on board, and increasingly on land, contribute greatly to the country's economy.

The entire, comprehensive exploitation of the sea through fishing and freight, has both given rise to, and been reliant upon, large-scale technological developments. Certain lines of development have had to be abandoned – for example, the pioneering Norwegian contribution to whaling, where the development of the harpoon led to the over-fishing of the South Arctic Ocean. But essentially there is a continual line of development from the viking longships right through to the modern, specialised coastal and ocean-going fleets, resulting from the collaboration between shipping companies, shipyards and research-and-development institutions. Equipping this fleet, with the instrumentation required by specialist fishing vessels and the technical equipment relied upon by the international transportation industry, has become something of a national speciality.

KVÆRNER

NORSK DESIGNRÅD

Ever since the Viking era, Norwegians have developed a sense of strict aestheticism in shipbuilding.
Above, top: The elegant Gokstad-ship.
Above, centre: An advanced and specially constructed ship for the transportation of gas.
Above, bottom: The most modern type of catamaran is capable of reaching speeds in excess of 40 knots.

Architecture and Construction

There is much evidence that large buildings from earlier times were built not only of stone and brick but also of wood. Naturally, the remains are largely of stone, which better resisted decay, fire and water damage. An exception to this are the so-called stave churches, wooden constructions dating back to the 11th century. Whilst stone never secured a strong position in Norwegian building tradition, in the period up to the 13th century, almost 1,700 stave churches were built. Elements of both Christian and heathen tradition were included in these buildings. The result was a construction of simple magnificence, their exteriors as exotic as their interiors were calm. Their most remarkable feature, however, is their resilience; those not burned or demolished, have remained in good condition for over 800 years. Modern experts have posited three reasons for this resilence; firstly the exclusive choice of building materials, which were of a much higher quality than today; secondly, the method of construction, which was especially well suited to withstand snow and wind; thirdly, small but important structural innovations which protected the timbers from the effects of climate. The stave churches were not isolated examples of the building practices of the era, which were characterised by a definite sense of style and excellent craftsmanship. These traditions have lived on to our own time.

In a country as dominated by mountain and fjord as Norway, the building of roads has always presented the most demanding challenge. The national road network has been gradually expanding for over a thousand years, but more systematically since the middle of the 16th century. The ancient roads are particularly impressive when one considers the equipment available at the time. From the middle of the last century, railway construction came into the picture, and the need for moderate inclines and gentle curves led to the wide development of both bridgebuilding and tunneling techniques. Both the laying of the Trondheim Line, and even more so the line to Bergen with its branch line out to Flåm, represent engineering of a very high calibre.

Modern technology has revolutionised both road, bridge and tunnel construction. It is now possible, technically and economically, to cross the coastal fjords with both conventional bridges, suspension bridges and tunnels. With the completion of the ferry-free coastal road in the

West of Norway, the country will really become a land of bridges and tunnels. Modern construction plant, full profile drilling and modern concrete technology have made it possible to bind together a country whose geography earlier rendered it little more than a series of isolated islands and villages. Norway is today recognised as amongst the world leaders in tunnel- and concrete-technology.

Perhaps the most impressive examples of Norwegian construction technology are the gigantic concrete chassis for the North Sea oil platforms, some of which reach a height of more than 300 metres. The calculations involved in designing these vast edifaces has only been made possible by relatively recent advancements in computer technology, but the actual production presents logistical and engineering challenges hitherto unknown in the construction industry. The platform base, often with oil and ballast tanks integrated into its structure, is first cast in a dry dock and afterwards towed out to the deep arm of a fjord, which serves as the construction site for the huge pillars. These are built in a gliding shutter, or casting-frame. The entire structure is gradually sunk deeper and deeper into the water, so as to maintain a reasonable working height. A construction such as this requires massive reinforcement and concrete of the highest quality to withstand both structural stress and the effects of corrosion. But even the oldest platforms show little sign of damage. Placing the deck of the platform, which can weigh up to 50,000 tons, onto the pillars is a highly demanding operation; leverage is enhanced by pumping out large ballast-barges positioned below the deck during construction.

Energy, Raw materials and Processing

The real industrial breakthrough in Norway at the beginning of this century was related to the harnessing of the country's hydro-electric potential, and its use in manufacturing energy-intensive products such as artificial fertilizers, metals, and wood and pulp products. In the course of the last 20 years, the arrival of oil and natural gas has secured Norway's position as, pro rata, the most energy intensive of all the industrial countries. In addition to being plentiful, these resources are environmentally friendly. Hydro-electric power is in a category of its own. Natural gas, which Norway has in very large quantities, gives off considerably less pollutants, including carbon dioxide (CO_2), than either coal or oil. Today, Norway's three most important exports are oil, natural gas and aluminium produced by electrolysis.

Hydro-electric Power

There is a long tradition of hydro-power; a direct line can be drawn from the water-driven mill-wheel, used for grinding corn, via the water-powered sawmills – which, with their multi-bladed saws could be very large indeed – to the modern hydro-electric power-station. The development, this century, of the large power-stations represented a technological and logistical achievement of the highest order. Amongst the pioneers the name of Cristopher Kars Kielland looms large – his career is without parallel in Norway. From 1905 to 1950, he was associated with what were then the largest power stations in the world, including those at Rjukan and Mår. All of his projects were characterised by brilliant technological and economic planning, and completion within very tight schedules. As a contempory commetator put it; «He created wealth for Norway to an extent which few of the country's citizens could even dream of».

The Norwegian hydro-electric system is today considered one of the very best in the world, and Norwegian technology is implicated in the whole system, from the construction of dams and reservoirs, the laying of penstock, the design of power stations, the production of turbo-generators and high voltage pilons for transmission cables and mains control. The integration of different aspects of the plant via mountain tunnels, the use of such things as high pressure tunnels and subterranean power stations, etc., have become Norwegian specialities. This technology provides both financial income and security.

Before the use of high voltages improved transmission techniques, energy-intensive industries were situated in close proximity to the power stations. This was, in many ways, a continuation of an old tradition, and has influenced the distribution of heavy industrial sites throughout the country. Today, all power stations are integrated into a national grid, thus creating one of the largest integrated supply networks in the world, which is also connected with the supply networks of our neighbouring countries. One of the system's special features is its storage capicity, through a comprehensive system of reservoirs, which ensures supply even in dry years. Each person in Norway has 3 kilowatts of power at his disposal at all hours of the day, throughout the year. No other country in the world has such a large proportion of its power supplied solely from hydro-electric sources.

SAMFOTO/J.B. Olsen/R. Sørensen

An Industrial Vision

The largest of the power stations built in Norway at the beginning of this century formed part of an industrial vision associated with Sam Eydes, a pioneer of international calibre, blessed with access to Swedish and French capital. Eydes recognised the world's need for artificial fertilizers, especially nitrates. Nitrogen constitutes 78 % of the Earth's atmosphere, but this mostly exists in molecular form which plants cannot utilise. The molecules must be split and nitrogen atoms allied with, for example, hydrogen, and attached to ammonia or salts which plants can then absorb. This process is extremely energy-intensive. Originally, Sam Eyde utilised an electric arc for the first phase, thus introducing the need for large quantities of electricity.

Norsk Hydro a.s., founded by Sam Eyde, is today the largest privately owned company in Norway, and artificial fertilizers remain one of its main products.

The pioneering work with artificial fertilizers lead Eyde and other like-minded visionaries into energy-intensive electro-chemical and electro-metallurgic industries. Norway is today one of the leading producers of carbide and other electro-chemical products.

KNUDSENS FOTOSENTER

High quality wood has been the basis of an important industry in Norway. Exports of wood have throughout centuries been a vital part of the Norwegian economy. Late last century, the wood-processing industries really got started and paper- and wooden products have since played an important part in Norwegian exports.

Energy and Wood Materials

There is, of course, a connection between energy and raw materials generally. The traditional raw-material industry in Norway is forestry. The country has always been well endowed with currently popular woods such as pine, fir and birch, but also with older, stronger types such as oak and beech. High quality timber has always been readily available. One wonders how it was possible, with just an axe and wedge, to produce the fine, even planks used by the vikings for shipbuilding. Water-powered sawmills and circular saws, were gradually developed from the middle of the 15th century. Export of logs, planks and boards became a mainstay of the economy from around 1550. Even today, it is still an important trade.

The long fibres of the slow-maturing Nordic tree-family make them well suited for the production of paper pulp. This pulp, produced simply by grinding cleaned logs of appropriate length, became a common, energy-intensive industry from around 1860. Later, the aspirations of the industry expanded to include all qualities of paper, manufactured partly from the mechanically produced wood-pulp, partly from chemically processed wood-chip. Today, approximately 10 million cubic metres of timber are felled annually, from which is produced some 1.8 million tons of paper and cardboard in addition to the export of around 700,000 tons of wood pulp.

Naturally, ancient traditions of carpentry provide the basis for the modern wood-products industry, which in turn has contributed to the continuity of the old traditions. It has also given rise, not least in the Møre region, to a modern furniture industry with an impressive record of exports. Norwegian textiles have also contributed to this development.

Metals from Norway

Norway is rich in metal ore, though in concentrations so low that mining can easily become unviable.

The tradition of metal-production, particularly of steel, began with the historic extraction of bog-iron. During the reign of the Danish King Christian IV, the monarch's tireless initiative lead to an influx of mining technology from Germany, resulting in the establishment of new mining communities around smelting works, variously engaged with copper and silver production. In this context, Kongsberg Silver Works (1624) and Røros Copper Works (1644) developed into important industrial centres.

Only a moderate amount of mining – of iron, copper and zinc occurs in Norway today. Since the deposits are so thinly spread, the industry is very sensitive to market fluctuations and many old mines and mining communities have been abandoned. Despite this, the export of iron ore, partly in the form of pellets, is still of some importance. Norwegian steel-making traditions grew from its simple origins to consist of a large number of traditional ironworks, based on Norwegian ore, often with their own foundries. Today, all steel production is based on scrap-iron and is centred on a mini steel-works in the town of Mo i Rana, in Northern Norway. The scrap is melted down in an electric oven and subsequently cast into iron billets, or rolled either into reinforcement rods for use in concrete-production, or sheet-iron sections.

Light Metals

Even though primary production of metal from ore is modest, the processing of mainly imported raw materials is more widespread. This industry, precipitated by the country's plentiful energy resources, is a mainstay of the Norwegian economy.

Aluminium production in Norway has a long history. Originally, the principal raw material was blue clay, which had a large aluminium content. Later, bauxite won favour internationally, and Norway fell into line. During the Second World War, the demand of the aero-industry for a tough, lightweight metal for use in aeroplane manufacture, led the German authorities to draw up plans for an enormous increase in Norwegian aluminium production. This development was set in motion in places like Årdal and Sunndalsøra, where conditions were favourable for the building of power-plant. The Germans were denied the chance to realise their plans, which were later, however, far outstripped by Norwegian initiatives.

Today, aluminium is produced through electrolysis, using imported aluminium oxide derived from the mineral bauxite, found in large quantities all over the world. An electrical current is run through a fusion plant containing mainly aluminium oxide, which divides the oxide from the aluminium. The three largest aluminium producing companies in Norway are Hydro Aluminium A/S, Elkem Aluminium A/S and Sør-Norge Aluminium A/S.

SAMFOTO/Trygve Bølstad

The power-consuming aluminium-extraction industry in Norway is sizeable, and Norway has a 20 %-share of the European market. Products as the one in the picture, made at Norsk Hydro's installation at Karmøy, are sold world-wide.

Semi-manufactured aluminium-electrolysis products, such as rolled-blocks, bolts, plates and wire, are Norwegian specialities. Although some degree of final processing does occur in Norway – for example, the manufacture of automobile parts – this is mostly carried out closer to the final market place, in rolling- and pressing plants. Norsk Hydro, in particular, owns a number of such plants abroad.

The production of each kilogram of aluminium requires 15 kilowatt-hours of energy, mainly for the electrolysis process, but also in the production of electrodes and in casting. Norway produces some 6 % of the world's aluminium, equal to 20 % of the total European output, the country's clean energy sources affording it considerable natural advantage.

Another light metal produced in Norway through electrolysis is magnesium. 20 % of the total world production of magnesium is produced in Norway, by Norsk Hydro A/S, who in addition operates a large subsidiary in Canada. Magnesium, like aluminium, is very much a metal of the future, owing to its lightness and strength. Demands for cuts in energy consumption promise increased use of light metals, especially in automobile manufacture.

Norway is a major global player, both relatively and absolutely, in one particular energy-intensive field, namely ferro-alloys (ferro-silicon, ferro-manganese and ferro-chromium) and silicon metals, all by-products of steel production and aluminium alloying. Norway controls an approximately 32 % share of the world market in the major product, ferro-silicon, and dominates the European market completely. Production occurs in large electric smelting ovens in a large number of smelting works spread throughout the country according to energy supply. Elkem A/S is the market leader, with smelting works abroad, and a research and development department which has made important contributions to the technology itself.

Norway in the Oil Age

The origins of Norway's oil industry are discussed in the next chapter. Since oil was first discovered, over 30 years ago, Norway has seen a revolution in all areas of oil and gas technology, be it in exploration, extraction, processing or marketing. These developments have been strongly influenced from outside but now the country stands firmly on its own legs, with three large national oil companies, various internationally successful engineering firms, and an industry based on traditional shipbuilding producing structures and modules for all purposes, from gigantic oil platforms to subsea installations manned by advanced robo-technology.

The process began with seismic exploration, originally by detonating explosives under water and registering the echoes from the rock strata with microphones and seismometers. The Norwegian oil industry has played an important role in the development of this technique, using air-cannon as a sound source and long strings of microphones (streamers), often several in depth, with subsequent electronic processing of the data. Constant advances are being made in the process of three-dimensional subterranean imaging, and it has already assisted greatly in the mapping process, as well as reduced uncertainties about the next phase of the work, namely exploratory drilling. As oil-speak still puts it, «Oil is where you find it».

Norway made an early contribution to exploratory drilling, in the form of so-called semisubmersibles, literally semisubmersible drilling platforms, and later developed drilling ships which could also be equipped for exploration and initial production. Drilling techniques themselves are the result of almost 100 years experience in the U.S.A, which came to the North Sea with the American and French oil companies. Nonetheless, Norway's contribution to exploratory drilling has been considerable, not least in the building and operation of a service fleet, allowing Norwegian seamanship to develop whole new areas of expertise.

SINTEF

The multiphase-transportation through pumps treating mixtures of oil, gas and sand, constitutes a relatively new technique. The research institute SINTEF, has developed new systems, some of them with the use of full-scale models.

Once oil or gas deposits are located, there follows painstaking logistical, financial and technical evaluation and planning before the actual development can begin. With investment levels of up to 30 billion kroner per platform, it pays to be certain! Various platform concepts are considered. There is a wealth of possible alternatives – concrete or steel base, a variety of floating structures – to choose from. The engineer's imagination is taxed to the utmost, in calculating the structures' strength and cost. The deck of the rig alone can weigh up to 50,000 tons, housing a hotel for up to 300 people, in addition to the drilling unit and a chemical factory for separating sand and water from the oil. If, in the first phase of production, any gas found is NOT pumped back into the ground, it must immediately be directed away from the platform via a pipeline. Oil can either be taken away by pipeline or temporarily stored in tanks – which might form part of the concrete platform-base in order later to be transferred to a cargo ship (flexiloading). The running of an oil production platform can be compared to that of a large and complicated processing-plant, with extreme demands being made, not least, to matters of security. Materials and procedures must be capable of coping with «the hundred-year wave», that is the most unthinkable situation. An important element of oil and gas production is the transportation infrastructure which has been developed, including oil and gas pipelines to Great Britain, Germany and Belgium, and a fleet of oil-tankers together with flexiloading facilities at sea. The established system of pipelines, which crosses among other obstacles the 300-metre-deep Norwegian Trench, is a major technical feat in itself. Bringing oil ashore over highly exposed beach zones presents a particularly difficult problem.

New Challenges

The extraction technique briefly described above, does not represent the culmination of development in the field. New concepts are being developed continually. Three particularly important areas under research are: the use of underwater installations in developing new oil fields; phased transportation systems for oil, gas and water; and horizontal drilling. Underwater installations will normally be built on a frame, or template, which is then anchored to the sea bed. The guides for the drilling equipment will be mounted on this frame, with room for ventilators and controls. Oil and gas are removed via attached pipelines. The placing, start-up and control of such an installation by remote robo-technique, at depths of anything up to 300 metres, is a challenge of staggering proportions. Developments of diving technology continues in parallel with those of robo-technology, with pressurised diving now possible down to a full 300 metres. A number of these underwater installations can be attached to a single platform, which will reduce the costs of expansion by minimising the number of platforms necessary in any given area. An extensive use of phased transportation, with pumps able to handle a mixture of oil, sand and water, will further advance the concept of underwater installations. The mixture can either be stored on a smaller platform, prior to tranfer to oil terminals on land where separation can take place, or be transferred directly to the terminals from the underwater installations.

Phased transportation is a relatively new development, to which Norway has made a considerable contribution, not least through the provision of a large full-scale simulator at the SINTEF research institution, in Trondheim.

Horizontal drilling is also a relatively new technology. Tangental drilling from vertical bore-holes has long been practiced. Use of this method means that a single platform can cover a large subterranean area. Now, a technique of horizontal drilling has been developed, affording great accuracy. The cutter-head must be positioned and operated with great care and the bore-hole secured against collapse. Horizontal drilling will facilitate, for example, exploitation of the narrow, but extensive layer of oil present in the enormous Troll Gas Field. This layer of oil is only a few metres deep, and impossible to extract economically with vertical drilling techniques.

Maritime extraction technology is by no means at the end of the road, and Norwegian teaching institutions, engineering firms, and not least the oil industry itself, are all dynamically engaged in the challenges it presents. In general, maritime technology is a rapidly expanding field.

For as long as there has been a coastal population, the abundance of fish has been exploited. The catches with primitive tools were not great, but sufficed to uphold a minimum standard of living.

Many of the biggest trawlers process the fish on board. The Alaska Ocean is among the biggest factory trawlers made, constructed at the Ulstein/Hatlø shipyard in Sunnmøre. The trawler fishes off the Alaskan shores.

ULSTEIN/Per Eide

KNUDSENS FOTOSENTER

Today, the methods of fishing are altogether different, the most efficient tool probably being the trawler. The huge trawlers sweep the sea bed, and catches are sometimes enormous. Some are expressing concern, however; greed may result in an empty ocean.

HUSMO-FOTO

HUSMO-FOTO

Drying of fish is a centuries-old practice. Dried cod, and other types of dried fish, have for the most been for export, but have also been a supplement to the Norwegian diet.

SAMFOTO/Pål Hermansen

The coastline of Norway is at its most hostile during the winter months. At an early stage in history the system of lighthouses was developed, and smaller and larger lighthouses became abundant along the coastal waters. Despite modern equipment, coastal traffic and fishermen depend on the blinking lights, as seen here provided from the lighthouse at Lyngør.

HUSMO-FOTO

Norwegian salmon is sold throughout the world, and much is flown out to the foreign markets. SAS carries 1000s of tons of fresh salmon to fish markets around the world.

The salmon has been seen as the aristocrat of fish, rare and expensive to most people. Then fish-farms were set up and frozen salmon became abundant in supermarkets. Above all, it has become a major export product.

The fishing of salmon was for the longest time an exclusive domain for the wealthy, who bought the fishing rights to many rivers. Today, the fish in fish farms are as large and tasty as the river-salmon.

OLA RØE

HUSMO-FOTO

OLA RØE

Fish farms have been set up all along the coastline. In many places the breeding of salmon has become an important supplementary source of income to many fishermen and farmers. The larger fish farms are often operated by private companies or cooperatives which also process the meat by smoking or marinating the fish. The salmon is then sent to the market in appealing packaging. Fish farming is risky business, with bad weather, algae-attacks and diseases being important risk-factors.

The most outstanding contribution to architecture is the stave church, built 600–800 years ago. The constructions remain impressive to this day and age, as do their durability. Some of the churches are still well preserved, more than 800 years after they were constructed. Right: Borgund Stave Church.

KNUDSENS FOTOSENTER

Naturally, the construction of bridges has long traditions in Norway, with its spread population, and fjords and rivers in abundance. Many of the old wooden bridges, constructed by practical men and primitive tools, are still in use. Modern traffic demands more solid constructions. Norwegian engineers have done pioneering work when it comes to the construction of bridges. Concrete construction are sometimes beautiful, as seen in Måløy.

STATENS VEGVESEN

HUSMO-FOTO

HUSMO-FOTO

HUSMO-FOTO

Norwegian church architecture still attracts the interest of many. Since the last war, churches throughout the country have earned international acclaim, such as the «Ishavskatedralen» («ice-sea cathedral») in Tromsø, drawn by the architect Inge Hovig.

Fires have through the centuries made ashes of many cultural heritage sites. Buildings were mostly made of wood and once they caught fire, little could be done to save them or their contents. Some buildings survived, and not only stave churches, but old farmhouses. On these sites, the finest carvings are to be seen, as on these portals in Åmotsdal. The durability of the wood is one of the most remarkable features of these cultural remains of the past.

The modern drilling machines are powerful and technologically advanced. «They eat rock,» comments one of the workers at Jostedal-skraft.

SCAN-FOTO/Morten Uglum

The construction of tunnels has been an act of necessity in a country like Norway, and Norwegian engineers have done pioneering work in several fields. The construction of huge tunnels were needed in the process of creating hydraulic power, in order to bring the water from the basins to the power stations.

Right: The huge tunnels built in connection with the Ulla Førre development were one of the largest undertakings in Norwegian power development.
Below: The modern power plant is built inside the mountain. Water drives the enormous turbines which produce the electricity.

SAMFOTO/Tore Wuttudal

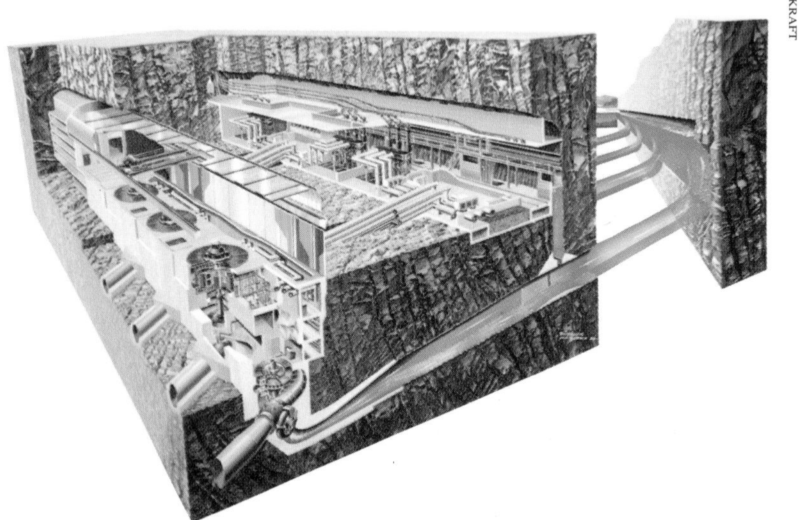

STATKRAFT

HUSMO-FOTO

As impressive as the power stations and tunnels, are the great dams which are needed to hold back the huge masses of water. Picture: The Sakarias dam in Tafjord was built in such a way as not to impare its beautiful surroundings in the Sunnmøre region.

HYDRO

The availability of cheap energy is what has made Norwegian aluminium production possible. The production process is particularly powerconsuming. Traditionally the raw-materials would be shipped off for processing abroad. Today, however, aluminium production is well established both at home and at Norwegian-owned plants abroad. Left: Norsk Hydro's installation at Karmøy.

Various fields of high technology have been developed in Norway. The development of maritime power cables is one area of technology in which Norway and Alcatel STK excel. The breakthrough came with the development and installation of power cables along the Skagerak sea bed, making the transfer of electricity from Norway to Denmark possible. The company also installed the world's longest maritime power cable, across the Gulf of Bothnia.

SIMRAD

The Simrad company has developed a multiple beam echo-sounder which covers larger areas. It interprets approximately 30 individual beams hitting the vessel. Maps are made with extraordinary speed and exactitude.

OCEANOR

Oceanor surveys the ocean via satellites. Buoys planted in the ocean measure things like currents, wave activity, and temperatures. The measurements and observations are transmitted to a terminal on shore which compile and process the information of importance for e.g. shipping and oil industry.

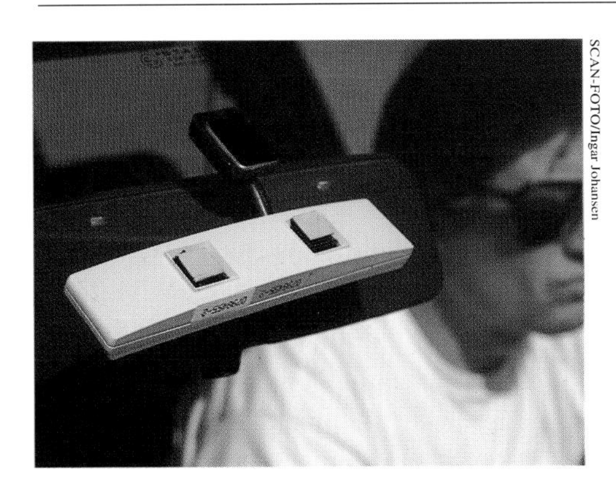

SCAN-FOTO/Ingar Johansen

Road tolls are becoming widespread. The development of a system of toll payment system that should not hinder the flow of traffic, was the challenge facing the little electronics company, Micro Design, in Selbu. It came up with «Kø-fri», or «Queue-free», a system by which all vehicles carrying a small electronic reflector can be identified, even at high speeds. The reflectors contain a PIN, which is transmitted to a computer terminal. If driving without a reflector, a videocamera photographs the car registration number. «Queue-free» is being used in several areas in Norway, and is currently being marketed internationally.

HUSMO-FOTO

SCAN-FOTO/Ingar Johansen

MIRIS

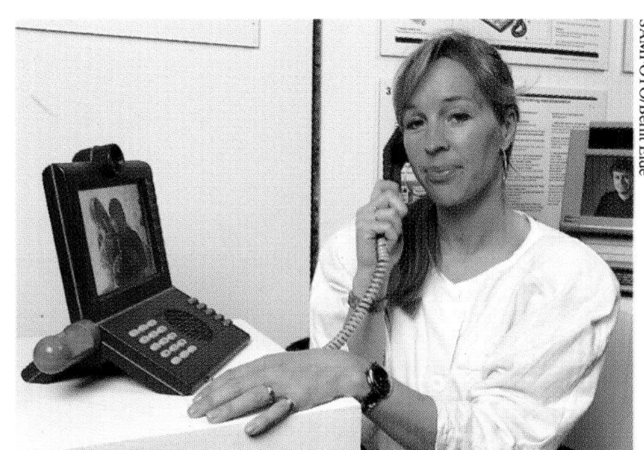

SAMFOTO/Bernt Eide

The telecommunications industry has been at the forefront of systems-development. The development of the video telephone (picture above) is one area of research in which Norway has an edge over others. The company, Miris, has developed a simple system of identification. A thin wristband keeps constant track of the wearer's identity on the computer screen, a plus for security-conscious workplaces like oil platforms.

The examining of the heart and blood circulation through ultrasound is (right) important in evaluating cardiac and vascular activities, without surgical intervention. Vingmed Sound has further developed this system and supplies vital equipment for cardiac examinations. Today, it is a much used product in hospitals and with specialists. 95 % of their production is sold to foreign markets.

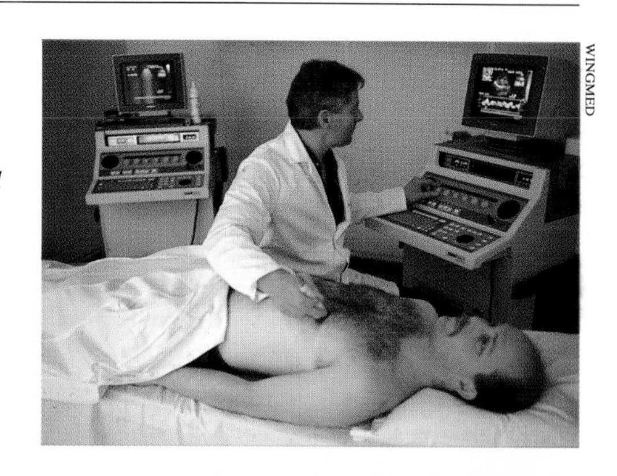

WINGMED

Professor John Ugelstad at the university in Trondheim, developed, in cooperation with the research institute, SINTEF, tiny plastic beads of exactly the same size. Using his method, the pellets can be made solid or porous, radioactive, and magnetic. They are of use particularly in medicine, where they can help remove unwanted cells in the blood system. For more than 30 years scientists throughout the world worked towards the development of these particles.

SAMFOTO/Svein Erik Dahl

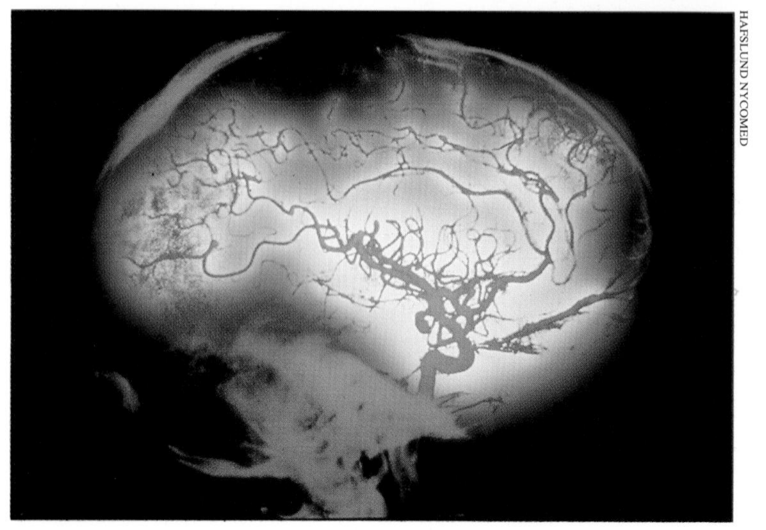

HAFSLUND NYCOMED

The pharmaceutical branch of Hafslund Nycomed has done pioneering work in the development of radiographical techniques. Isopaque, Amipaque, and Omnipaque are essential products in X-raying, and are sold throughout the world.

Advanced Technology

The term 'advanced technology' is problematic. All periods of history have boasted technological and artistic developements which seemed advanced, in their own time. For example, the pre-historic sword found at Svartemo, in Hægesbostad, a magnificent object with a gold-plated handle, representing craftsmanship of the highest calibre. Similarly, the Oseberg wagon represents masterly technology, craftmanship and artistry from the beginning of the 9th century.

Within that which we may term «current traditional activities», we find the most outstanding examples of technological achievement. It might be some detail of aluminium or magnesium electrolysis. Or the use of the unit system in designing complicated concrete marine structures. Or the design and construction of refrigerated tanks for transporting cooled gas, which need to withstand the most extreme thermal conditions. Or, a programmable knitting machine for making traditional Norwegian sweaters! Whilst we allow ourselves to be impressed by the latest technological advances, the traditional areas are often undervalued.

Norway is engaged also in advanced technology in the conventional sense of the term. But with a population of just over 4 million, it goes without saying that Norway imports up to 99 % of its new information and technology. In this context, Norway has benefitted from the tradition of openness and exchange, created not least by countries with seafaring backgrounds.

The country's four universities and large number of colleges of various calibre, play a central role in the import of new information as well as the creation new technology thinking. The students at these institutions number some 112,000, which means that at any one time over two school-generations are involved in higher education. In addition to the colleges and universities a number of special institutes have been established, especially in the technological sector, for the convenience of both the authorities and the business community. The authorities otherwise contribute a comprehensive support system for technological development, with the Royal Norwegian Council for Scientific and Industrial Research (NTNF) and its cooperative institutes, at the centre. The institutes of Defence and Telecommunications Research (respectively the FFI and TF) have also made considerable contributions to Norwegian technology with audacious development projects leading to the establishment of a number of advanced technology companies. A total of 1.8 % of Norwegian gross national product is reinvested in research and development, with approximately half of this figure provided from government sources.

KVÆRNELAND

A simple, and yet advanced product, is produced by Kverneland Klepp in Jæren. Picture: A reversible plough with an automatic rock extraction mechanism.

No 'Locomotive' Product

Norway manufactures a wide variety of advanced technological products. Lacking what might be called a single 'locomotive' product, as found in other countries, Norwegian products have become niche-products within mechanics, chemicals, medicine or electronics, often in various combinations. Normally, the developments occur within the relevant industry, with participation from academia and the institutes. The Norwegian shipping industry has developed a highly innovative research mileau.

Below, are brief examples of these advanced-technological niche-products, though the list is by no means exhaustive.

Ploughs for the World

From the machine-industry firm Kverneland Klepp A/S comes the reversible plough with automatic stone extractor, an apparently simple, but nonetheless advanced product. The plough is light and strong. The automatic stone extractor has made it a popular product worldwide, with more than 12,000 units produced annually.

The Magical Dr. Dahl

No Norwegian has been responsible for more advanced technology products, principally machine products, than the legendary Dr. Odd Dahl. First, his participation as a pilot in Roald Amundsen's 1922–25 expedition, and the later repeated demonstrations of his extraordinarily constructive talent, have turned Dr. Dahl into, literally, a fairy-tale figure. His inventions stretch from the first high-voltage energy installation to rockets and launching ramps at the Norwegian rocket site at Andøya. Between these two extremities, he was the principal designer for two Norwegian atomic reactors and, for a while, the chief designer at the International Atomic Research Centre (CERN), in Switzerland.

The wizard Odd Dahl, is a Mythical figure in Norwegian science. He has developed advanced medical equipment, rockets, and launching pads, and was chief designer of two Norwegian nuclear reactors.

Medical Electronics

The use of electronics for medical purposes is a highly important area for Norwegian niche-products. Ultrasound examination represents a simple and effective method of evaluation of the functions of the heart and circulatory system which avoids the need for surgery. The ultrasound probe both sends and receives acoustic signals from the internal organs, creating an acoustic image of the heart's functioning during blood circulation. With the development of the CFM-750, VINGMED Sound A/S has increased the value of ultrasound image-diagnosis by combining image-formation with measurement of the blood-flow parameters. The CFM-750 provides a complete flow image in which details of heart contraction and blood circulation are presented in accurate measurements. CFM-750 is utilised both in hospitals and by specialists. VINGMED Sound has achieved a considerable international market, with a 95 % export rate.

Oceanographic Monitoring

The company OCEANOR (Oceanographic Company of Norway) has developed an oceanographic monitor known as SEAWATCH. Sensors on a number of bouys measure meteorological parameters such as flow, waves, aquatic temperature, etc. This information is continually sent, via satellite, to a terminal on land, where it is processed and placed at the disposal of the public authorities, fishing industry, tourist industry, etc. The oceanographic bouys contain, among other things, sensors developed by the pioneering company Aanderaa Instruments A/S.

Instruments for subsea mapping are another Norwegian speciality. Traditionally, mapping of the sea bed is carried out by a vessel, equipped with an echo sounder, passing over a particular area, with the depth being recorded along the vessel's course. A map is then drawn on the basis of this information. The Norwegian company Simrad A/S, has 40 years of experience in subsea acoustics. The firm has developed a multi-ray echo sounder (the EM 100), which makes it possible for a vessel to reconnoitre a wide area by allowing it to receive echoes from up to 30 sounders ranged on either side of it. Appropriately processed, this information facilitates the making of highly accurate, detailed maps of the sea bed. With extra equipment, the range of the reconnaissance can be increased from 2 to 8 times the depth.

Across Sea and Fjord

In the specialist area of underwater energy-transfer cables, Norway has set numerous world records, through the activities of Alcatel STK A/S. The breakthrough came with the laying of a 250 kilowatt DC cable across the Skagerak. The first of these was laid in 1976, connecting the power supplies of Norway and Denmark. Since the supplies of these two countries are so dissimilar, a connection between them is extremely advantageous. Subsequent to this first pioneering project, a series of other world records have been set, including in the 1980s the development and laying of a number of 525 kilowatt AC cables, with a capacity of 2400 megavolts, out to Vancouver Island, in Canada, and in 1989 the laying of the world's longest underwater energy cable over the Gulf of Bothnia. A cable connecting New Zealand's North and South Islands is now in preparation.

Avoiding the Queues

Recent years have seen an increase in the operation of toll bridges, tunnels, motorways and ring roads. One of the major challenges has been to develop a simple payment-system which avoids obstruction of traffic flow. The firm Micro Design A/S, in Selbu, has developed a flexible system, dubbed 'Queue-free', which identifies an individual moving car equipped with a simple passive reflector. Essentially, the system consists of a passive electronic chip which is attached to the front windscreen of the car. This chip contains an identification number. This chip is illuminated by the light from an antenna suspended above the road; the identification number is recorded by a computer system which notes all passing traffic, and can process the information for any purpose. Any vehicle passing without a valid chip has its registration number photographed by a roadside camera.

'Queue-free' is a unique solution to a difficult problem and the system is now being marketed internationally, after its success at a number of sites in Norway.

From Tape recorders to Computer Technology

In 1952, the technical mileau in Norway was particularly moribund. Yet, in that year Tandberg Radio Factory unveiled its remarkable high-quality, medium price-range tape recorder. This was then further developed, through a series of new models up until 1978, and captured a large market, particularly in the USA. Today, Tandberg Data A/S occupies a position at the cutting-edge of mass-produced precision mechanics and magnetic-head technology, specialising in data storage systems. The company's latest product is a 26 track, 6mm band, with a capacity of 525 Megabytes, giving a storage density of approximately 650 bits per. millimeter. To date, in excess of 500,000 units have been produced, principally for the export market.

In recent years there has also been considerable growth within those branches of Norwegian industry seeking a market for pharmaceutical products and medical aids, generally.

The Famous Pellets

Since 1950, chemists the world over have been trying to produce monodispersed particles – in other words, minute plastic pellets of exact mutual dimension. Though this was achieved in the weightless conditions of a satellite, the achievement had no practical application. Then, ten years ago, Professor John Ugelstad and his colleagues at the University of Trondheim and SINTEF – the largest research institution in Scandinavia – managed to develop a method for the production of compact or porous pellets capable of being rendered either radioactive or magnetic.

Amazing at it might seem to the layman, these pellets, or granules, have any number of applications, principally in the field of medicine. Being all of precisely the same size, their behaviour is utterly predictable; for example, in their affinity for diseased blood cells needing treatment or eradication. In this context, magnetised pellets are allowed to attach themselves to the cells in question, which can then be extracted with a magnet, along with the pellets. The company Dyndal A/S now markets these monodispersed pellets for diagnostic or therapeutic use throughout the world.

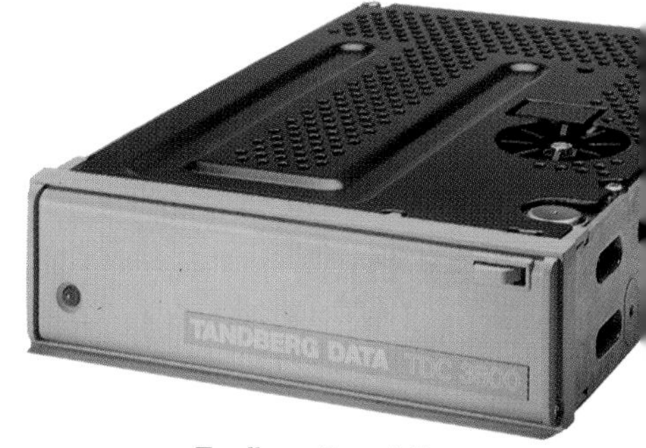

Tandberg Data A/S produces unique computer storage components. Their models have superior storage saturation levels and more than half a million units have been produced of their latest model.

Leaders in Health and Nutrition

Apothekernes Laboratorium A/S was established in Oslo in 1903 for the production of domestic medicines, but has since expanded into advanced-technology products such as antibiotics based on advanced microbiological processing (fermentation). One of the company's most important brand products is Bacitracin, the main application of which is as a supplement in animal feed. Over 99 % of this product is produced for export, and in addition the company has established a large production plant in the USA. Apothekernes Laboratorium A/S is the largest producer of this particular antibiotic in the world. In addition, the company has adapted its fermentation processes for the development and production of fish vaccines, consequently becoming the largest supplier of vaccines for the fish farming industry. The company also holds a 50 % stake in the aforementioned Dyndal A.S.

From Energy to Contrast Fluids

The Hafslund Nycomed concern is essentially, extensive internal restructuring notwithstanding, an amalgamation of the former Nyegaard & Co., a well-known pharmaceutical firm, and the energy and metallurgy company, Hafslund A/S. In the Norwegian context, Hafslund Nycomed is a large concern, with around 3,000 employees, an advanced-technology pharmaceutical company deriving stability from its participation in the energy industry. The concern is active within the area of image-formation techniques, therapeutic aids and pharmaceuticals generally. One of its core products is the x-ray contrast fluid Isopaque and its derivatives Amipaque and Omnipaque. Dr. Hugo Holtermann played a central pioneering role in the development of contrast fluids.

Technology for the Environment

Over the past decade, industry has become increasingly more conscious of its relationship to both the interior and exterior environment. Not least, the demands made upon the aluminium industry, relating to the discharge of flouride and corrosive materials, have been considerably tightened. The company A/S Norsk Viftefabrikk, a division of the multi-national Flakt group, specialise in filtration systems for the aluminium industry which recycle flouride, and have achieved international success with the delivery of 90 systems to 15 different countries. These systems are capable of cleaning and recycling waste gases from about 40 % of all the plant in the world. A purification and recycle rate of 99.8 % of flouride is not unusual. The systems recycles over 100,000 tons of flouride every year, which would otherwise be released into the atmosphere to the detriment of plant and animal life.

Last, But Not Least . . .

In 1972, engineer Tore Planke's popular invention was first introduced, thus solving one of the endemic problems of shopkeeping, the world over. The sorting of returned deposit bottles and cans, and the calculation of total amounts repayable to the customer, is by definition both time and space intensive. The answer to the problem lay in an electronically operated machine fitted with a photo-cell and counter device. Tomra Systems A/S, of Asker, discovered the solution in advanced image-identification, and a Norwegian family effort became an international success.

Towards the Future

In Norway today, approximately 1.9 million people, of a total population of just over 4 million, are in regular employment. Industry accounts for 333,000 of these (1988 figures), dealt into the following headings:

Oil extraction	20,000
Food products	54,000
Textiles, clothing	12,000
Timber products	28,000
Wood processing, graphics, publishing	48,000
Chemical products	25,000
Mineral products	11,000
Metals	22,000
Engineering industries	110,000
Miscellaneous	3,000

Industrial employment levels have been in decline in recent years, due to increased surplus purchasing power related to the oil activities, which has in turn increased employment levels in the service sector.

Relative to its Gross National Product, Norway's levels of both import and export are high. Roughly speaking, 50 % of all products are exported, and 50 % of all consumer items are imported. The Norwegian economy is closely integrated with that of the rest of the world, especially Europe.

The principal export articles are, in %, (1989 figures):

Mineral oils	37.7
Aluminium	7.7
Natural gas	7.6
Fish	4.7
Cardboard and paper	3.5
Ships	3.0
Nickel	2.6
Pig iron, specular iron	2.4

The principal import articles are, in % (1989 figures):

Ships and boats	15.8
Clothing	4.3
Computerware	3.8
Instruments	2.5
Paper and paper products	2.4
Telecommunication equipment	2.2
Plastics, raw materials and semi-manufactured articles	2.2
Cars	1.8
Furniture	1.7

A glance at this table reveals that the Norwegian economy is still dominated by primary products, and that the oil dependency is high. This picture, however, is balanced by the importance of Norwegian exports in shipping services.

The great challenge facing the Norwegian economy, is to reduce oil dependency, increase exports and make the home market of processed goods and services more competitive, particularly in relation to high technology. In this regard, the shipping sector is an example to follow. Progress is also to be found in recent developments in the energy consuming industries, as well as in the creation of high technology niches in many new areas. The competitiveness of Norwegian goods and services has increased greatly over the recent years, and there's currently a high level of activity in our market places. The wage settlements of the recent years have contributed towards only a modest inflation and better competing conditions. But the Norwegian economy depends on a positive global economic development.

The avarage level of prosperity in Norway is high, creating a challenging situation. It demands a high level of performance from every individual in society. In an ever-altering world, this requires great flexibility and readiness to make extra efforts, if needed. Industrial history tells of many daring enterprises. *That* is still the challenge.

When Norway Became an Oil Nation

Leif T. Løddesøl:

SCAN-FOTO/Per Svensson

Leif T. Løddestøl (b. 1935) is the director of the Wilh. Wilhelmsen-group, a shipping company with interests also in offshore activities. He is a trained lawyer and, working for the Foreign Office, he took part in the making of Norwegian petroleum legislation as well as in the negotiations on the partitioning of the North Sea. He has been the head of the legal branch of the Norwegian Shipowners' Association and later became the executive director of Den norske Creditbank (Den norske Bank).

The so-called oil adventure arrived unexpectedly, but once they were shown to exist, Norway secured control of resources on the Continental Shelf with a comprehensive body of legislation. Initially, there was bitter protest from the foreign oil companies, but finally they were obliged to accept the strict Norwegian licensing regulations. Norwegian companies developed advanced technology for offshore oil production and our expertise is now employed in many countries throughout the world.

The flaring of oil and gas sends billows of fire and smoke out over the North Sea from the Nordtrym oil rig. It's a fascinating, but also potentially dangerous sight requiring strict adherance to safety measures.
Right: Drilling for oil requires sturdy drilling heads.

PHILIPS PETROLEUM

HUSMO-FOTO

The North Sea is not always a hospitable place. During the autumn and winter storms, the wind howls around the rigs and giant waves sweep across the decks. The many supply ships are designed to cope with harsh weather conditions, nevertheless, manouvring in an agitated ocean is often a demanding task. Right: Norman Skipper on her way back from the Ekofisk field.

HUSMO-FOTO

HUSMO-FOTO

Fishermen feared offshore oil activities would devastate catches. They soon discovered that fishing was even better in the vicinity of the rigs.

The drilling equipment looks simplistic enough, but in fact they are exponents of the most advanced equipment in drilling technology. Below: Haugesund has been a part of the oil adventure since the very beginning. Numerous rigs have been brought in for overhauling at Haugesund Mek. Verksted.

STATOIL

HUSMO-FOTO

HUSMO-FOTO

STATOIL

Every man and women have their specific tasks on the oil platforms. Controls are continually carried out according to checklists, precision being of vital importance during the drilling process. Despite the huge proportions of the equipment, precision is a prerequisite.

The building of the International Court of Justice in the Hague, Netherlands.

SCAN-FOTO/Billedsentralen

In 1965 it became evident Norway would extract oil from the North Sea. The Minister of Industry, Karl Trasti (right), and the state secretary at the Foreign Office, Jens Evensen, are briefing an audience and pointing out how the sea had been divided into blocks. Years before this, Norway secured its exclusive rights on the Continental Shelf and adopted legislation and regulations accordingly.

NTB

The Negotiations on the partitioning lines were complicated, and a few of the conflicting issues were decided by the International Court of Justice. Jens Evensen was later appointed judge to the court.

SCAN-FOTO/Billedsentralen

When, in the 1960s, the possibility of oil on the Continental Shelf first arose, a would-be expert on the subjet was heard to say, «If we find oil in Norway, I'll happily drink it». For decades, Norwegians had transported, refined, blended and exploited this valuable commodity, but the idea that we should find our own source of oil on Norwegian territory was considered so outlandish that if we did, we would indeed be happy to drink it.

Such was the general attitude. However, in the 1950s, when the large gas deposits were discovered on the outskirts of Groningen in the Netherlands, and significant quantities of petroleum products were found in what were relatively recent geological formations, certain people in certain circles began to speculate on the possible presence of similar circumstances in the North Sea. A cautious search was begun.

Those responsible for this developement were primarily the oil companies, who unleashed their geological bloodhounds, in the face of passivity and ignorance from the authorities. The legal position was unclear. Whilst it was true that oil exploration on the Continental Shelf had been under way since World War Two, and the rights to the American shelf had been proclaimed by the U.S.A in the Truman Doctrine of 28th September 1945, in the early 1950s, there still existed no general legal framework. In fact, the entire legal position with regards to the offshore areas and the ocean bed was singularly ill-defined. Countries argued hotly about fishing rights and rights to free passage in international waters, but very few were concerned about the Continental Shelf.

The legal position was so unclear, and the potential for conflict so real, that an International Conference on 'The Right to the Ocean' was convened in Geneva, in 1958. Here, a great number of conventions were passed, controlling rights to the exploitation of resources both in the waters of the sea and in the sea bed off the coasts of individual countries. This was not before time. A number of legal cases had already arisen, amongst others a dispute over fishing zones between Great Britain and Norway, brought before the International Court of Justice in the Haag. For Norway, as a fishing and shipping nation, the question of fishing rights and the rights to free passage stood at the very top of the agenda. But, when it came to oil, Norwegian geologists had little belief in the presence of oil off the Norwegian coastline.

STATOIL

STATOIL

The first oil, mud and rock samples to be extracted, were well guarded. The miniature bottles were in great demand by souvenir hunters.

Annexation

Then, the unexpected happened. International oil companies approached the Norwegian authorities requesting clarification as to who owned the rights and who could grant permission for the start of oil exploration on the Norwegian Shelf. Whilst no one knew precisely the answer to this question, the Foreign Office felt a twinge of responsibility; anything to do with oil companies must surely fall under the general heading 'international' – not least when they were operating within areas where Norwegian rights were unclear, and clashed with those of other nations. If this was not Foreign Affairs then nothing was. The Foreign Office applied at once to the problem.

In doing so, it took the unprecedented action of formulating a new Norwegian law. True, it was only a short law, a few paragraphs merely, but it was followed up by a Royal Declaration stating Norway's sovereignty of the Continental Shelf off the country's coast. The law was based on the middle-line principle, ie, that the North Sea should be divided along a line, mid-way between the relevant states.

The Foreign Office was elated. Norwegians had not experienced such annexation since the viking era. Of course, the focus was not so much on the possible discovery of oil or gas as on the securing of as broad a range of rights as possible. It could not do us any harm.

This, however, marked the start of the real 'oil adventure'. The Oil Law was passed in 1963, when the explorations off the coasts of Britain were already well under way. The area off the Norwegian coast constituted a territory many times the size of the country itself, and its economic potential quickly stirred us into action. Suddenly, it was a question of getting going as quickly as possible.

Regulations

The Royal Declaration of 31st May, 1963, proclaimed Norway's jurisdiction over the Continental Shelf. This revolution was followed up on 21st June, 1963, by the law governing the exploration for, and exploitation of, subterranean resources. This law emphasised that these resources belonged to the Norwegian State, and the right of the King to grant access to their exploration, and eventual exploitation, to either Norwegian or foreign companies or individuals.

The law governing the Continental Shelf was a new phenomenon within international law. It was perfectly acceptable that those parts of the shelf which lay within a country's territorial waters should belong to the state in question, but the question was, what laws should apply to the sea bed beyond the territorial limits? These ocean areas are, after all, open waters, that's to say, open for all and sundry. But it does not necessarily follow that the same legal framework applies to the actual bed of the ocean. Eventually, the notion that the ocean bed should belong to the nearest state whose coasts it adjoined, won through.

It was particularly President Truman's aformentioned Declaration of 28th September 1945, which established the guidelines for the attitudes of the various implicated states to the Continental Shelf question. This Declaration proclaimed that the natural resources contained in the Continental Shelf off the coast of the U.S.A belonged to the United States and came under American jurisdiction and control. It further stated that the Declaration only applied to the actual shelf, ie. the sea bed and subsurface, and that the waters above the shelf would continue to function as international waters.

A succession of states had subsequently followed the American example and passed similar proclamations, and the discussion on the Continental Shelf areas at the 1958 Conference on International Waters in Geneva, ended in the convention's decision that «the coastal nations shall exercise sovereign rights over the Continental Shelf areas with regard to the exploration for, and exploitation of, the said areas' natural resources.»

It continues, «the coastal states' rights over the continental shelf areas does not alter the status of the overlying waters as international waters, nor to the air space above these waters.»

The Convention came into effect during the summer of 1964, and, today, the claim of the coastal states viz a viz the continental shelf areas – ie. sea bed and subsurface – is legally binding, also in the eyes of international law.

Norwegian state jurisdiction extends «as far as the depth of water allows the exploitation of natural resources, notwithstanding other prevailing coastal limits, nor extending beyond the middle-line in relation to other states». Nowhere is the North Sea too deep to «allow the exploitation of natural resources», so in accordance with the Norwegian Proclamation, Norwegian sovereignty extends all the way to «the middle-line in relation to other states».

So what does this Norwegian sovereignty actually include? The practical application of these principles had to be clarified in negotiations with neighbouring states. Agreement with Great Britain was reached and ratified in 1965.

The parallel negotiations with Denmark were difficult. The question of a limit with Sweden was later solved, whilst discussions with the Soviet Union about demarcation in the Barents Sea – although the parties have moved closer in recent years – have still to produce any agreement.

The negotiations were frequently dramatic. The nature of Norway's coastal line meant that Norway gained control of huge areas. Had significant oil deposits been discovered before the demarcation negotiations were completed, they would almost certainly not have led to such a favourable result for Norway.

Other demarcation disputes ended up at the International Court of Justice in the Haag, which chose to build on slightly different principles, but by then Norway's rights had already been established in law.

The negotiations had resulted in a considerably expanded area of sovereignty for Norway. A small nation had gained greater reponsibility and, by the same token, greater potential. The question remained, how would we cope with this in the future?

The Licensing System

The laws contained in the Royal Resolution of 9th April 1965, regulated the parameters and progress of exploration and extraction. The regulations operate with two different types of license, an Exploration License and an Extraction License.

An Exploration License allows the licensee to undertake closely specified exploration of large areas. The License does not give the licensee exclusive rights or priority to exploration or exploitation of any deposits which might be discovered, nor is drilling allowed during this phase.

An Extraction License gives the licensee the right to undertake further explorations leading to eventual extraction. At this stage, the licensee is granted exclusive extraction rights, and others must keep away. In return for this, however, the licensee is placed under a variety of obligations, the aim of which is to ensure that thorough exploration is undertaken, and to make it impossible for speculators to operate. One of these obligations is the fulfilling of a programme of work. In addition, a system of taxes and excises, and propriet prerogative further inhibits speculation.

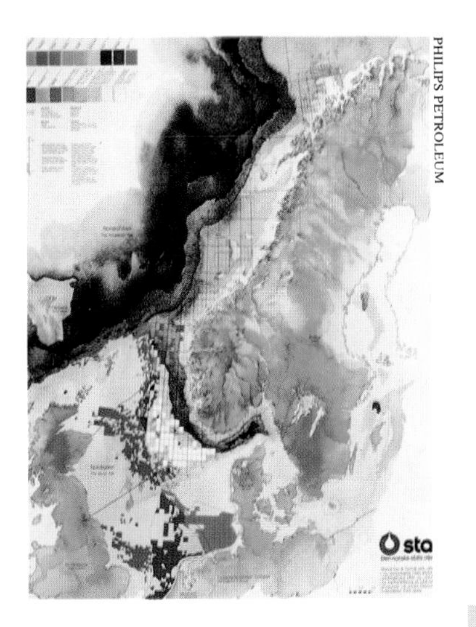

PHILIPS PETROLEUM

Innumerable charts have been made over the years, showing the resources in the North Sea.

The whole licensing system is constructed with the aim of attracting serious operators, and discouraging speculators. It is highly important that the licensees be properly qualified to fulfill the complicated tasks ahead of them. The danger of pollution was one of the first considerations confronted; it was vital that the oil industry did not advance at the expense of traditional industries, such as fishing. Norway wished to retain proprietary control of the new industry.

The oil companies were not particularly impressed by this package. Could they really be expected to accept so much in the way of obligations and control? In reality, the answer to this could only be given when the Norwegian authorities saw how many applications it received for Extraction Licenses.

Throughout the process, the authorities had consulted the oil companies. There had been a continual dialogue about what rules and regulations were necessary and appropriate. This procedure lay entirely beyond the scope of previous Norwegian administrative practice, but the authorities inexperience of such negotiations were matched by their determination to keep control of the industry. It was made abundently clear to the oil companies from the word go; if they didn't like the conditions being laid down, they would just have to go elsewhere.

The oil companies, on the other hand, were concerned both with political stability and the fact that any eventual oil fields needed to be in close proximity to potential consumer areas. They also found the new data coming from the North Sea Basin extremely enticing, and decided to pursue a policy of flexibility and cooperativeness. How deep their interest really lay could not be properly established until after the first round of negotiations. In the event, the answer was clear enough. The oil companies could live with the licensing conditions; the licenses were issued – and the Norwegian oil-adventure was seriously under way.

What is Petroleum?

For Norwegians, the word 'petroleum' is a rather strange word. In the text of the law, it is used to describe all petroleum products, first and foremost oil and gas, which are by-products from the process of decomposition of organic materials trapped in sedimentary rocks.

Oil exploration began at the turn of the century with surface drilling in areas where geologists and other experts could reasonably indicate the possible presence of significant deposits. Luck was an important resource for these early pioneers. Their knowledge of geology was limited and the techniques of extraction primitive. Even if they struck oil, it might be pressurised, and difficult to control. The business was both risky and expensive and usually offered more in the way of disappointment than joy. On the other hand, a real 'strike' could bring enormous rewards, which made the oil industry as attractive to gamblers as to businessmen.

A good deal of oil and gas has been found in benign conditions, mostly in the U.S.A. But, as a rule, large oil deposits tend to be found in less hospitable corners of the globe, where climatic conditions are difficult and transportation problematic. The desert areas of the Middle East, the Sahara and Libya are interesting examples of this tendency.

In seismic searches for oil, sound waves are bounced off the rock to reflect the transition from one layer of rock to another. The signals provide information about the shape and size of the strata.

Given that 70 % of the Earth's surface is covered with water, it follows that restricting drilling activity to dry land, reduces the chances of oil discovery correspondingly. It was therefore only natural that the oil companies should gradually begin to direct their search for new sources of oil towards the sea. New techniques were perfected in the Gulf of Mexico. The drilling rigs that had stood on land, slowly crept out into the sea, extending their legs downwards to the ocean bed. The further they came offshore, the more difficult drilling from them became.

Gradually, a semi-submersible rig began to be developed, which floated on pontoons just beneath the surface of the water. The drilling deck was raised well above the water by legs extending from the pontoons. With these platforms, stable conditions for drilling in deep water became a possibility.

Dry land drilling was originally developed by the Americans. But as Norway's oil-deposits were confined to the sea, the semi-submersible platforms were what was required. Their subsequent development represents an interesting collaboration between American drilling and Norwegian marine technologies.

The search for oil involves a variety of detailed explorations to identify potential sites of oil deposits. But the only way to determine the content of the 'pocket' is by drilling. The North Sea oil industry has stimulated the development of a series of new techniques. Marine drilling is so expensive that the preliminary exploration must be as thorough as possible. Consequently, considerable focus has been directed to these techniques, which are improving all the time, as are drilling techniques. In fact, the North Sea has become one great laboratory for new oil-technology which are subsequently employed all round the world. New oil deposits will be discovered further and further out to sea, in deeper and deeper waters, thus increasing the demand for more advanced exploration and extraction technology.

By drilling several wells the reservoir's size and extent is established.

For this reason, it is not only the oil companies which have shown interest in developments in the North Sea. Entrepeneurs in all fields are drawn to the challenge posed by the oil-industry, not least within the Norwegian technological community, where, in the 1970s and 80s, the opportunity offered by developments on the shelf, led to a sharp rise of the number of new Norwegian engineering and technological companies, offering stiff competition to their oversees rivals operating in the area.

National Control of the Oil Industry

Norway is a young nation. Despite our long coastline and international industries within shipping, chemicals and aluminium production, we have a great impulse for independence, especially with regards to control over what we think of as 'national resources'. In many ways we are an insular people, and from the beginning we ensured the existence of a licensing system which limited foreign ownership and exploitation of these resources.

As soon as the annexation was carried out, and Norway had secured what it considered was the maximum sovereignty over the Continental Shelf, work began on a legal framework for the area. It was soon realised that the traditional licensing laws could not be applied to the new situation. Neither were the mining laws of much use; they applied to a completely different kind of commoditity, and to a specifically land based industry.

In accordance with the principle of national control, material relating to petroleum-law in other countries was collated. The Norwegian embassies were engaged in this task, but in addition meetings were set up with representatives of private industry and the oil companies.

The message was quite clear – the faster you help us to educate ourselves in petroleum law, the faster it will be possible for us to establish Norwegian pertroleum law. Help us to gather the necessary material, come with suggestions and opinions, but don't try to deceive us! As a consequence, Norwegian civil servants received a lightening course in pertroleum law. But what was the rush?

The answer to this was the lack of clarity in international law pertaining to the Continental Shelf issue. The more watertight the Norwegian legal structure was, the more secure our rights would be. The British were already ahead of us on this matter; their legal framework was firmly in position and their oil industry well under way. A legal system applying to the main areas of the North Sea would create greater security both for the individual countries involved and the companies which wished to operate on the Continental Shelf.

Therefore, it was natural to base Norwegian petroleum law on the British system, and as usual the British authorities were willing and open to discussion. After many a training session in London, we were ready to formulate our own laws. During this whole period, the administration was able to function relatively freely within the political mileau. The oil industry had yet to acquire any party-political dimension.

It was decided to present the first draft proposals as a Royal Resolution, in order to make alterations easier if it was found that the difficult balance between freedom and control had not been satisfactorily struck. The system of excise and duties also presented difficulties. Speculators were to be excluded. After effective exploration, areas should be returned to proprietary jurisdiction. A system of gross excise was introduced and tax regimes established. Not everything could be solved immediately, but the decision was made to proceed, despite insecurity on a number of points.

Generally speaking, the oil companies are not comfortable with such situations, but they were willing to take a chance in order to be able to get going. Also, I believe it's fair to say, a relationship of trust had developed between the relevant parties, such that they all felt secure that their views would be treated with reasonable understanding, despite the lack of some detailed clarification.

Parallel with the developement of the legal framework, work was also begun on the question of demarcation. It might seem a relatively simple task, to establish a middle-line between countries, but such was not the case. From what point should such a line be calculated from? Whilst the British coastline is virtually island-free, the Norwegian coast is thick with islands, great and small. The Norwegian view was that these, and not the mainland, should provide the basis of any calculation, and it is interesting to evaluate the effect of this point. Many of the richest oil fields are situated in the border areas with other states, and the positioning of these borders has had an enormous consequence for Norway.

The boundary with Denmark presented particular problems. The use of the middle-line principle, which states that any point on a continental shelf belongs to the nearest nation, would assign enormous areas to Norway, including areas in the south of the North Sea which the Danes meant were their perogative. But Norway came out of these negotiations very well indeed, even though the Danes were decidedly disgruntled when their negotiations on the same principles failed to win them the advantage with Germany.

The so-called Norwegian Trench, a deep crevice in the Continental Shelf quite close to the Norwegian coast, also raised some problems. Would other countries try to insist that Norway's rights ceased at the Norwegian Trench? Norways' argument – that this was a geological anomaly which could not be taken into consideration – was eventually accepted.

In retrospect, one can speculate as to how international and national legal frameworks were established so quickly, when the subject under discussion was as important as oil. One of the main reasons, certainly, must have been the uncertainty as to whether there really was oil in the North Sea, or, if there was, to what extent conditions would make it possible to extract.

On the other hand, there was an undeniable willingness by all parties, to get the process under way. If petroleum resources were discovered in this part of the world, it would create a much healthier balance in international energy politics.

For Europe, the advantages of having an energy source under our direct control were obvious. But for this to be achieved it was necessary for national rivalries to be put aside, so that no time be wasted. The willingness of the British to cooperate on this was an important factor in the success of the enterprise.

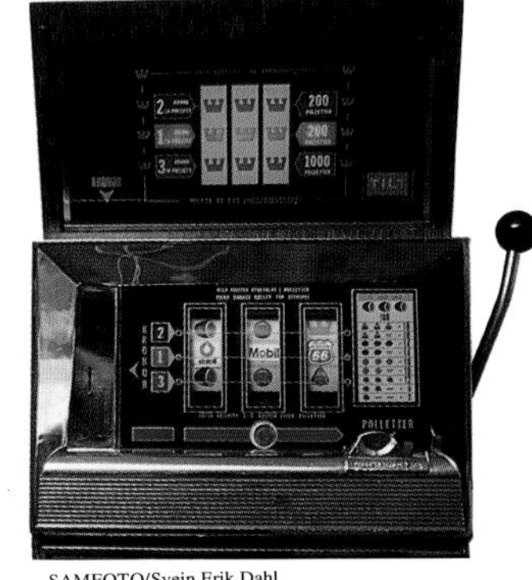

SAMFOTO/Svein Erik Dahl

The slot machines are played by the petroleum workers during their spare time, the only difference being that instead of apples and pears, company logos grace the wheels.

Hydro, Saga and Statoil

Norwegian business interests became engaged early in the process. First and formost, it was the larger shipping and industrial companies which became aware of the potential. This awareness arose partly by chance, but partly also through the offices of foreign companies wishing to become involved, who considered that alliance with a Norwegian partner would strengthen their profile with the Norwegian authorities.

This view was probably influenced by Denmark's choice of a completely different licensing structure. Already in the inter-war period, the shipping company A.P Møller had won exclusive drilling rights in Danish waters, which was later extended to include the Danish sector of the Continental Shelf. In other words, the Danes staked everything on one national company which would later issue licenses to international companies, as it saw fit. Some Norwegian firms hoped for the adoption of a similar solution by Norway.

In the Norwegian context, there were two particular groups that showed active interest in the Norwegian Continental Shelf. One was Norsk Hydro, in collaboration with various French parties. The other was a syndicate of important Norwegian companies within the industrial and shipping sectors, under the general leadership of Elkem. These Norwegian companies were involved in all the legislative discussions and gained valuable knowledege from the process. The authorities, on the other hand, never seriously considered the Danish model. They wanted to create a competitive regime involving many different companies, thereby attracting considerable economical resources and expertise into the industry. To draw in Norwegian companies was considered important; if there were resources to be found on the Continental Shelf, the advantages ought to accrue to Norwegian industry directly through participation. At the same time, one was talking about a huge investment programme, well beyond the capacity of Norwegian industry alone.

Already, at this stage, it was understood that the oil industry would require the development of various support industries in areas where Norway had considerable expertise. It was not difficult, for example, to imagine Norwegian shipping involving itself in the ferrying services required, and perhaps even in the construction of the oil rigs themselves. If Norwegian technology, which in many respects was well advanced, could be drawn into oil-exploration, capital outlay could be greatly reduced. If we could build a domestic market for Norwegian maritime expertise and find new applications for our technological expertise, we might well see an internationalisation of Norwegian industry, with enormously positive consequences for the future.

Norwegian companies, often in association with overseas partners, were therefore well represented amongst the first batch of licensees, in 1965, including Hydro and the forerunner of the Saga Petroleum, the Norwegian Oil Consortium. Following the first license issue, the discussions continued as to how the state might involve itself more directly in the process of oil exploration.

A decision on this was eventually reached in connection with the second license-issue in 1969, and in 1971 a special commission recommended a state oil company be established. The following year, Norwegian parliament voted unanimously for the creation of Statoil. Meanwhile, the Saga oil company gradually emerged from the amalgamation of a number of important Norwegian companies.

As a result, Norway ended up with three national oil- conglomerates, centred on Statoil, Hydro and Saga, all three of which have achieved political acceptance, and developed into considerable companies in their own right. Of course, there has been discussion as to whether or not a small country like Norway can support three such conglomerates, but the fact is that all three companies have broadened their expertise and applied themselves to areas well beyond the Norwegian Continental Shelf.

The regulations governing Norwegian participation have been, and remain, under continuous discussion, but there is no doubt about the participation of Norwegian oil companies in all future developments. By the same token, neither is there any question of a complete 'Norwegianisation' of the country's Continental Shelf area. The presence of international oil companies is

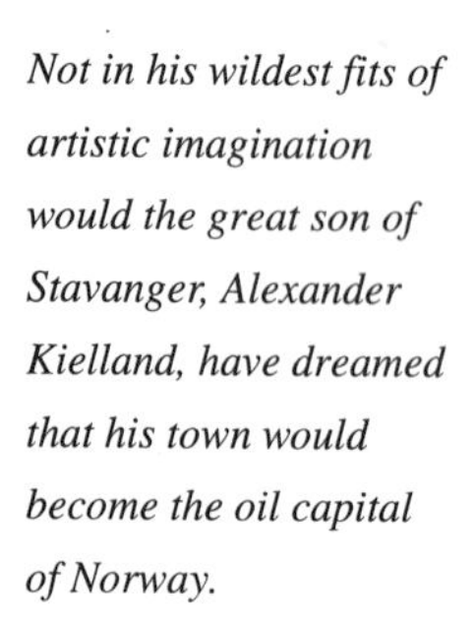

Not in his wildest fits of artistic imagination would the great son of Stavanger, Alexander Kielland, have dreamed that his town would become the oil capital of Norway.

HUSMO-FOTO

considered essential, and this will be reflected in all future lincensing rounds. There are many of these companies, and the oil industry in Norway is deeply influenced by the mix of Norwegian and international companies.

Stavanger – Norway's Oil Capital

At the beginning of the 1960s, Stavanger was a town on the retreat, with traditional industries in steep decline. But it could also boast more than its fair share risk-taking business people, who recognised the new possibilities ahead. As a result, Stavanger has become the undisputed oil capital of Norway.

Not only do many of the oil companies have their central offices in Stavanger, the town also hosts numerous oil related conferences and technological exhibitions, which have helped Norway achieve an elevated position in the international oil community. Originally, there had been great hopes that the oil industry would spread its activities to other sections of the Norwegian coast, but although this has occurred, it has been on a much smaller scale than had been envisaged.

On the other hand, both Mid- and Northern Norway are currently engaged in oil ex ploration, with clear social and economic consequences for the areas concerned. The industry has led to huge employment creation, and platform workers now commute to the North Sea from all over the country.

Whilst many of these workers have come from the shipping sector, others have come from technological industries which had been in decline. In 1977, women first found their way onto the rigs. The conclusion is quite clear; the North Sea has become an important source of employment for engineers, technicians, economists, caterers, health workers and many, many others.

The remote spots along the fjords entered a new era, the farmhouses seemed to have shrunk next to the colossal rigs. Right: From the construction of the Gullfaks B in Vats, in Ryfylke.

HUSMO-FOTO

Some of the first oil rigs to be used in the North Sea, were built at Aker Mek. Verk, located in the centre of Oslo's harbour basin.

HUSMO-FOTO

Later, concrete platforms were built. The huge foundations were constructed in the deep fjords, surrounded by the beauty of the mountains.

HUSMO-FOTO

Haugesund has a tradition of ship-building. It was natural that the town came to actively take part in the new oil era.

The expertise within the oil industry has expanded steadily, and the people in charge of the drilling equipment have to be meticulous in their work, even if the equipment is of huge proportions and very heavy.

KNUDSENS FOTOSENTER

FOTOJOURNALISTEN AB/Victor Lenson Brott

HUSMO-FOTO

The assembling of the various units to form an «oil city» is not only an admirable piece of engineering, but also demands experience and expertise on the part of the many workers with specialised skills.

HUSMO-FOTO

The mounting of the huge stays are of particular importance, as the big installations are to resist the «centennial wave», in other words, be able take the worst storms and hurricanes.

Within the sectors, the platforms are relatively close to one another.

HUSMO-FOTO

Virtually every activity and disposition can be monitored in the large control room.

HUSMO-FOTO

HUSMO-FOTO

HUSMO-FOTO

The coupling phase draws to a close, as the eastern wall is put in position in the EKO-FISK sector. Aboard the towing boats, barges, and rigs everyone knows exactly what his or her task is.

This is the centre of the EKOFISK sector, from which all the different bridges and pipelines to the various installations can be seen.

OLA RØE

The helicopter flight to the platform area is matter of routine. Not long after arrival, they are ready to go on shift.

HUSMO-FOTO

The bedrooms are light and practical.

HUSMO-FOTO

There's a need for relaxation between the shifts.

HUSMO-FOTO

It's the cooks responsibility that everyone is satisfied.

FOTOJOURNALISTEN AB/Victor Lenson Brott

The dimensions of the cranes are extraordinary (right). Note the people on deck.

HUSMO-FOTO

A permanent doctor and hospital is a natural prerequisite.

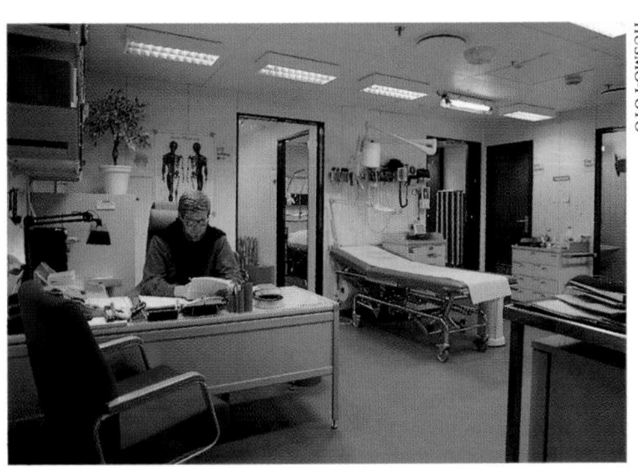

HUSMO-FOTO

The helicopter returns and the workers travel home for a well earned period of vacation from work.

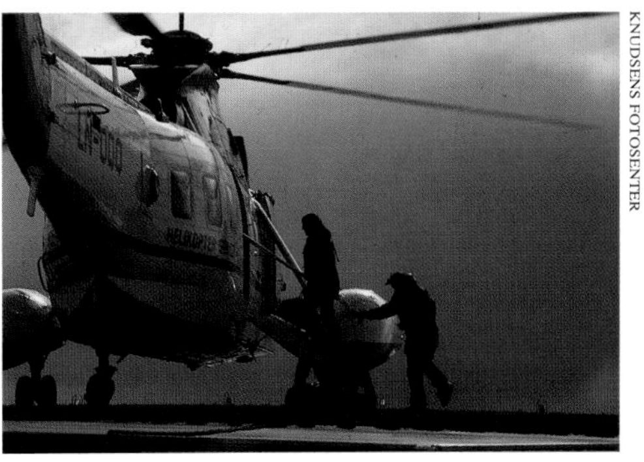

KNUDSENS FOTOSENTER

The large deck is generously sized for recreational activities.

HUSMO-FOTO

HUSMO-FOTO

There's nowhere like the North Sea for a place to hang one's fish up to dry, but the catches aren't always great.

HUSMO-FOTO

To cope with the masses of dirty laundry, the washing capacity has to be great.

HUSMO-FOTO

The Rise of the Supply Industries

When the oil-industry establishes itself in a new locality, it requires a number of services, offering potential for both large and small local businesses. The industry, however, is a demanding partner, both in terms of product-quality and price. Competition is tough, and international. Also, some oil companies may wish to maintain established relationships with former suppliers. It was important that international oil companies arriving in the country developed a knowledge of Norwegian trade and industry. Many local supply-industries, including many related to shipping, could boast long and distinguished traditions, as well as a great potential for development of their particular expertise.

Many Norwegian companies saw the potential of the new situation. The engineering industry quickly engaged itself in the construction and repair of supply-ships and oil rigs, as did the shipping industry. The cyclic nature of the oil industry appealed strongly to the venture-orientated shipping firms, who could smell both the challenge and the possibility of this decidedly 'shipping-related' development.

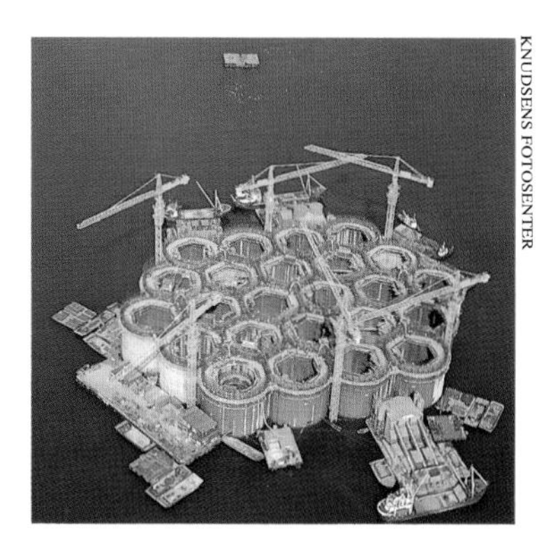
KNUDSENS FOTOSENTER

The casting of the concrete foundations for Statfjord B.

Engineering companies were also quick to realise that oil offered them the potential for overseas expansion.

A completely new type of oil-platform would be needed – enter the Norwegian concrete industry?

The whole initiative would need financing – a role for Norwegian financial institutions?

These questions, and their like, were asked in all areas of the Norwegian business community. Some believed oil would provide an easy route to wealth and success. Others were more sober in their assessments, and they were to be proved right.

Competition was hard and progress was much slower than some had estimated. There were problems of overinvestment, forcing many a crestfallen retreat. But a few managed to survive, by exploiting the possibilities that presented themselves and reinvesting in new areas of activity. From the very start, the cyclic nature of the industry has meant that success has come as much by dint of good fortune as expertise.

Those who have made it through this difficult phase, however, now possess advanced technological expertise which, tried and tested under the most extreme conditions imaginable, can now be applied all over the world.

This expertise is regularly exhibited at the bi-annual trade fair, in Stavanger, which attracts thousands of people, both from Norway and abroad. Norwegian maritme companies have a leading position in the offshore market place; activity on the Norwegian Continental Shelf accounts for 10 % of world demand for offshore products and services; Norwegian shipping companies own 20 % of the international drilling and commercial-shipping fleet, over 80 % of which operates way beyond the Norwegian shelf. Future developments offer exiting possibilities and challenges for Norwegian and international business, and, with the annual conferences on the future of the petroleum industry at Sanderstølen, Norway has become a meeting place for oil-professionals from all over the world.

Consequences for Norway and the Norwegian Economy

It was not only the Norwegian business community that saw the possibilities offered by the oil industry in Norway. The authorities were also aware of the huge consequences for the public purse; the State not only owned the shelf, it also set the levels of taxation. What is perculiar to the Norwegian oil industry is that the largest share of its profits end up in the hands of the Norwegian State. As a consequence, Norwegian state revenues have increased enormously, as has the potential for social spending by politicians. The international price of oil has, therefore, become one of the central parameters for any Norwegian finance minister, and the oil revenues in effect underwrite mainland-Norway's deficit.

Of course, this has, inevitably, led to a rise in expectations amongst the population as a whole, and an increase in the ambitions of the country's politicians. An ever increasing number of problems were to be solved by the state, and mentally, at least, the oil revenues were used up many times over before they had even been collected. Perhaps worse, they effectively postponed some highly necessary changes of attitude in the Norwegian business community.

In a small country, an overdependence on such revenues creates a number of complications, not least over investment, and the resulting high levels of inflation, which places great strain on the oil revenues.

Such a developement was perhaps inevitable. But even here, we have now entered a period of sobriety. The fall in oil prices brought about a rapid understanding of the importance of a cost-effective production base, and the undesirability of unbridled consumption of resources, notwithstanding high levels of income.

Now the first phase of the oil-adventure is over and, as we begin to look forward to the next, it becomes clear how much we have learned from the experience. It would seem obvious that the oil resources will continue to be substantial at least the next hundred years. They will certainly continue to provide the state with considerable income, and inspire our business endeavours. From this point of view, the oil has been good for the country.

By the same token, history shows that societies without natural resources are often the most successful. They are obliged to develop their human resources, instead of simply relying on unearned income. The Norwegian challenge lies in using the oil revenues correctly, as an inspiration for other initiatives.

Quo Vadis

Even though, from time to time, the world might be saturated with petroleum products, in the long term, oil is going to be in short supply. The North Sea has shown it contains substantial quantities of oil, and events of the past decade have underlined the importance of a stable political climate.

Also, consumer centres have become more accessible. There is, therefore, no doubt about the importance for the energy situation in Norway, and industry generally, of the presence of oil on the Norwegian shelf. There is every reason to suspect that subterranean reserves will last for at least another 50 years. I my opinion, this is more likely to be closer to 100 years. Not only are the estimated reserves greater than previously supposed, they will also be exploited with increasing efficiency. Today's high levels of oil extraction will, therefore, continue for a long time to come.

Techniques in the North Sea are continually developing. We are becoming more proficient in our use of infrastructure, in terms of current processing and transporation systems. New drilling and production techniques makes it possible to exploit smaller oil fields. The costs involved in exploration can be reduced through the use of three dimentional seismography, and other techniques. Through agitation, reservoirs can provide greater yields, and much else besides. Petroleum products will be discovered along the entire length of the Norwegian coast, presenting exciting challenges to both national and international initiative. Norway has always had strong energy resources. That these are now even stronger, provides us with a good foundation for industrial development. The sea covers 4/5 of the Earth's surface, and the nature of techniques developed in the North Sea will allow them to be utilised in other sea areas.

The petroleum industry is perhaps just one episode in the life of the country. For thousands of years we managed without it, and we will do so for thousands of years to come. The age of oil will last no more than perhaps a couple of hundred years – and the product itself will acquire increasingly advanced applications. Its importance as an energy source will be reduced. What IS the best long term use of oil – both by Norway and the world? Perhaps oil steaks will be on the menu of the finest restauraunts in the course of a few short decades?

STATOIL

Celebrations, as the oil was first found along the coast of Northern Norway.

The Statfjord A – platform (right) in its first autumn storm. Below, the supply ships are struggling with the giant waves, but still, they're on a steady course. The crew on these ships are sailors with a long experience from the North Sea.

HUSMO-FOTO

HUSMO-FOTO

HUSMO-FOTO

KNUDSENS FOTOSENTER

Polar is a floating platform. Picture: In shallow waters in the Troll sector.

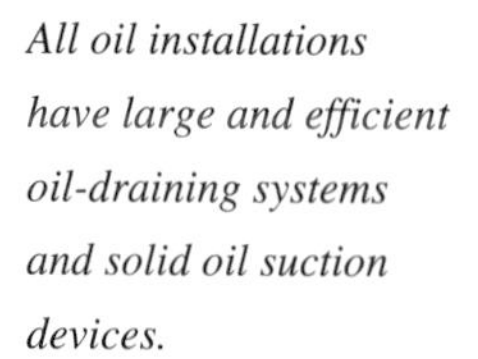

All oil installations have large and efficient oil-draining systems and solid oil suction devices.

Horizontal wells and the related services will become part of a well established technology with the move towards greater automation and robotisation.

The waves are measured with the help of laser equipment.

HUSMO-FOTO

Much of the oil being extracted from the oil fields is transported to the mainland through pipelines. One of the largest pipelines stretches to Emden, in Germany. This too, was a peaceful, and rural area being transformed into a busy industrial site. But there are still pastures left for the sheep.

Mongstad, in Hordaland, has had a long life of obscurity, but now, the biggest refinery in Norway has been built on the spot, by Statoil.

HUSMO-FOTO

HUSMO-FOTO

The dimensions of the pipeline at Emden are enormous, as seen here from the size of this newly installed ball valve.

HUSMO-FOTO

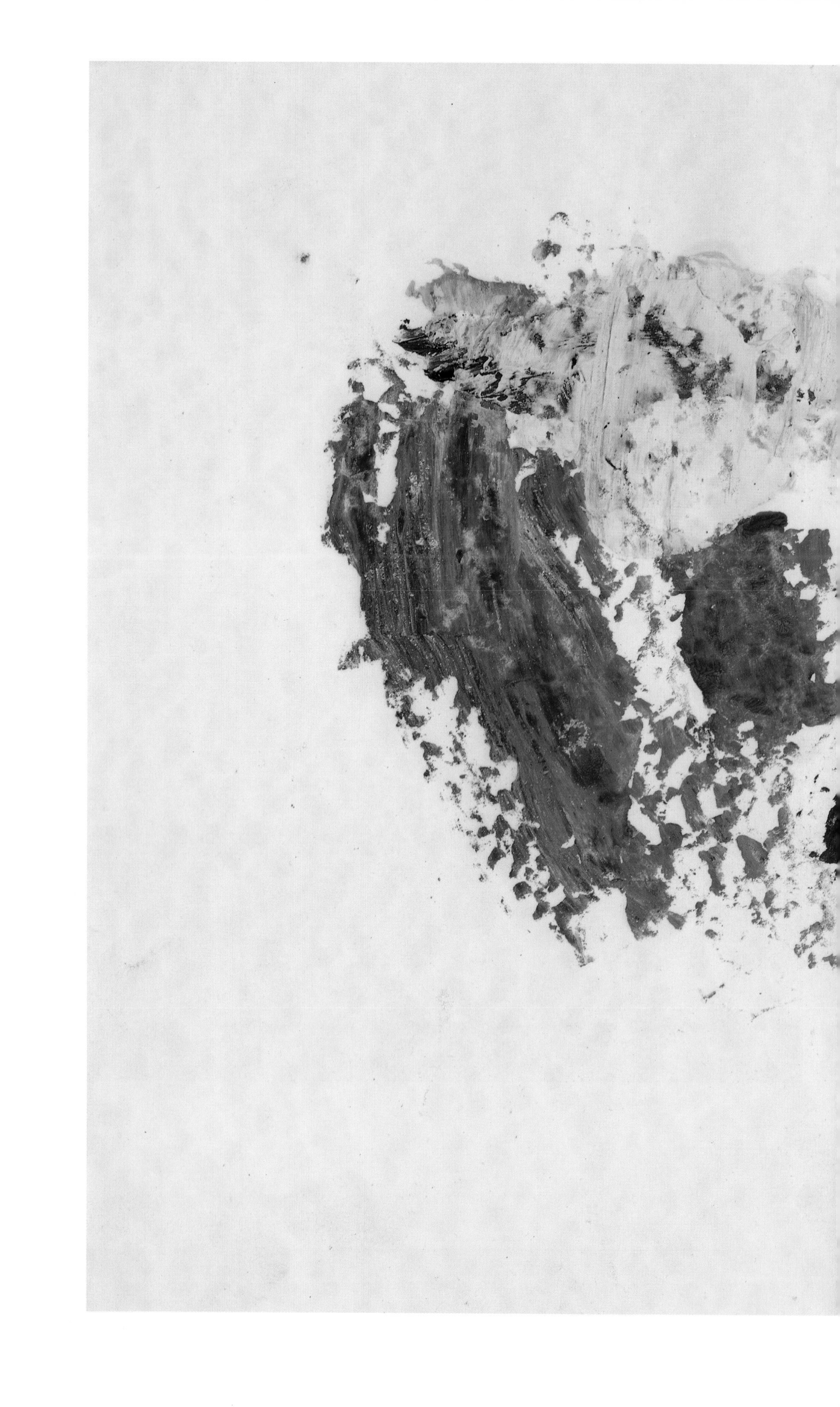

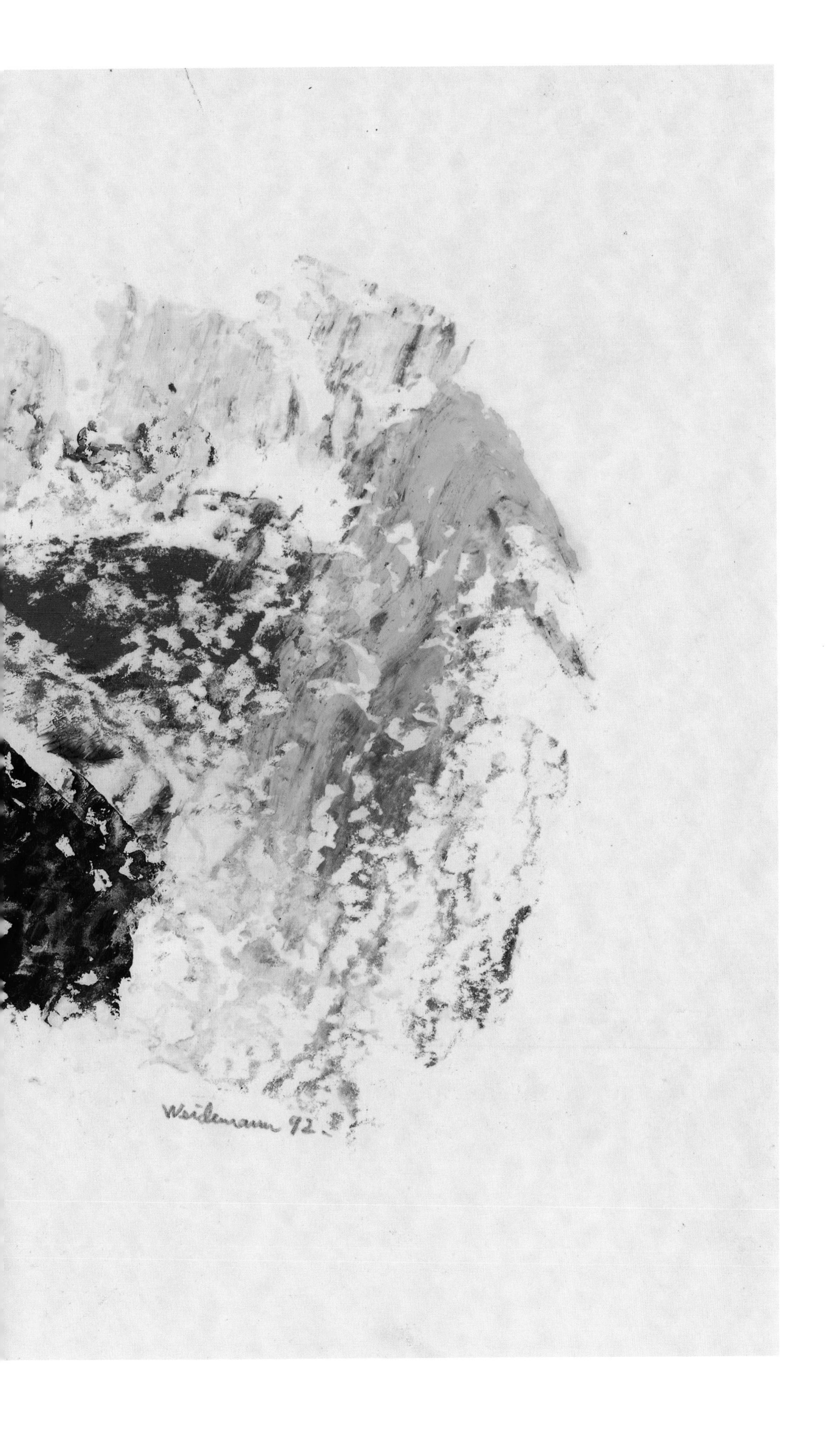
Weidemann 92

Norwegian Politics

Jo Benkow:

SCAN-FOTO/Trygve Indrelid

Jo Benkow (b. 1924) is a trained photographer, and has had studios in Moss and Bærum. After a very active period in regional politics, he entered parliament, Stortinget, in 1965. For the past few years he has held the position of president of the Storting. Among others posts, he has served as chairman of the Conservative Party (Høyre), and as president of the Nordic Council, (Nordisk Råd). Jo Benkow is also the author of several books; His memoirs of the late King Olav V, and his own autobiography both became best sellers in Norway.

Norway is a young state, but an old nation. Despite a 400-year union with Denmark, immediately followed by a further 90 years in union with Sweden, Norwegians have always identified themselves as a people. Neither their earlier greatness, nor the Norwegian Royal dynasty, was ever forgotten. In 1905, the Norwegian people chose their own king, Haakon VII. Both he and his son, Olav V, were remarkable People's Monarchs who helped create stability and strength for the country and its people. King Harald and his family continue in the same tradition.

They named him the red agitator, and the bourgeoisie feared him. . . Martin Tranmæl played a dominating role in the Norwegian labour movement for over two generations.

SCAN-FOTO/AKTUELL/Sverre A. Børretzen

SCAN-FOTO/Ingar Johansen

The national assembly was assembled at Eidsvold in 1814 and produced an independent constitution, the second oldest in the world. Oscar Wergeland's painting of the national assembly, hangs above the seat of the president of the Storting.

STORTINGSARKIVET

SCAN-FOTO/Knut Falch fra Stortingets 175-års jubileumsutstilling i 1989.

Three of the founding fathers at Eidsvold, Christian Falsen, Count Herman Wedel Jarlsberg, and Prince Christian Fredrik.

KNUDSENS FOTOSENTER

Carl Johan, King of Sweden and Norway, took part in the formation of the new Norway, which entered a period of growth both economically and culturally. His statue stands in front of the Royal Palace, overlooking the capital's main street, which bears his name.

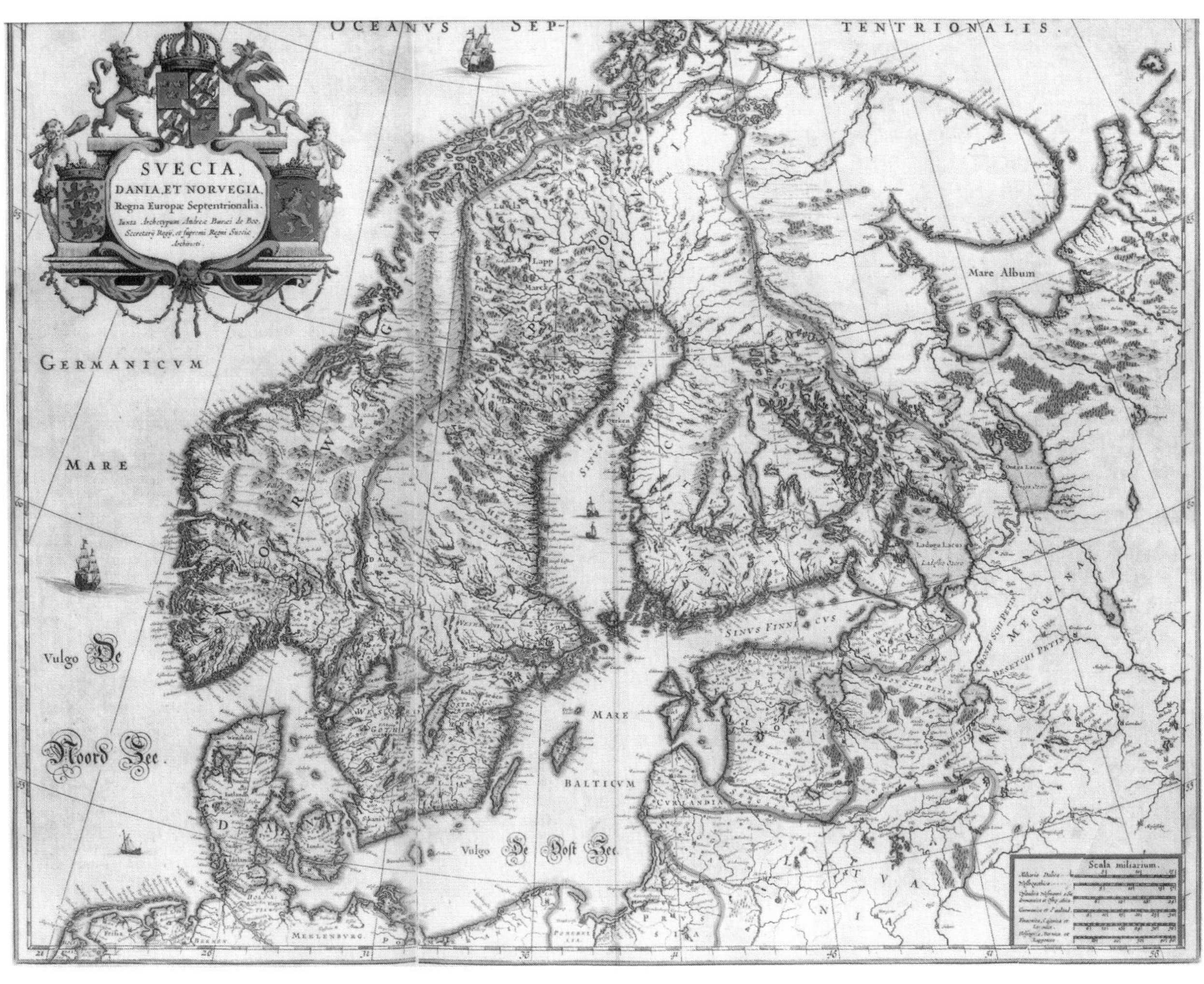

DEICHMANSKE LEGAT

The first naval map, drawn by Anders Bure, published in Amsterdam in 1635 in the work entitled, Svecia, Dania et Norvegia, Regna Europae septentrionalia.

The first hall of assembly for the Storting was placed in the Katedralskolen, Dronningensgate in Oslo.

Some citizens feared that the new assembly, the Storting, would have its «Freedom and Security» restricted. They established the voluntary organisation, the Rifleringen, so that the «old men in the assembly should enjoy safety and freedom when voting».

SAMFOTO

Giv — Akt!!!

Grundlovens § 85 lyder saa:

„Den, der adlyder en Befaling, hvis Hensigt er „at forstyrre Storthingets Frihed og Sikkerhed, gjør sig derved skyldig i Forræderi mod Fædrelandet".

Altsaa:

Gamlingen paa Tinge
skal faa stemme trygt og kjækt,
bagom Rifleringe
af vor unge Slægt!

Dette Skrift sælges for **10** Øre i „Nordmanden"s Ekspedition, Torvgaden 5 b.

When one has participated in political life for nigh on a lifetime, it ought to be easy enough to draw a picture of the Norwegian political scene. In fact, it is far from easy. One stands too close. The foreground details dominate one's mental picture, and crowd in on each other making it difficult to identify the salient points. Nothing has an obvious beginning or end. Every statement, one feels, must be qualified, because of a fear that any representation of the facts might do violence to reality. And despite all good intentions, such a picture cannot but be subjective. In Norway, more unites than divides us, and for this reason we value our disagreements, exploit them for all they're worth. If we did not, our political culture would surely lose such tension and nerve as it has, and the people would dislocate their jaws, yawning.

In modern terms, Norway is a comparatively new nation-state. The world first became aware of the country – in so far as it ever has been aware of it – in 1905, when the union with Sweden was dissolved. We ourselves consider independence to date back to 1814, when the National Assembly at Eidsvoll, drew up our Constitution. But even that event, as far as Norwegians were concerned at the time, was merely the reestablishment of 'the ancient throne of Adelsteiner and Sverre', the restoration of the ancient kingdom of Norway.

Which, in a way, it was. Norway had been a sovereign nation long before the moribund period following the Black Death forced us into a four hundred year colonisation by Denmark, and then a further ninety years of union with Sweden. Whether or not she could be said to have retained her status as a country whilst subject to Danish authority and jurisdiction, is something the experts still hotly debate. What is more important is that Norwegians never ceased to feel themselves a People, a folk. Besides, owing to the geological reality of the *Skagerak* and the *Kjøle,* there was never an effective amalgamation with our larger and stronger 'partners' to the south and east. Norway maintained its essential character of nationhood, which was always connected to a relatively well defined territory.

This national unity both had its roots in, and was strengthened by, a sense of social unity which has survived into the present time. A lack of social differentiation and strong class structure is reflected in the complexion of Norwegian politics and provides a key to understanding the country's political development and such political conflict as we find today. Political struggle and conflict has, of course, been part of the agenda for almost 200 years, but it is particularly noticeable how little this has concerned itself with actual developments of Norwegian society. Whilst the country slowly developed from being an essentially subsistence economy into a full blown industrial society, the politicians engaged themselves in the question of our relationship with our Scandinavian neighbours and internal administrative matters. Whilst our welfare state came into being, much earlier and more emphatically than in any other country, our politicians fought over questions of national linguistics and teetotalism! All the central mechanisms of society and state came into being, if not as a result of active collaboration, then certainly in the absence of any fundamental political strife.

NORSK FOLKEMUSEUM

Christian Michelsen, a shipowner from Bergen, was a brave and firm Prime Minister during the tense period of the dissolution of the union in 1905.

The Role of the Constitution

In these respects, Norwegian politics have followed the line of the National Assembly at Eidsvoll, in 1814, which gave the country its Constitution, the second oldest functioning constitution in the world. The Assembly was, of course, the scene of enormous struggles, both inside and outside the parliament building, but these had little to do with socio-economics. Foreign policy was the great divider, and also influenced the parties' position on other matters of conflict. The division was basically between those who wished to confront Sweden in a struggle for independance, and all that implied (even unto death, if need be), and those who preferred to win as much self-government as possible through a process of negotiation. These landowners, citizens, civil servants and few aristocrats were more or less agreed on the important questions of sovereignty, enfranchisement, conscription and civilian rights.

In many respects, the Norwegian Constitution was extremely radical for its time, but in others it was deeply conservative. Taking the various strands of contempory ideological thinking, it consolidated them into a political structure which belonged with the most progressive concepts of government in existence. At the same time, it built upon Norwegian social realities and historical context. The Constitution was to be a framework; the content would be determined by subsequent development, not fixed for all time by the legislators.

The Joint Programme – a modern parallel

One hundred and thirty one years later, the spirit of Eidvoll can easily be discerned in the Joint Programme of 1945. Again, this was a framework for future development incorporating elements of current political and ideological thinking. The Joint Programme signaled a broad-based, national concensus, encapsulating all political parties and population groups, about the main principles for future development, whilst at the same time leaving adequate leaway for subsequent negotiation. Thus, the Joint Programme became an influential force during a critical time.

Clearly, these two manifestations of national and social unity grew out of circumstances of a similar nature – the Kiel Settlement, and the German Occupation – and were shaped by similar challenges to the country – the resurrection of Norway as an independent state, and the reestablisment of the economy and infrastructure after five years of war.

Perhaps the consensus was a little artificial. Quite genuine disagreements were simply papered over with fine phrases. But the fact that such a consensus could be established at all – artificially or not – tells us some important things about the state of Norwegian politics. It tells us of the homogeneousness of the small Norwegian society, but above all it tells us of a society which views national consensus as a valuable political ideal. This is the ancient Germanic tradition of unanimity, which presupposes the existence of an objective truth which everyone shares a responsibility to achieve, in contrast the Anglo-Saxon tradition in which a conclusion is allowed to emerge from conflict of opinion, and trials of strength. The members of the British parliament sit facing each other, separated only by a distance of two sword lengths. Their Norwegian counterparts sit in a semicircle, arranged alphabetically according to their constituencies, in a magnificent party-political blend.

KNUDSENS FOTOSENTER

King Haakon VII was more than the symbol of national unity during the last war, he came to be the people's king. Monuments of him have been erected throughout the country, as here in front of the Bodø City Hall.

The People's King

Nothing else in this century has better symbolised the national consensus than the Norwegian Royal Family. This was able to build on a strong tradition that had been preserved even during the various unions. During the Union with Denmark, the King was referred to as 'our father in Copenhagen', and even during the more confrontational union with Sweden, the King always commanded respect and good will. Carl Johan XIV sits high up on his horse before the Royal Palace in Oslo, looking down the main street of the capital, which bears his name. Only at the very turn of the century, when the conflict with Sweden intensified considerably, did the monarch's popularity begin to decline.

Even so, with Haakon VII, the country gained something completely different and new. Even before he had mounted the throne, Haakon had made it quite clear that his wish was to be the People's King, at the call of the People and not just of the *Storting* (parliament), or of government. In the years leading up to dissolution of the union, republican sentiment had been on the increase. Consequently, against the better judgement of his closest advisors, the young prince demanded a national referendum on the matter. He had no desire to be king in Norway against the wishes of Norwegians. In the event, the peoples' opinion was clear enough – 79 % of them wanted him as their king. No one has ever had cause to regret this decision.

Rationally speaking, there can be little doubt, in this day and age the monarchy is an anachronism. Not least in our small, democratic, egalitarian country, where the distance between Royalty and subject required to preserve a romantic aura is all but impossible to maintain. But the fact is, in Norway, first King Haakon, and later King Olav, have managed to create for themselves a mixture of institutional respect and personal confidence, currently upheld by the new King, Harald. Between them, they have developed a constitutional monarchy in full and harmonious accordance with our system of government and parliamentary democracy. Aided by nothing other than their own determiniation and genuine appeal to all areas of the population, they have laid the foundation for a modern monarchy.

In recent times, our attitude to monarchy as such has changed character. Its old power and mystique is gone, though not all. The figure of the king has assumed a different role for us.

Our view of the King himself has remained strangely unaltered. It is possible for us to have a dispassionate and at times even critical attitude to our consititution, but this does not affect our particularly Norwegian relationship with the king. Totally unabashed, this otherwise reserved and modest people, indulge in a celebratory monarchism that appears completely at odds with their national character and tradition.

But this willing subservience, so foreign to the Norwegian mentality, does have an explanation. In this way, we are able to celebrate our love of country. By cheering the royal family, we have an outlet for our desire for fellowship, around a figurehead we have no need to feel obliged to argue over. In the middle of our arguements and quarreling, in a time of internal and external conflict, it is useful to have something, and someone, to gather together around. The power of the monarchy may be weakened, but its strength has, if anything, been increased.

Clearly, the people's attitude to the King has an effect on the King's own understanding of himself and his role.

It is, for example, remarkable that anyone – least of all a king – could achieve the kind of position within society as the one held by the late King Olav.

In no other country has Axel Sandemose's *'Janteloven'* ('The Law of Jante') been otherwise so vehemently adhered to. The first of these 'laws' – 'Thou shalt not believe that you are anything special' – applied to everyone except King Olav. The people wanted him to be something special – and he obliged.

The notion that the whole concept of monarchy is a fundamentally undemocratic anachronism, has been resoundingly disproved. Indeed, I would contend that the three Scandinavian kingdoms are bearers of a more authentic democratic tradition than all those countries that have rid themselves of their monarchies in the name of democracy!

The figure of the King belongs both in fairy tales and to reality. Our historical, and mythological image of kinghood has been expanded in a way that stimulates the imagination.

Our royalism is not merely the result of a historical tradition. Just as importantly, it grows out of contradictory human inclinations which alter with circumstances. We all carry inside us the need for autonomy. We wish to be independent individuals – not obedient tools of authority. If those in power infringe our human rights, we are provoked to resistence and rebellion. If the rebellion develops into a general melee, this could be catastrophic. Even in the struggle for freedom and equality, we require leadership. Deep in our consciousness, there exists a need to subject ourselves to a leader whom we can respect, trust and follow, through thick and thin – a leader who will always fight our cause. This is the kind of figurehead a king can provide, and indeed was, and is, provided most successfully by King Haakon, King Olav, and King Harald. They have manifested the content and nature of the ancient concept of kinghood.

But the need for monarchy and a king-figure is not based primarily on rationality or expediency. If we view the phenomenon from the limited point of view of rationality, the monarchy is, undoubtedly, anachronistic. But the motivating forces that have resulted in the Norwegian monarchy's unique position, are completely different. It is a matter of a complex of feelings, not easy to define, but which are linked to the intangible, irrational, even superstitious and naive world of fairy tales, so important to us as children. Norwegian monarchism has become an extension of childhood, when the monarchy had already established its permanent place in our affections as an unshakable point of reference which it never even occurred to us to question.

King Haakon's line consists, to date, of three kings, all of whom have understood that their position relies entirely on the patronage of the people. This understanding of the limits of their power has, parodoxically, afforded our kings a political influence which has been of great importance to the government of the day and the democratic development of the country as a whole.

Previously, even after the decline of absolute rule, a royal line could survive despite one or more generations of inadequate rulers. History is littered with examples of this. Today, the situation is different. The monarchy would be hard pressed to withstand an undistinguished monarch, who might limit him, or her-, self to the minimum ritual activity, or even take liberties beyond those defined by constitution and tradition. A modern king who offends the sensibilities of his subjects could well unleash demands for change more dramatic than would previously have been the case. The time of absolute monarchy is passed. Power now lies with the people.

Monarchy, then, is not justified by rational or logical argument, but by feelings. Nonetheless, the monarchy has proved to have the best arguments on its side, especially if we are to judge by actual experience. In the end it is a matter of taste whether we heed the heart or the mind in this matter. My personal feeling is that the Norwegian monarchy exerts a strong appeal to both heart and mind!

In Norway, the monarchy has turned into an anachronism we all wish to preserve – at any price – precisely because, of course, it is NOT an anachronism at all, but a particularly useful arm of the state which has served us extremely well. It has provided us with the stability and security necessary for the growth and development of the nation as a whole, both its institutions and individual citizens. Continuity and historical context have been the hallmarks of our royal family.

SCAN-FOTO/Arkiv

SCAN-FOTO/Arkiv

King Haakon VII, chosen by the people by an overwhelming majority, was crowned in the cathedral in Nidaros in 1906. At his side, Queen Maud, and on the large picture, the Royal Court gather around the Royal Couple.

KNUDSENS FOTOSENTER

Chr. Michelsen, the Prime Minister, welcoming King Haakon, with Crown Prince Olav on his arm, at his arrival by boat in the capital in 1905. Picture, right: A small albeit happy Royal Family at the Royal Palace, and below, the new heir to the throne, Harald, at about the same age, with his grandfather and father, King Haakon VII and Crown Prince Olav.

KNUDSENS FOTOSENTER

NTB

King Olav V wanted the blessing of the Church and in 1958 he was blessed in the cathedral in Nidaros by the bishop, Arne Fjellbu.

SCAN-FOTO/AKTUELL/Sverre A. Børretzen

Before and after the blessing of the church, King Olav toured the country.

SCAN-FOTO/Billedsentralen

SCAN-FOTO/Knut Skarland

SCAN-FOTO/Hans Olav Forsang

When Olav V, a true king of the people, died in February 1991 the entire nation was in mourning. Thousands of mourners gathered leaving lighted candles or flowers on the large Palace square.
Right: From the funeral.

SCAN-FOTO/Olav Olsen

SCAN-FOTO/Jan Greve

King Harald gives his oath to the Storting, with Queen Sonja at his side.

SCAN-FOTO/Knut Falch

The bishop, Finn Wagle, blessing King Harald in the cathedral in Nidaros in June 1991. Queen Sonja was also blessed by the Church. In the background, the Bishop Andreas Aarflot, who led the sermon, and the then dean of Nidaros, Tor Singsaas.

THOR MELHUS

As in 1906, pictures were taken of the Royal Family surrounded by their court. The photographs were taken at Siftegården, the royal abode in Trondheim.

KNUDSENS FOTOSENTER

When the Storting assembled in the autumn of 1991, King Harald declared it open, with Queen Sonja and Crown Prince Haakon Magnus at his side.
The new monarch declaring the start of the Storting session.

SCAN-FOTO/Tor Richardsen

During the royal tour, the Royal Family was met by the spontaneity and warmth of the people, sentiments that were reciprocated. In spite of a strict schedule, the royals took time off to talk with the young and the old.

SCAN-FOTO/Knut Falch

A royal photograph on the occasion of the Crown Prince Haakon's 18th birthday.

Formation of the Party System

Between 1814 and 1884, Norway can justifiably be seen as a 'bureaucratic' state. Political leadership lay safely in the hands of a government appointed by the king, undisturbed by democratic process, and, with the exception of a few representatives of the economic ruling class, recruited exclusively from the ranks of civil servants. Whilst the rural communities made up the bulk of the electorate, they had little opportunity to make their influence felt. One of the reforms eventually introduced, however – the establishment of local self-government and an annual meeting of a national parliament (the *Storting)* – strengthened the rural hand, which finally came into its own with the introduction of a full blown parliamentary system of government, in 1884.

The same year saw the founding of the two main political parties – *Høyre* (literally, the Right, or Conservatives) and *Venstre* (the Left, or Liberals). Whilst the Conservatives attracted the support of the civil servants – who naturally tended to be more positive to the union with Sweden – the opposition Liberals was a coalition of disparate groups, first and foremost the farming community, but also the more liberally inclined members of the business community, intellectuals and the urban middle class.

As with all coalitions (whether between, or within parties) the frictions within the Liberal Party soon became apparent. An unofficial division into radical and moderate wings occurred already in the 1890s, and with the introduction of a universal franchise for men in 1898, the party began to face increasing competition from *Arbeiderpartiet* (the Labour Party), which had been founded in 1887. The previously vertical socio-economic division of the electorate between town and country, now began to flatten into something more horizontal. In reality, it became impossible for the Liberals to choose a political path which could bind together such contradictory views. But, assisted by tradition and an electoral system which strongly favoured a two-party system, the party managed to maintain its dominent position until 1918. By then, the Conservative and Labour parties' share of the vote had grown to such an extent, and the election results had become so unreasonable, that electoral reform was inevitable. The Liberal's fate was effectively sealed. Their radical social line proved unattractive to the rural communities; at the same time, the Labour Party commanded the loyalty of the growing urban working class as well as the landless classes out in the districts.

The Political Axis

The convention in Norway is to range the parties along a left-right axis with a central line dividing the 'socialist' grouping from the 'non-socialist'. Thus, the Progress Party stands furthest to the right, followed by the Conservative Party. Bunched together around the centre post, as it were, we find the Christian Democrats, the Centre or Agrarian Party and the Liberals. To the left, come the Labour Party, the Socialist Left Party and, finally, the Communists.

How useful such an arrangement is is debatable. If the left-right division is seen as a simplified picture of the difference between laissez-faire and socialist ideology, then the fact is that most Norwegian political parties have no place on the axis at all! Only the Progress Party can properly be said to subscribe to laissez-faire thinking, in the same way that only the parties to the left of the Labour Party can truly be identified as 'socialist', despite the Labour Party's use of socialist as a kind of honorary-title right up until the last decade.

The axis is more useful as an indicator to the extent to which the various parties view the state as a possible organ for solving economic and political problems. By the same token, the axis also indicates the degree to which the parties see the growth of the power of the state as a problem, or even a danger, in itself. In this context, there are only two parties on the axis that properly belong to the right of centre – the Progress Party and the Conservatives. However, the distance between these two is, in many respects, as large as that between the two main traditional rivals in Norwegian politics, the Conservatives and Labour. Logically, then, it is perhaps the Conservatives who should be seen in the centre position, midway between the Progress Party on the right, and the Labour Party on the left. Though such an arrangement would undoubtedly provoke a storm of protest from the majority of politically-engaged Norwegians, of whatever persuasion!

Ideologically, though, it is not an unreasonable suggestion. Conservatism as an ideology was born of the struggle with liberalism and laissez-faire, and was seen right up until the late 1930s as decidedly pro-state. But, as a party, the Conservatives undeniably acquired much in the way of thinking and voters from the Liberals in the wake of that parties' increased radicalisation. As a result, the Labour Party became the dominent rival.

The underlying truth in Norwegian politics, is that the left-right axis line is remarkably short. Both ideology and political pragmatism have built on the essential homogeneity of Norwegian society, and pushed Labour and the Conservatives closer together than either of them would care to admit. This development eventually led to the foundation of new political parties. First the Socialist People's Party (now known as the Socialist Left), in 1961, attempted to redress the balance caused by Labour's drift the the centre, and later, in 1973, a party calling itself first Anders Lange's Reduction of Taxes, Duty and Official Encroachment Party (!), later edited itself down to the Progress Party. But even these populist parties of protest were soon infected by the moderation bug. From a position of ostracism by the political community at large, the Socialist Left Party was finally accepted into the fold sometime during the 1970s, and we may safely assume the Progress Party will also loose something of its ability to provoke – and excite – in the not too distant future, also.

The Cultural Axis

It is impossible to understand Norwegian politics if one sticks exclusively to the left-right model. As important – occasionally more so – are two other axes, one passing between town and country, the other of a cultural nature. The first of these is primarily a politico-economic division. The economy of the 'country' is dominated by agriculture, forestry and fisheries, and the problems of rural society were very different to those found in the business and service communities of the towns and cities. Furthermore, these differences were extremely marked until well into this century, though with the increase of the manufacturing base, the two communities began to be drawn closer together and, today, the notion of the 'country' as an electoral base has weakened, substantially. Rural self-sufficiency – which functioned without recourse to money, and formed the basis of the economic policy in the previous century – has disappeared completely, and the rise of a capital-based economy in both town and country has helped to substantially reduce the barrier between the two.

Norway's geography and topography have, on the other hand, meant a marked degree of isolation in the rural community. In the course of history, this isolation has led to a cultural diversity only partly based on differences of trade, but which nevertheless has contributed greatly to the continuation of the notion of a town-and-country axis in Norwegian politics.

This cultural axis is itself dominated by three issues: language disputes, the temperance movement, and Christianity.

Chapel versus Church

The State Church came to Norway with the Reformation – and stayed. The ministers were civil servants, appointed by the King, and characterised by their urbanity, university education, self-awareness and strong class identity. In the small towns and isolated villages the distance between these men and the simple faith of their parishioners could often be yawning. The wave of evangelism which spread through the country in the last half of the 19th century further deepened this divide. The place of the church, with its heavy, formal liturgy, was taken by the chapels, with their hymns and simple, fundamentalist, sermons by populist lay preachers. Here, people felt at home, and though the established nonconformist religious movements, like Methodists, Baptists, the Mormons and Quakers, all put down roots in Norway, they never achieved a broad following. The chapels largely followed the Lutheran tenets of the state church, but in a language and social context more appropriate to rural society.

This fundamentalism also found its way into the towns, especially the small coastal towns, but also, via the migration of workers from the countryside, into the larger industrial towns

Throughout the summer, Christian festivals attract huge crowds of people. One of the most popular gatherings is held at the Pentecostal movement's centre, at Hedmarkstoppen, close to Hamar.

KNUDSENS FOTOSENTER

Harriet Backer's oil painting «Barnedåp i Tanum kirke» from 1892. The painting is on exhibition in the National Gallery.

NASJONALGALLERIET/Jaques Lathion

One of the outstanding psalm writers, M.B. Landstad, with his wife Mina.

SCAN-FOTO/Arkiv

and cities. Not surprisingly, a broad-based movement of this sort eventually acquired political significance, tending to strengthen with its support those parties in opposition to the political and cultural Establisment.

One of the most significant political by-products of this fundamentalism was teetotalism. In Norway, as in other countries, industrialisation gave rise to many social problems. One of these, which often served to worsen the effects of the others, was a growing alcohol abuse. The old, official temperance movement was replaced by a more aggressive teetotalism emanating from the low-church community. During the First World War, Norway introduced a complete ban on the sale of alcohol, which was only lifted, in 1927, after a long and hard battle involving the collapse of several governments! The scars of this battle run deep, and even today the question is not without a considerable political dimension.

Following the dissolution of the union with Denmark and establishment of a new union with Sweden, in 1814, strong nationalistic tendencies emerged in Norway. 'Norwegianness' became a fashionable, if somewhat unhistorical, reaction to both the years under Denmark and the union with Sweden. Written Norwegian had been, naturally enough, formed by those that most used it, that is to say the urban-based government officials and economically advantaged. It was inevitable that it should acquire certain qualities from Danish. The gap between this and the vernacular, especially as it had developed in the more isolated areas of the country, had become quite considerable. This language barrier also contributed to the division between town and country and between the different socio-economic groups within the population. And it was against this background that Ivar Aasen's 'The Grammar of the Norwegian Folk-Language' (1848) and 'The Dictionary of the Norwegian Folk-Language' (1850) lay the foundations for the development of a new Norwegian language, which became a bitter bone of contention in Norwegian politics for more than a hundred years.

The Liberal Party, given its opposition to the state bureaucracy, afforded the natural umbrella for these cultural-political trends. But in fact the state bureaucracy was in decline already when the Liberal Party was founded, and once this rallying issue was settled, the balance between urban and rural culture and between the Liberal and Conservative parties could no longer be maintained. The urban conservatives inclined towards the Conservative Party, and the weaker economic groups, both in the towns and the countryside, gravitated towards Labour. The Liberal's lost much of their appeal to the agricultural community and in 1920 the Norwegian Countrymans' Association turned itself into a political party, The Agrarian Party, who quickly replaced the Liberal Party in the districts. The increasingly urban character subsequently assumed by the Liberals resulted in a weakening of their contact with the low-church movement, which also formed its own party in 1933, the Christian Democrats.

Thus the Liberals lost control of the last element of the power base which had guaranteed them such a dominent position in Norwegian politics. Its attempt to create a position for itself as 'party of ideas' in the centre floundered on the fact that they were more or less duplicating the role ofother political groups. The centre, already crowded, was destined to become more crowded still.

The lack of room for manoeuvring in the centre, – if indeed there is any at all – has always severely limited the scope of so-called 'centre alternatives', or 'alliances of the centre'. But there are other reasons also why neither the Agrarian Party (now renamed *Senterpartiet* – literally the Centre Party) nor the Christian Democrats can simply claim a place at the centre of the political axis. Both of them nurture political aims incompatible with true centre politics, which in effect means that their claim to centrality is nothing more than a flag of convenience, allowing them to support either Conservative or Labour governments, whichever currently offers them the best chance of pushing through their own particular agendas.

The Women's Awakening

This might be the natural point at which to focus on the single development in Norwegian society which has probably had the most far-reaching and permanent effect on the political culture of the country, namely the changing role of women.

No country has much to boast about in regards to the historical position of women in its political landscape, but Norway can perhaps claim to feature 'least worst' in what is admittedly a miserable record.

A limited vote for women was first introduced in Norway for the 1901 local elections, and this was extended to the national election, in 1907. By 1910, universal franchise was established for council elections, and for national elections in 1913. Only three countries – New Zealand, Australia and Finland – have bettered this record. The first Norwegian woman to sit in the *Storting* was Anna Rogstad, who sat as a deputy member in 1911, though we had to wait unti 1921 for Karen Platou to be elected as the first full women member of parliament. From 1927 until the Second World War, the *Storting* could always number one, and in two periods, two women amongst its full members. In 1914, four women were elected as deputy members, and this figure rose steadily to reach a total of 21 in the last election before the outbreak of war in 1939. However, none of these achieved particularly high positions on the party lists, such that of the 64 women involved, only 14 of them ever experienced actually taking their seat, and then for a few days only. Women were in reality no more than decorations on the political lists and few, if any, came within striking distance of a role in national politics. Nearly all of them were nominated from the urban constituencies, and more than two thirds of them represented either the Labour or Conservative parties, the largest parties in the towns, and therefore entitled to most deputy members.

KNUDSENS FOTOSENTER

Large parts of the population have felt more at ease in chapels, rather than churches, and all over country chapels have been erected where popular preaching takes place.

After the war, there was a modest increase in the amount of women representatives – six in the first period, and seven in the second. But the number of women deputies increased enormously, with fifty percent in 1945, to over a hundred percent in 1949, and over two hundred percent in 1953. This trend continued throughout the 1960s, by the end of which decade there were 14 full women representatives in the *Storting*.

But it was the so-called 'women's coup' in the 1971 local elections which really got things going. Encouraged by the feminist movement, women activists mobilised a candidate replacement campaign (replacing male candidates on the party lists with females) which achieved sensational results. Though in some ways, it must be said, the achievment was more apparent than real. Nationally, the percentage of female representation on the councils was increased only from 9.5 % to 14.8 % But in three of the largest counties, Oslo, Trondheim and Asker, the election actually put women in a majority position on the councils, whilst six other counties returned between 40 and 50 % of women councillors. In terms of voter-choice, not a lot had actually happened; very few voters crossed party lines in favour of specific women candidates, and most of the candidate-replacements occurred within the framework of the party lists. As the vast majority of voters tend to keep within these party lists, the success of the campaign can be seen to be more a triumph of organisation than anything more fundamental.

But the psychological effect of it was massive, both amongst the party leaders and women themselves. The parties became worried about losing both votes and public sympathy, and the women were in a position to make demands. In the 1973 National Election, the number of women representatives rose from 14 to 24, and four years later this figure became 37. It currently stands at 58.

A more or less parallel development has occurred in the composition of governments. From 1945 to 1963, only one woman was to be found in the cabinet, safely positioned as either a consultative minister, or Minister for Family and Consumer Affairs, or, exceptionally, put in charge of Social Affairs. The centre-right coalition government of 1965 broke new paths with the appointment of a women to the post of Minister of Justice, thus increasing the female presence on the cabinet to two, a situation previously only achieved for a seven month period in 1955. It was 1973 before any further improvement; three women cabinet ministers, in the Justice, Social and Communications ministries. A further advancement occurred when Gro Harlem Brundtland took over as Prime Minister in 1981, with four women ministers, but the real revolution had to wait until Mrs. Brundtland's second government, which included eight women amongst its ranks.

NTB

When the era of Danish domination ended, demands for a separate Norwegian language emerged. Ivar Aasen founded the new Norwegian language.

NORSK FOLKEMUSEUM/Wilse

After the dissolution of the union in 1905, Norway got its own Liberty Bell. It hangs in Akershus Fortress.

The abolishment of the union was made public from the pulpit in the Church of Our Saviour, Vår Frelsers Kirke, Oslo, to an audience, «listening in utter silence», as put by one of the newspapers.

NORSK FOLKEMUSEUM

The participation in the plebeiscite of August 1905 was overwhelming. When photographed, the solemn election committees would often carry catching national slogans with them to have in the background.

The celebration of the 17th of May in 1905 attracted huge crowds, and in the many speeches of that day, nationalism flourished.

But the situation was still tense, and Norwegian forces were mobilised and put on alert along the Swedish border.

SCAN-FOTO/Arkiv

NORSK FOLKEMUSEUM

SCAN-FOTO/Ingar Johansen

KNUDSENS FOTOSENTER

The greatest celebrations during the National Day, which attract thousands of visitors, take place in the capital. The singing children's procession ends in front of the Royal Palace, at the end of Karl Johansgate, and the Royal Family greeting the children from the balcony is met by a warmth and devotion rarely matched elsewhere.

KNUDSENS FOTOSENTER

On their way to the Royal Palace, the children pass in front of the Storting, where the president is greeted, as he stands on the balcony of the assembly.

SCAN-FOTO/Jan Greve

Few countries can match the degree of popular participation seen during the national day in Norway. Parades and flags to be seen everywhere, as here on Svalbard (left).

In 1905, the year of the dissolution of the union, the celebration of the 17th of May was particularly great in Bergen, the home of the Prime Minister, Chr. Michelsen.

Their eyes filled with expectation, the children pass in front of the balcony of the Royal Palace, where the royals are gathered.

SCAN-FOTO/Arkiv

KNUDSENS FOTOSENTER

Henrik Wergeland was the man to make the 17th of May a day of celebration. Monuments of him have been erected in many places, and they are often bestowed with flowers, at the beginning of the celebrations.

SCAN-FOTO/Ingar Johansen

ARBEIDERBEVEGELSENS ARKIV

The Storting sessions used not to last as long as they do today, and most issues were decided by a general vote, rather than through committee works.

SCAN-FOTO/Arkiv

The building which houses the Storting was completed in 1866 and the hall of assembly is at the centre of the rotunda. As the number of representatives have risen, the space has become restricted. But there is still enough room in the corridors and on the galleries.

SCAN-FOTO/Knut Falch

Two speakers of authority. W.F.K. Christie played a dominant role in the national assembly in Eidsvold. The present president, Jo Benkow.

SCAN-FOTO/Knut Falch

SCAN-FOTO/Jan Greve

Today, we can safely assume that both the emotional and political prejudice against women's involvement in politics have been very greatly reduced. Soon, I'm sure, they will be altogether a thing of the past.

A New Political Agenda

The assumption by women of their proper place in political life is not an isolated phenomenon. It is just one – particularly positive – example of how public opinion has, for better or worse, wrested the political initiatve away from the hands of the political leadership and party apparatus. The deciding factor in this change has been the increasing role of television, which entered the political arena seriously during the King's Bay debate, in 1963. Four days of dramatic parliamentary debate, culminating in a government crisis and the first centre-right government for 27 years, naturally stimulated enormous public interest. Politicians became 'media personalities', either as heroes or villains, and as such of intrinsic interest to the general public. Radio and the press followed up the phenomenon, and suddenly both media and politics became conscious of the role Public Relations had to play. Not all issues had audience appeal. Ideally, they needed to be relatively simple, with a dramatic element connected to a few key players. The effect of this new media-created climate was further enhanced by the parallel development of what we might call 'gallup democracy'. The position of the various parties could be monitored by the weekly public opinion polls, which in turn were supplemented by the parties' own research and the pollsters' constant pulse-taking of the electorate's views on both issues and personalities.

SCAN-FOTO/Knut Falch

A new generation in the Parliament. From left Sylvia Brustad (Labour) Paul Chaffey (Social Left Party) Karita Bekkemellen (Labour) Tor Mikkel Wara (Progress Party) John G. Bernander (Conservatives) and Tor Inge Akselsen (Labour).

Inevitably, these developments also had an effect on the electorate, and the 1960s and 70s saw the loosening of traditional party ties. Elections campaigns, which until then had functioned more or less as 'alarm clocks', reminding the voters to cast their vote for the same party they had always voted for, suddenly became dramatic events upon which one was required to make judgement. A successful showing, especially on television, could gain a politician thousands of votes for his particular party, overnight, a fact which, not surprisingly, had a corrosive effect on politicians' sense of responsibility. For whatever one can say about responsibility, exciting or dramatic it is not! At a time when the old party loyalties have all but disappeared, and a newly elected member of parliamnet needs to begin working on his or her first day to ensure reelection next time, political life has lost much of its calm and dignity. No one can take an extended career in politics for granted any longer, and certainly not by simply towing a party line. Individual initiative is an absolute necessity, whether in support of, or at odds with, the policies of one's own party. In fact, all the better if it's the latter, with the resulting media coverage and public interest. On the other hand, one's reelection and political future does not lie in the hands of the individual, alone. If the party's position declines, not only can this affect one's electoral chances, it can also make a mockery of one's dream of a cabinet position. Party presentation, therefore, is vital. And in these personality-obsessed times, this boils down to the presentation of the party through its leadership.

It is not possible for all the leaders to win at every election. No party can deliver on all its promises or follow up all its initiatives. And one clear side-effect of our reader- and viewer-friendly democracy is the growth of public contempt for politicians as a breed. Whether or not this will give rise to a new breed of politician remains to be seen. But we cannot ignore the fact that the realities of political life will, in the long run, effect the kind of person that is attracted to the profession, for better or for worse.

The time, however, when 'The old men of parliament vote peacefully inside/ the defensive ring our young provide' is long passed as the members of the *Storting* become ever younger, and the electorate that hires and fires them becomes ever older. No less than seventy four members of the present parliament were elected for the first time at the last election – those they replaced having fallen either at the 'spring cull' (the party nominations) or the 'autumn cull' (the election itself).

Changes in Government

After the establishment of parliamentary democracy, the average life of a Norwegian government has never been long. In the days of the two-party, first-past-the-post system, up until 1922, the conflict over the union-issue, and the splits within the Liberal Party, led to few governments surviving the prescribed three-year term. With proportional representation, the period up to the Second World War, the average fell to around eighteen months, (not including the reconstructions following the deaths of Prime Ministers Halvorsen and Kolstad).

The war saw a considerable increase in stability. The government of Prime Minister Nygaardsvold lasted for ten years, until the end of the war, and after four months of so-called national government, the country entered its first, and so far last, period of stability with successive Labour Governments lasting up until 1963. Subsequently, there was a period of minority rule, with twelve different governments lasting an average of two years each.

From 1884 until 1922, Norway operated a two-party system without achieving the kind of stability it may have wished. The electoral reforms of 1922 put a stop to this development. The Labour Party, which was on the verge of taking over the Liberal's role as the party of the majority, suddenly had further to go to achieve overall majority, whilst the delay of the disintegration of the Liberals led to the transfer of support to the new Agrarian and Christian Democrat parties, instead of *en bloc* to the Conservatives.

What might have happened in the late 1980 and 1990s, were it not for the further electoral reforms of 1988, is anybody's guess. Prior to 1988, a series of centre-right coalitions had created a new political climate. The development of a nationwide mass-media network had weakened the mobilising force of the old political issues of language, temperance and religious fundamentalism. Economic development had softened the divisions between town and country. The electoral groups bound to agriculture and fisheries had become so numerically insignificant that their energies would have been better employed within either the Labour or Conservative parties than in trying to function as a party in their own right with a negligible parliamentary power base.

But the adoption of a mathematically fairer electoral system has effectively put a stop to further development toward a two-party system, and presumably condemned Norway to years of weak and short-lived governments. It will also strengthen the Labour Party's position as the most obvious party of government, being the largest single party, and boasting the most effective party discipline – though this has proved somewhat fallible from time to time. Whilst the centre-right is obliged to form a coalition to ensure any kind of majority, the Labour Party can usually expect to be able to govern alone, albeit as a minority government. Clearly, given the limitations inherent in any coalition – and always presupposing that a coalition is possible in the first place – the centre-right will remain hard pushed to present itself as a credible alternative to a Labour Government. This is certainly the experience of the Conservative Party, whose voters consistently pose two equally strong, and virtually irreconcilable, demands on the party: firstly, that it should follow a firmly conservative political line and, secondly, that is should guarantee the success of the coalition. This is not the demand of the party's supporters, alone. The Conservative Party is not in a position to present a government alternative without the cooperation of other centre-right parties. There is, consequently, a very real danger that the party will be condemned to eternal opposition. The other centre-right parties face an easier task. Their attitude to government, and that of their supporters, is principally orientated towards their own particular 'hobby-horses'. This allows them infinitely more freedom of movement outside the left-right political axis.

There are few tasks more difficult for a Norwegian politician than trying to explain the dividing lines in his country's politics for a interested foreigner. As a rule, he will stretch his powers of articulation to their limits, yet still have to be satisfied with, at best, a resigned nod from his listener. One has to be born in Norway to understand why such a small, unusually homogeneous society needs 7 or 8 political parties. Nonetheless, our historical traditions will probably ensure the continued flourishing of our national political flora, if not forever, certainly for the forseeable future.

At the liberation of Norway in May 1945, the Nygaardsvold cabinet, that had governed in exile, in London, during the war years, was replaced by a coalition government, led by Mr Einar Gerhardsen. After the elections in the autumn of 1945, he formed his first Labour government, and the party stayed in power until 1963.

NTB

The Lyng government only held power briefly in 1963, but after this the Conservatives started serious attempts at getting into a government position. In 1967, the non-sosialists could once again form a government, and since, the Conservatives and Socialists have alternated being in a government position. At the elections the margins have often been very narrow. Right: The third Gro Harlem Brundtland government.

NTB

NTB

NTB

The referendum on EEC-membership in 1972 engaged every Norwegian. At the count, the TV-barometer pointed towards a 50–50 distribution for the longest time, before finally showing a comfortable leading margin for the No vote. Electioneering is good televison entertainment. The debate between the party chairmen is watched by «everyone», as here from the elections in 1989.

SCAN-FOTO/Jan Greve

SCAN-FOTO/Tore Berntzen

SCAN-FOTO/Nils Bjaaland

SCAN-FOTO/Jan Greve

Three of the strong-willed party chairwomen in Norway, in 1992. Anne Inger Lahnstein (left) of the Senterparti, the Agrarian Party, Kaci Kullman Five of Høyre, the Conservatives, and the skiing Prime Minister Gro Harlem Brundtland, whom is also the leader of the Arbeiderparti, the Labour Party. The debates often get heated when the three meet.

KNUDSENS FOTOSENTER

KNUDSENS FOTOSENTER

Høyres Hus (above) and the Folketeater-building on the Youngstorg square, are the headquarters of the two largest political parties,

Weidemann 92

Norway's Cultural Heritage

Yngvar Ustvedt:

Yngvar Ustvedt (b. 1928), Ph.D., has been with the Norwegian broadcasting corporation, NRK, working on matters of art and society, since 1962. He was, for many years, the editor for cultural affairs for NRK Radio. He has held several teaching posts in Oslo. For three years he also worked as a teacher of Norwegian language and literature at the Sorbonne University in Paris. He is the author of several works on the history of literature as well as contemporary history.

The history of the Norwegian people is divided into a number of distinctly dissimilar periods. The Old Norwegian culture emerged during the High Middle Ages, between the years 900 and 1300 AD. This was followed by the «Four Hundred Year Night», when Norway was reduced to a Danish colony and its own culture was conspicuous by its absence. With the political liberation of the 19th century the country experienced an unparalled cultural renaissance. Norwegian cultural heritage had survived centuries of Danish domination in the folk arts and culture of the people.

UNIVERSITETETS OLDSAKSAMLING

The Snartemo sword, previous page, is among our finest grave findings. Its handle is covered in gold and silver. The sword was discovered in a chief's grave, at Hægebostad in the county of Vest-Agder. The chief carrying the sword was found lying on a bear's rug and covered with two coloured wool blankets.

KNUDSENS FOTOSENTER

KNUDSENS FOTOSENTER

KNUDSENS FOTOSENTER

KNUDSENS FOTOSENTER

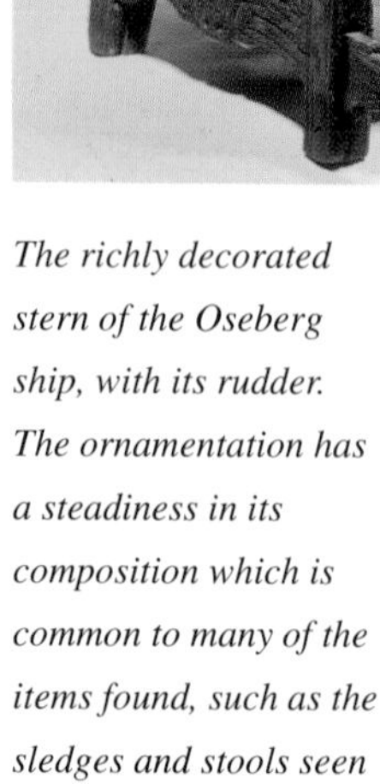

The richly decorated stern of the Oseberg ship, with its rudder. The ornamentation has a steadiness in its composition which is common to many of the items found, such as the sledges and stools seen in the picture.

The finds in Oseberg, not far from Tønsberg, are considered the richest finds ever in Norway. The Oseberg ship is almost 22 metres in length and 5 metres wide. The excavations unearthed a unique collection of equipment, not least a wagon and four sledges, in addition to the jewelry, household furniture, tools and spearheads.

KNUDSENS FOTOSENTER

UNIVERSITETETS OLDSAKSAMLING

It was a prominent woman who was buried in Oseberg, in the mid 9th century. The woman is possibly Queen Aasa, the mother of Halfdan the Black and grandmother of Harald Fairhair. One has found that Harald Fairhair used the same type of ships and sledges that were found in the Oseberg graves. The findings of the ships, in Oseberg, Gogstad, and Borre constitute the bridge between the sagas and the history of our artistic heritage, that starts with these finds. The Oseberg find is richer than the ones in Gogstad and Borre, and are amazingly well preserved, as seen from the picture of the wagon from Oseberg.

The Viking sagas are an important part of our literary and cultural heritage, Snorri's «The Sagas of the Viking Kings of Norway» being the most monumental. The illustrations are taken from the luxurious J. M. Stenersen edition, first published in 1899.

One of Christian Krohg's most famous paintings, the Discovery of America by Leiv Eriksson.

KNUDSENS FOTOSENTER

SCAN-FOTO/Arkiv

KNUDSENS FOTOSENTER

Rose painting is a deeply rooted tradition, mostly applied on wooden bowls, but in ancient times also on walls and cupboards.

KNUDSENS FOTOSENTER

A beautifully decorated goblet, or drinking cup, from the collections of the Folkemuseet. Right: A bridal crown from Osterøy. Under: One of the colourful national costumes.

NORSK FOLKEMUSEUM

O. VÆRING

JARLE KETIL ROLSETH

Adolph Tidemand was fascinated by the motive of «Grandmother's Bridal Crown». In all, he produced five paintings where the grandmother and the three children are exactly the same. The five paintings were all sold abroad, but later three of them were returned, one to become a part of the collection at the Royal Palace.

Building sections dating from before the 12th century, are preserved in the Garmo Stave Church, which has been moved to Maihaugen in Lillehammer.

KNUDSENS FOTOSENTER

The western wall of the cathedral in Nidaros, with its apostles, saints, and kings. In the middle, the large rose window which provides the interior with a beautiful light.

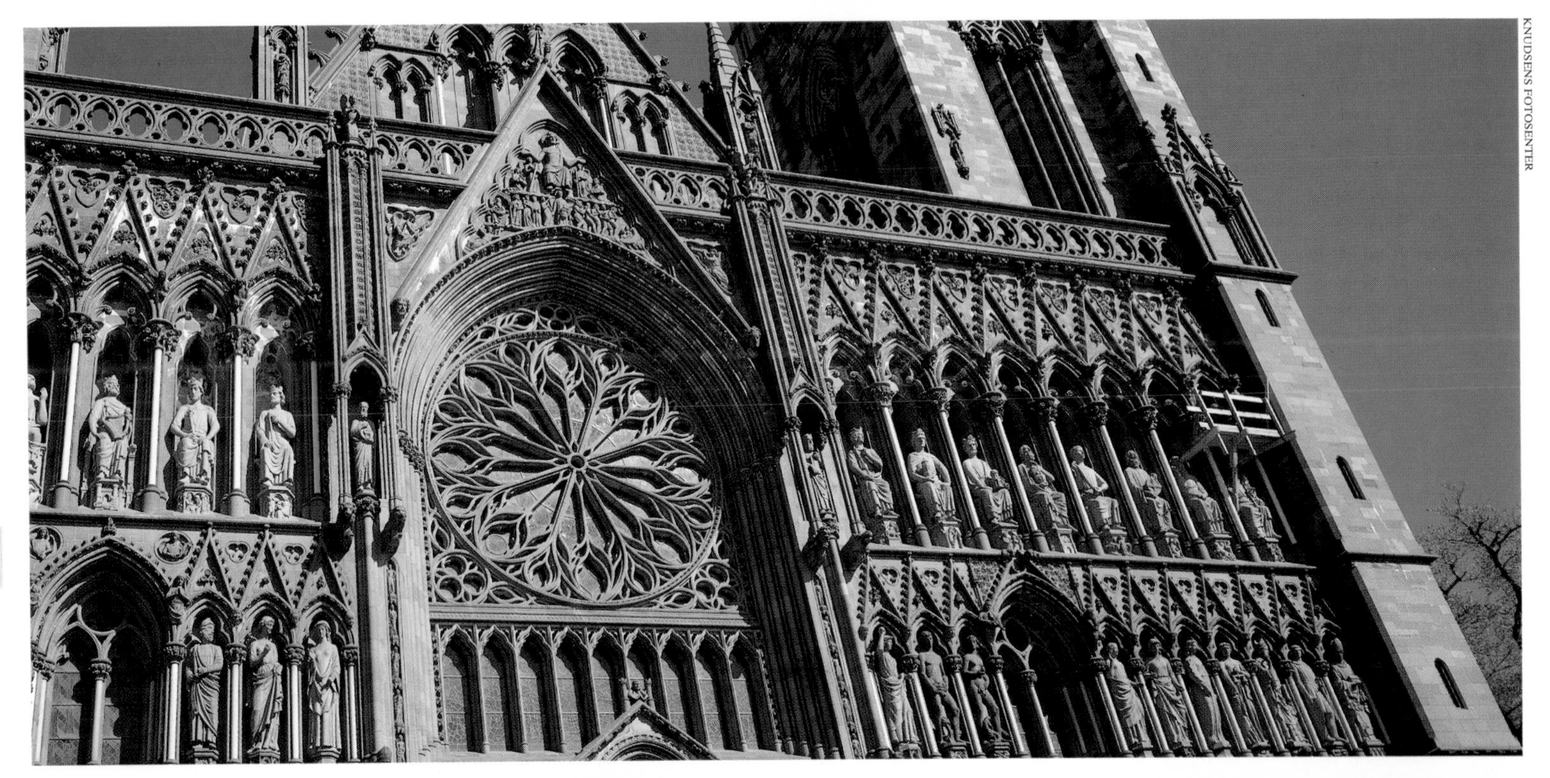

KNUDSENS FOTOSENTER

KNUDSENS FOTOSENTER

Picture, right: Parts of the interior in the Uvdal stave church are well preserved. Picture, above: Wooden sculptures from the Viking era.

KNUDSENS FOTOSENTER

In Norway, as in other western countries, it is a common assertion that the maintenance of our cultural heritage is of the utmost importance. We must do all we can to ensure the survival of the Norwegian character, it is said, both by the authorities and leading public figures. The increasing internationalisation of society demands that our attention be turned to our national identity. Thus, the inclusion in Norwegian educational law of a clause obliging our schools to build upon the national cultural heritage. Likewise, the state broadcasting company's statutory obligation to nurture our ancient culture and ensure its continuity through the generations. In fact, official cultural life as a whole is committed to this oft mentioned cultural heritage. The seminal Cultural Report of 1974, the purpose of which was to define guidelines for all Norwegian cultural activity, states that «we must ensure favourable conditions for the growth of our own cutural heritage in the future».

Fine words, indeed. But what, in reality, lies behind them?

Nothing, no doubt some would say. The schools abandoned culture, in all its perspectives, long ago; the mass media is dominated by news, current affairs and standardised international entertainment. Radio and television have not served the cause of culture as many intellectuals and 'culturalists' might have hoped. Though this does not stop every new programme director or head of broadcasting declaring that the mass media's greatest mission is to afford people access to their national heritage. Again and again, the cry goes up for the protection of our national character and the preservation of the Norwegian cultural heritage.

But, what IS cultural heritage?

Previously, and especially before the war, there was a tendency for spokesmen and writers to use the label as a convenient catch-all. Everything that had occurred in the course of history as a consequence of people's confrontation with the environment – not just art, poetry and religion, but also such things as costume, agricultural implements, items connected with play and leasure, and all the other myriad institutions of everyday life – all this has been defined as our cultural heritage.

More recently, the expression has been used with rather more precision. Nowadays, it is used in reference to the culture of the past – books, pictures, sculpture – but also religion and ancient traditions. When we speak of 'Jewish heritage', we refer to the totality of surviving Jewish tradition.

In Norway, the phrase cultural heritage has always referred to something specifically Norwegian, and contains within it a notion as unique and inexplicable as it is real. Its context lies within the span of our history, the character of which differs from that of most other European countries in that it separates into a number of distinctly dissimilar periods. During some of these – extremely long – periods Norway can hardly be said to have had any culture to inherit at all; for many hundreds of years we languished as a Danish colony, as part of Danish culture, and, indeed, in terms of cultural heritage, the 13th, 14th and 15th centuries simply didn't occur for Norway. By contrast, the remarkably rich and varied old Norwegian culture developed almost exclusively during the Middle Ages, between the years 900 and 1300. It was during this period that our specifically Norwegian cultural identity was forged.

Norway was late in joining the developments of the Middle Ages. For a long time, Norwegians were barely more than nature-children, practically without any heritage at all, cultural or otherwise. Whilst Pericles established democracy in Athens, we struggled with Stone Age farming methods. Whilst Ceasar created the Roman Empire, it was all we could do to survive from one day to the next in our tiny, windowless huts.

The one thing we had, though, was boats; ships which carried us to foreign lands, where, in the fullness of time, we perfected the arts of rape and pillage. Fortunately, this was not all our Viking ancestors learned from Europe. There, they came into contact with religion, the articles of statehood, with art and poetry. And, suddenly, Norway arrived – as a nation in its own right. A land like any other in Europe, and before long, on a par with the best of them.

We acquired bishops and priests, monasteries and monks. Kings and queens. We built churches and towns, acquired merchants and aristocrats, learned men, poets, musicians, woodcarvers, artists and saints. A rule of law of the highest quality was observed. In art and poetry, Norwegians developed a position which can only be described as peerless. Norwegian and the Norse languages gave rise to a blossoming of poetry and prose, unparalleled in any other European language. As eternal evidence of this we have the Sagas and legends, just as the magnificent stave churches give evidence of our building prowess, and much else.

Then, as suddenly as it began – it ceased. Completely.

A darkness spread itself over Norwegian society and culture. No more books or poems were written, no more churches were built. Literature was silenced. Our great personalities died out. History, the life of our society, turned grey and dull.

Then for hundreds of years, Norwegians existed in a state of virtual suspended animation. Their sole preoccupation was survival. The people slept a deep, deep sleep. «Norway resembles an old widow, leaning on her staff, barely able to walk», wrote one of the very, very few who bothered to put pen to paper during this period, one Absalon Pederssøn Beyer. How right he was: 14th century Norway was decrepit and moribund, a land cloaked in cold, impotence and hopelessness. A land without a future.

And then, in the mid-19th century, a miracle; the country awakens, and experiences a cultural renaissance without parallel. In one area after another, talented men and women emerge to create a life for the country, with achievements in the arts and sciences which strike the rest of the world dumb with amazement. This small people, who for four to five hundred years had produced no cultural development worthy of mention, suddenly creates a culture so varied and energetic, so rich and vital that it has been justly compared to the more famous Italian Renaissance. Suddenly, Norway could boast world famous scientists, lead by Nils Henrik Abel; poets, of the calibre of Henrik Wergeland and Bjørnstjerne Bjørnson; in the theatre, Henrik Ibsen, of course; musicians Ole Bull and Rikard Nordråk; the composer Edvard Grieg; and so many talented visual artists that one can barely count them all.

How can we explain this cultural and intellectual miracle, which burst forth in 19th century Norway? Certainly not according to any Marxist theory of historical development; the material circumstances underlying Norwegian intellectual development had not altered in any significant degree from pre-1814. What HAD happened, on the other hand, in 1814, was that Norway had rid itself of the yolk of Danish colonialism, and could at last step forth as a free and independent nation-state. The consequence of this political event, its inspiration to the country's artistic and cultural life, simply cannot be underestimated.

Nonetheless, as an explanation for the sudden and violent change in the character of Norwegian intellectual and cultural life, it is not entirely satisfactory. Political liberty might be a condition for such an extraordinary development, but it does not explain it. Perhaps there is no explanation? Perhaps the Norwegian renaissance will always retain something of its fairy tale-like mystery?

Whatever: at this point in our history, Norwegian cultural heritage made its grand entry.

Because, what all these poets and artists, writers, critics and scientists did, was to direct their steady gaze at the past. That's not ALL they did, of course. But a powerful, collective fascination with the old Norway, with the last culture to dominate the land, asserted itself in them all. From there they drew their inspiration, their courage, initiative and creativity. Without more ado, they leapfrogged over the dead centuries, ignoring the victims of the so-called Four Hundred Year Night, to forge a link with those they considered to be their true ancestors.

«Our Norway and the Norway of the Ancients are like two half-circles which join most perfectly,» said Henrik Wergeland, famously. «The intervening years are but a false link we sweep away to allow true union. We leap across these years; these Norwegians, we neither respect nor love: in time they may stand closer than the Ancients, but not in spirit. When we talk of the old Norway, it is of the Ancients we speak. We gaze across to them, as one mountain peak to another, without once letting our eyes drop to the dark valley between.»

Of course, one could say – as indeed it HAS been said – that such leap frogging of history is impossible. Nonetheless, it is a fact that the cultural heritage of what we might call the Old

Norway, became after 1814 a vitally important source of energy in Norwegian intellectual life. Enthusiasm for the Old Norway, respect for the size and breadth of the saga-period, laid the foundation for the new Norwegian culture. Poets and artists, historians, critics and commentators – even they needed something to counterbalance the vestige of the Danish period. It was a matter of life and death. It was a matter of self-respect. Pride. «Independence's own sense of honour», as Bjørnson described it in reference to the creation of his historical dramas – his ancestoral gallery. And many others would have described it thus. Everyone was fumbling for their heritage; in the saga-period they discovered a Norwegian cultural life they could acknowledge and be inspired by.

Contempory culture in Norway was so depressingly Danish; the literature, music, painting. Even the language was Danish. But the artists wanted to be Norwegian, and so they became. The inheritance from the Middle Ages spoke of a Norwegian identity, a Norwegian language. These were taken up, and forged into the foundation of all that was to follow.

The manner in which this was done was often crassly patriotic in the extreme, as when Wergeland and his cohorts clad themselves as Vikings and publicly declared Snorre's Saga as Norway's new Bible. But the campaign also had its quieter and gentler moments, particularly in the hands of the poet Welhaven and his circle. It was Welhaven, not Wergeland, who wrote the famous words:

«Farmer, your native soil is a holy land;
what Norway was, she must be once more –
upon the land, and the sea, and in the people.»

In their different ways, Wergeland and Welhaven dreamt of filling the huge void at the centre of Norwegian culture, desiring as close and heartfelt a relationship between the old and the new Norway as possible. How successful they were in this, is another matter. Neither Wergeland's historical poems nor Welhaven's ballads can be said to be amongst the most widely read works, today. But in their time and place, they passed a certain muster: the poems gave evidence of our golden past, and presented the old culture and values as ideals worthy of aspiration.

The first post-1814 generations had no real notion of the precise nature of their Norwegian heritage, and they were well aware of the fact. All the more reason, they argued, to sing its praises as loudly as possible, whilst throwing oneself into the study of the saga-period, in order to reclaim it for the present. They collected and studied everything pertaining to the old Norwegians, from before the arrival of the Romans with their foreign culture and ideas. Linguistic researchers applied themselves to the Old Norwegian and ancient Nordic languages, historians excavated all they could find on the way of life in the old Norway. And the people lapped it up.

At the epicentre of this whole process stood the historians, not least P.A Munch, one of the great driving forces of the Norwegian renaissance, whose monumental work, 'The History of the Norwegian People' was an inexhaustible inspiration to his contempories. In his time, Munch was the most learned man in Norway. He had an intimate knowledge of the Ancient Norwegian sources – the Eddaic poems, sagas, land surveys, laws – and was dedicated to sharing his knowledge with anyone and everyone who would listen. And there was no shortage of those. P.A Munch was more than just a historian and scientist, he was also something of a fantast and dreamer, which perhaps explains his great influence on the cultural life of his time. On the basis of his writings about the Norwegian Middle Ages, poets composed historical dramas that are still performed in the Norwegian theatre today. Linguists, historians, politicians – all were influenced by Munch.

His hypothesis was that the Middle Ages were still alive and well in Norway; and that living evidence of this was to be found in the villages and rural areas. The old Norwegian language, for example, was still very much evident in the regional dialects, and on the basis of this, in Munch's opinion, could and should be restored in its entirity. Every area of folk-tradition, but especially folk song and tales, bore testimony of the spirit and tone of the ancient society. It was simply a question of freeing them.

Norwegian cultural heritage, in other words, was alive and well in the Norwegian people themselves. It had simply hibernated during the long winter of Danish rule, in the arts and crafts of ordinary people. There was more than enough here to draw upon.

And drawn upon it was. Indeed, it was veritably dragged into the light of day, by activists in the most disparate fields. Asbjørnsen and Moe, Olea Crøger and M.B. Landstad made a comprehensive collection of traditional folk tales; Ivar Aasen travelled the length and breadth of the country, codifying the remains of the old Norwegian language in the various dialects; Ludvig Mathias Lindeman concentrated on folk music – spending decades travelling around, collecting melodies and airs that had been preserved unchanged through the generations from the Middle Ages.

And these activities fed directly into the new developments of the Norwegian renaissance – Ibsen's and Bjørnson's dramas, Ivar Aasen's New Norwegian language, Richard Nordråk's and Edvard Grieg's music. The old Norwegian culture formed the bedrock of the new.

True enough, there was eventually a reaction against National Romanticism in Norway. The unbridled enthusiasm for linking up with the culture of the past gave way to an attitude more critical of the inflated claims of a Norwegian Golden Age. A certain sceptism arose.

Nevertheless, the culture of the saga-period and the Middle Ages continued to exert a dominating influence on Norwegian intellectuals. Time and again, in both literature and music, we notice the way these ancient national impulses combine with current influences from Europe, to produce masterpieces.

Would Olav Duun or Sigrid Undset, for example, be imaginable without their specifically Norwegian heritage? A novel such as «The Juvik Folk», the style of which is so closely related to that of the sagas, is surely nothing if not a form of renewel of the sagas?

Sigrid Undset began her writing career with a novel in the saga style, 'The Saga of Viga-Ljot and Vigdis'. True, it was never published – it was rejected by the director of the Gylendal Publishing House with the advice to «Forget the historical novel; it's beyond you.» (This, to the eventual writer of one of the cornerstone works in Norwegian literature – the historical novel-cycle 'Kristin Lavransdatter'!)

«I think the reason I understand our own time as well as I do – or at any rate SEE it as well as I do», she later wrote, «Is because, from my earliest childhood, I've had a sort of living notion of an earlier time to compare it with. Strip away the layer of concepts and ideas belonging to your own time, and you find yourself in the Middle Ages.»

But the heritage from the Middle Ages didn't only lay the foundations for the 19th century Norwegian renaissance, it has also inspired the artists of our own century to great and audacious works. Even in the work of artists and poets who apparently have nothing to do with these traditions, we see traces of the influence. A writer such as Sigurd Hoel, for example, was happy to admit his indebtedness to the past, not least the Middle Ages. «The Sagas, folk-tales and songs function as an eternal basis of health in Norwegian intellectual life», he once wrote. «It's necessary to distance ourself from these sources, and often; we have to orientate ourselves outwards. The world changes, time doesn't stand still. But, every now and again, following our skirmishes with the new, we notice how our artists and thinkers follow their instincts to return to that which will always be Norwegain, and therefore natural and real for us, to renew their energies. The folk-tales and Sagas – which themselves were the result of an exchange between local and foreign energies, are, for better or for worse, the most thoroughly Norwegian things we can lay claim to»

Cultural heritage – the phrase has become so overused that for many that's all it is, a phrase, all too easily pressed into service whenever a speech must be delivered or a policy formulated. It is the same with 'Norwegian' or 'our national characteristic'.

But what does it actually signify? Where do we SEE this heritage? What is it about Norwegian art and culture that characterises it from that of other countries? What exactly is it that divides us from everyone else?

It is not easy to find an answer to these questions. But neither is it impossible. There are, undeniably, elements in Norwegian literature and art which leave us with the impression of ha-

Ivo Caprino, an artist of diverse talents, has created a fairy-tale park by the Hunderfossen waterfalls, where well known tales are presented. In the picture, Veslefrikk with his fiddle. Large picture: From the tale «The Princess that no one could outwit». Below: A scene from the «The Widowed Fox».

HUNDERFOSSEN FAMILIEPARK/Normann

HUNDERFOSSEN FAMILIEPARK/Normann

SCAN-FOTO/Arkiv

SCAN-FOTO/Arkiv

HUNDERFOSSEN FAMILIEPARK/Normann

The two great Norwegian storytellers, Jørgen Moe, painted by Chr. Olsen, and, left, Peter Chr. Asbjørnsen, painted by H. J. F. Berg.

Ole Bull (1810–1880) was a violin virtuoso who knew the secrets of his instrument better than any. He was adored during an age of romantic exultation and celebrated around the world. He spent much time in America and became an honourary citizen of New York. But in 1880, at the age of 70 he died in his summer house on the Lysøen island, close to his birthplace, Bergen. His native town has erected a statue of him, made by Stephan Sinding.

KNUDSENS FOTOSENTER

SCAN-FOTO/Arkiv

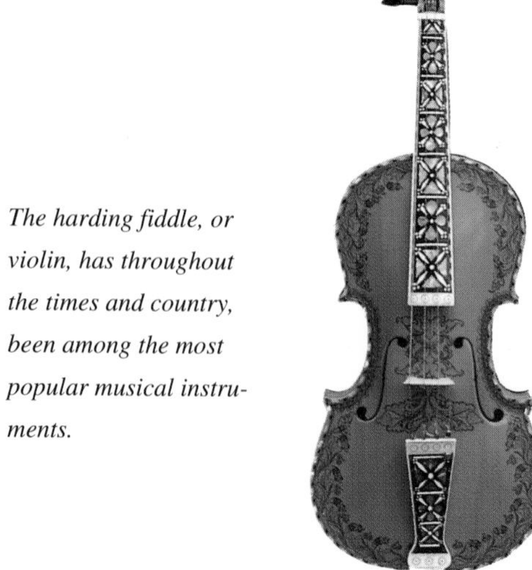

The harding fiddle, or violin, has throughout the times and country, been among the most popular musical instruments.

KNUDSENS FOTOSENTER

KNUDSENS FOTOSENTER

The Niels Henrik Abel monument, sculpted by Gustav Vigeland, was unveiled in the Royal Park in 1908.

KNUDSENS FOTOSENTER

KNUDSENS FOTOSENTER

KNUDSENS FOTOSENTER

The Grand Café used to be a meeting spot for the artists of the capital, and many of them can be seen on Per Kroghs's large wall-painting. Below: Some of the renowned statues in Oslo. From the left: Henrik Wergeland by Brynjulf Bergslien, J. S. C. Welhaven by Gunnar Utsond, Petter Andreas Munch and Rikard Nordraak by Gustav Vigeland.

KNUDSENS FOTOSENTER

KNUDSENS FOTOSENTER

Camilla Collett (1813–1895) wrote one of the first social commentary novels in Norway, «The Governors Daughters,» in 1854. It is a daring and defiant book, defending the rights of women, and full of attacks on the male dominated society. Ibsen, Lie, and Kielland all showed great interest in the book, which influenced parts of their work. In her later books, Camilla Collett displays a more outright agitation for the cause of women's liberation.

SCAN-FOTO/Arkiv

SCAN-FOTO/Arkiv

Sigrid Undset (1882–1949) was also preoccupied with women's position in society and her novel «Jenny», providing a realistic description of the erotic dilemma, led to a heated debate. However, it was her gigantic mediaeval novels that made her one of our greatest novelists and earned her the Nobel Prize in 1928.

ving heard the voice of a whole people. Something that binds both classical and contempory Norwegian writing with the sagas and the Eddaic poems. But how do we DEFINE these? Although one hesitates to isolate individual characteristics, or to attempt to define them in terms that may betray their complexity, one ought at least to try!

It has long struck me, that all Norwegian writing, down the ages, has leant strongly in the direction of individualism. From the very beginning, it would seem, Norwegian literature has functioned as an appeal to the individual; as a collective protest against the destruction of the individual.

Let us take, for example, the numerous depictions of doggedness in the saga-literature; the stubborn, intractable loners who stand on their principles and refuse to give in to force. They tell the story of an individual who, above all, wishes to remain true to him or her self; of men and women who refuse to bend to any threat to their individuality. Proud people, struggling to preserve their humanity. To take just one example – the speech delivered by the yeomen's leader, Asbjørn of Medalhus, to King Håkon Adelsteinsfostre when the latter tries to press the yeomen of Trøndelag to abandon the old faith. Snorre reports it thus:

> «King Håkon, the first time you held your parliament here in Trondheimen, we accepted you as our king and you granted us this land, and we believed we had heaven itself in our hands. But now, we no longer know whether you meant to give us our freedom, or enthrall us in this strange manner. Do you wish us to abandon the faith of our forefathers? True, they were finer men than we, but their faith has helped us, also. We have shown you much devotion, even to accepting your word in matters of property and law. It is our wish to keep these laws that you pronounced, and with which we agreed – all yeomen consent to this. We all wish to follow you and have you as our king, so long as any here in this parliament still lives, and as long as you, as king, act reasonably and do not demand more of us than we can deliver. But if you insist on pursuing this matter to the point of violence and force against us, then we have all agreed to abandon you and take another leader, one who will leave us in peace with our faith. And now, King Håkon, you must make your choice, before this parliament adjourns».

Defiance and obstinacy in the face of annihilation of the individual, with all its implications, is typical of many of the Norwegians we meet in the sagas, and elsewhere in Norwegian literature. The appeal of the individual would seem to command an important, indeed inalienable, position in our cultural heritage.

We find it in Wergeland:

> *«But whisper it not quietly*
> *Truth's friend must not be be sacrificed*
> *In all things, be yourself!*
> *This is the art of victory!*
> *As wild flowers between the stones*
> *You must stand, yourself alone.»*

We find it also in Welhaven, Vinje, Bjørnson. Henrik Ibsen's relationship to the individual is truly passionate. His entire creative output was concerned with the conflict between the individual and the masses, between the human being and the troll. The contrast between 'self-reliance' and 'self-satisfaction' is one of Ibsen's central preoccupations. He never tired of acclaiming the individual, even if sometimes negatively, as in Peer Gynt. In many ways, Peer is a travesty of Norwegian individualism, its negative and false manifestation. Similarly, Holdberg's Erasmus Montanus is also one against the masses, but to comic effect; he is also a caricature of the emphatic individual.

Suffice to say, classical Norwegian literature is full of individuals, portrayed with both pathos and passion. Indeed, it occurs so often, and so sincerely, that we are obliged to accept it as an important element in our heritage. A writer such as Hans E. Kinck – who employed this tendency more than most – emphasises that our feelings of individuality equate with our innermost dreams. Kinck is contemptuous of those who lack such feelings, who lack any sense of their inner selves – opportunists, salesmen and pedlars. Kinch despises these Norwegian types, in exactly the same way as Ibsen despised soldiers of fortune and status-seekers such as the lawyer Steensgård, or Peder Mortensgård; people who lack what Kinck called 'the spark of the ideal' – character, integrity.

It is not hard to provide examples of the way in which successive generations of Norwegian poets and writers have been inspired by the notion of the upright individual's struggle with all that threatens his individuality. They are to be found wherever one looks. Dip at random into almost any book you care to choose, and you will find them. Right up to, and including, our own time, this notion has exerted its influence on Norwegian art and culture, lying, as it does, at the very centre of our culture heritage.

The battle of Hafrs-fjord, in the county of Rogaland, where Harald Fairhair seized power over huge parts of Norway, is commemorated in Fritz Røed's momument, «Sword Into Mountain».

KNUDSENS FOTOSENTER

JARLE KJETIL ROLSETH

The staging of histori-cal plays is part of the Olympic arrangements. The Viking ship, Saga Siglar, is one of many models built during the past years.

SCAN-FOTO/Rolf B. Gundersen

The moving of old houses is an elaborate operation. Below, the Jørstad farm, which now stands at Maihaugen, as a part of the collection, De Sandvigste Samlinger. When disassembled, every plank or board has to be accurately marked.

LILLEHAMMER FOTO OG BILLEDARKIV/Jarle Kjetil Rolseth

LILLEHAMMER FOTO OG BILLEDARKIV/Jarle Kjetil Rolseth

Den Nationale Scene in Bergen is rich in its theatrical traditions, whereas Det Norske Teater in Oslo (far right) is the most modern in the country.

KNUDSENS FOTOSENTER

KNUDSENS FOTOSENTER

SCAN-FOTO/Erik Poppe

Liv Mildred Gjernes, known for her applied art, has found her sources of inspiration in the mediaeval traditions.

Four great artists

Lars Roar Langslet:

SCAN-FOTO/Ingar Johansen

Lars Roar Langslet (b. 1936), M.A. in the History of Ideas, is a commentator on cultural affairs for the daily, Aftenposten. Since the early sixties, he has been an acclaimed writer on matters of culture and the arts, and the author of numerous books. For many years he acted as the ideological spokesman for the Conservative Party, Høyre. In 1969 he became a member of parliament, Stortinget, and in 1981 he was appointed Minister of Cultural Affairs, in the Willoch government.

Internationally, impressions of Norway and of the Norwegian character are principally determined by the work of four great artists; Henrik Ibsen, Edvard Grieg, Knut Hamsun and Edvard Munch. All four drew on similar historical and cultural sources, and a comparison of their work can prove extremely fruitful. Here they are presented by the writer and former Minister of Culture, Lars Roar Langslet.

Opposite: «Fjelland-skap med Foss» by J. C. Dahl. The painting from 1873 is exhibited at the National Gallery, Nasjonalgalleriet, in Oslo.

JOHAN BRUN

In world population terms, Norways' four million-plus inhabitants constitute the merest drop in the ocean. Though occasionally it has struck me as an advantage that we are not more – four hundred million Norwegians is an unbearable thought, even for a Norwegian! Fortunately, our barren strip of a country at the northernmost edge of Europe provides neither the space nor the means to support so many people. Our national character has not been formed in densely populated, historic cultural centres; as one of the poets put it, «Loneliness has shaped our mentality».

Norway's nature has inspired all of the «four masters». Picture: Vindafjell in the county of Hedmark.

Nevertheless, this small people, in a country where the power of nature has often made us feel smaller still, has managed to create a culture to make the rest of the world sit up and take note.

For cultural activity is measured by different yardsticks than most other areas of human enterprise: in culture, the bottom line is quality – not quantity, and even a small people may create something which resonates, worldwide.

Significantly, Norwegian culture flourished most energetically, and had its greatest impact on the world, during periods of our history when our contact with the world was most vibrant. In particular the High Middle Ages and the bare half-century from the 1860s until the 1920s; the long centuries between these productive bursts were characterised by almost total isolation and estrangement from the world.

The cultural blossoming in the High Middle Ages was prepared for by the Vikings. Implements and jewelry from this period possess great beauty and style, though the Viking's most beautiful creations were their longships, excavated quite recently from ancient burial mounds. Perfect, slender lines and rich decoration make these unique cultural and artistic monuments, offering vivid insights into ancient principles of construction and navigation. Not unsurprisingly, the longships constitute one of the country's most popular tourist attractions.

But, symbolically, the longships also function on another level. Norwegians have long sea-faring traditions; our wild mountain areas and long, extreme winters made land communications extremely arduous and dangerous, and the sea provided the main artery of communication and the principal route of cultural exchange with the outside world.

Following pressure from the rest of the world, both ecclesiastical and secular, the Vikings' raids finally came to an end and Norway's integration into the cultural, political and economic development of Europe quickly accelerated, utilising a network of international contacts and influence far broader than was formerly believed. The pilgrims' way to the shrine of Norway's holy king, Olav Haraldsson, at the altar of Nidaros Cathedral, was a popular route, and the Church was the major energising source of cultural development. Olav The Holy, 'Norway's Eternal King', was admired throughout Christendom, even represented on one of the pillars of the pilgrims' church in Bethlehem.

The highest literary achievement of the High Middle Ages was the Sagas. Even today, this uniquely fresh and fascinating literary body of work, retains the power to inspire a sophisticated modern poet like the Argentinian, Borges. Originally composed in Iceland, then virtually a part of Norway, the spare, concentrated form of the sagas has served as a model for many modern Norwegian poets and writers, and provided Henrik Ibsen and Bjørnstjerne Bjørnson with material for their historical dramas. Sigrid Undset's saga-inspired novel-cycle about Kristin Lavransdatter and Olav Audunssøn, is one of the unsurpassed masterpieces of Norwegian literature.

The architectural and artistic heritage of the Middle Ages is seen most vividly in the wooden stave churches, Gothic and Romanesque monasteries, cathedrals, sculptures and reliefs, together with the great wooden buildings, with elaborately carved interiors, which characterised Norwegian rural culture down the centuries. The prototypes of a typically Norwegian building and craft tradition first saw light of day already in the Middle Ages.

The folk-song and music which so inspired Norwegian composers in the 19th and 20th century, not least Edvard Grieg, can also be traced back to this period. Beneath the lilting, melancholy tunes and melodies, one senses the resonances of both Gregorian Chant and the harsher rhythms of rural ring dances.

This creative explosion, however, was followed by a national catastrophe. In the middle of the 12th century, the Black Death wiped out two-thirds of the population and completely de-

destroyed the economic and cultural independence of the country. Under the rule of successive Danish monarchs, Norway gradually became a cultural backwater. The Norwegian language was even replaced by Danish – (although it assumed a certain 'Norwegianness' by combination with the dialects of southern Norway.)

The Union with Denmark lasted until 1814. By then, the need for independence was long since been awakened. It was the Middle Ages, Norway's great past, which was to provide the prototypes for the subsequent cultural renaissance, described elsewhere in this book.

This so-called National Romantic revival had strong connections with contempory European cultural movements, and laid the foundation for the unique cultural developments in Norway in the second half of the 19th century and first third of the 20th. The country's reputation as a cultural nation is above all linked to the greatest names of this epoch – Henrik Ibsen, Edvard Grieg, Knut Hamsun and Edvard Munch. In so far as people in distant parts of the world have any impression at all of Norway and Norwegian character, it is thanks to these four men, who form the main focus of this article.

It's not hard to see the circumstances of cultural blossoming in a small nation's struggle for independence. Artists wanted to use – or be used by – what might be called a 'nation-building ideology'. The task was to define a specifically Norwegian identity, which could engender and substantiate our cultural independence. Great artists thereby became the nations' spiritural pathfinders; there can be few countries in the world where poets and painters have played such a distinctive role in the formation of a nation's sense of self. It was the young Henrik Ibsen who wrote that his goal was to the inspire his his fellow countrymen to great thoughts! Neither was he alone in such ambitions.

But, that such an eruption of talent coincided so precisely with the need for it, can no more be explained by exterior circumstances than the fact that four such geniuses as Ibsen, Grieg, Munch and Hamsun should be fostered, sequentially, by a nation of so few people. Whilst fulfilling a national need for cultural self-confirmation, their art transcended national boundaries and turned them into international cultural figures.

It is perhaps easier, with hindsight, to see the truth in Gunnar Heiberg's aphorism, that «All good art is national. All national art is bad».

Programatic nationalism is as thin a veil for artistic crassness as any other ideology seeking to make art its servant, in whose name even good artists sometimes compromise their art. But whilst truly great artists always draw nourishment from their own specific historical, geographical and cultural circumstances, their greatness arises from their mysterious capacity to locate the universal dimension in their material, which renders it relevant across national or historical boundaries.

In the last century, when the challenge of national definition was more pressing than it is today, there was a tendency to overemphasise the introspective aspect of Norwegian cultural life, to undervalue outside impulses and links with other countries. But the greatest artists were more far-sighted, and Gunnar Heiberg relates a story which illustrates this. One day, he met Henrik Ibsen and told him he was preparing a polemic on Bjørnson's recent statement that Norwegian literature reflected the fact that the country was a basically a rural society. «Of course,», said Ibsen, eagerly, «That's quite right. It's a European culture. Our literature is European.»

We shan't examine Bjørnson's argument more closely here, though, suffice to say, it should not imply Bjørnson himself was a 'stay-at-home'. As with all our great artists of the time, he lived abroad for important periods of his life, was widely read, maintained a wide European correspondence, and followed European intellectual developments very closely. This tendency to look outward was in part due to insufficiencies at home; Norway lacked institutions of artistic training or education, publishers, galleries, etc, adequate for the needs of her artists. But there was also another reason. Norwegian artists then, to a much greater extent than now, saw themselves as members of a wider Scandinavian and European artistic community, affected by the same new impulses and insights as the rest of the continent. They were orientated towards a wider, European audience, and sought recognition beyond their country's borders.

Whilst the prevelance of national themes in their work was not due to any sense of parochialism, the national dimension soon began to change its character. 'Norwegianness' ceased to dominate as an ideological programme, becoming rather a common denominator for the contribution of our artists to the wider European context.

Henrik Ibsen (1828–1906) has a higher place in classical world literature that any other writer Norway has produced. His Norwegianness – in his temperament, his feeling for nature, his linguistic musicality, perhaps also his extreme ethical individualism – is umistakable. Yet he was also a European and a cosmopolitan; already in his own lifetime his plays were being read and performed all over the world. On the other hand, Ibsen's reputation has grown steadily, and today interest in his work, both at home and abroad, is more intense than ever.

The most Norwegian of his works – to Norwegians, at least – is 'Peer Gynt' (1867), a great dramatic poem which has assumed the status of national epos in Norway, on a par with Geothe's 'Faust' in Germany, and 'Don Quixote' in Spain. Written in a lively, sinuous verse, the play draws liberally on the mystical world of tales, myths, sayings, music and customs of Norwegian folklore. «The play is saturated in an atmosphere of fantasy and folklore», writes Daniel Haakonsen, and, for a Norwegian, it is hard to see how the play can either be translated or performed anywhere other than Norway. Yet it has been, and continues to be, repeatedly, with great success, throughout the world. Indeed, the leading British stage director, John Barton, has recently produced one of the best 'Peer Gynts' of our time at the National Theatre in Oslo, with Norwegian actors!

O. VERING

«Henrik Ibsen and the Beast» became a saying in contemporary Christiania. Every day, on his way from his apartment in Arbinsgate to the Grand Cafe, he would stop in front of the University and adjust his watch.

How can a play with such a specifically Norwegian frame of reference have any appeal for a modern audience in, say, China or France? The explanation must lie in the fact that Peer Gynt also functions as a univeral drama of human fate. In his anlysis of the play's ending, Daniel Haakonsen strikingly defines this marriage of dimensions; «As fantasy and reality merge into one, the fairy-tale world of the play recalls the Mediaeval Morality tale of Everyman, binding the characters to Fate, Providence, Judgement and Salvation.»

Generations of Norwegian school children have been force-fed the notion of 'Peer Gynt' as a searing satire on Norwegian weakness, boastfulness and flight from reality, with particular reference to events in 1864, when the other Nordic countries failed to assist Denmark in her war with Germany. «The Poetry of Indignation», as Koht, one of our leading literary critics, has dubbed it. It is certainly true that Ibsen began working on the play in a mood of profound indignation. But this must have evaporated somewhat as the artistic impulse overtook his need to castigate his countrymen. The shere vivacity of large sections of the play, the sense of fun and uplift, is difficult to square with the implications of a «Poetry of Indignation».

The same is true of the figure of Peer Gynt himself. The «Indignation» hypothesis accentuates the idea that Ibsen's target is Peer's great ability to cast himself as the hero of his preposterous stories. But in the play these scenes are undeniably the high points, in which Peer's creativity most clearly manifests itself. His decline into cheating and cowardliness, on the other hand, is underlined by a falling away of his visionary flights. The play itself refutes the 'Indignation' hypothesis; it is Peer Gynt's creativity which lies at the root of his greatness.

Not least, 'Peer Gynt' anticipates a theme Ibsen was to take up with corrosive clarity in his later works: that of the Artist, pushing life to one side in his fixation on his own creative development, consummating the tragedy through the destruction of himself and others. Peer himself is saved – by a redeeming mercy from on high – in one of the play's many parallels with 'Faust'. This salvation is linked to the notion of a liberating transformation which releases the individual from «the vessel of the self», and humanity from the «The signboard of the Master».

A similar transformation is found in Ibsen's other great poetic drama – 'Brand' (1866). Pastor Brand is a man livng under great tension, as strict and strong as an Old Testament prophet – the complete opposite to Peer Gynt. He demands 'all or nothing'; that one should never 'go round about', even when it means pushing aside the mitigating power of love; until, dying in the Ice Church, he feels 'the crust', or scab, about him burst. The last words of the play – «He is Deus caritatis – the God of Love» – is both a judgment and a prophesy.

Ibsen's reputation in world drama was first established, however, by the long cycle of so-called realistic plays, written in his later years. In these plays, which all have a clear 'sociological' dimension to them, Ibsen dissects the 'bourgeois family' both as way-of-life and social institution, often within the context of a Norwegian provincial setting. But the primary focus of the poet's bitter-sweet concern is the essential human tragedy inherent in the breakdown of an individual's freely-chosen personal ideals. In Ibsen, this 'claim of the ideal' is balanced against a fundamental personal responsibility for the consequences one's choices bring about in one's own life and other people's. It is not enough to legitimise one's good intentions: the result of one's actions outweighs any other considerations.

This 'realistic form', so-called, constitutes the framework of a very conscious dramatic structure, with a magical centre of poetic symbols, (which gradually assumes a more dominent role in Ibsen's oeuvre), and a finely tuned sense of narrative rhythm and musicality. The exhaustively detailed stage directions also fulfill a symbolic function. With his quasi-realistic, contempory dramas, Ibsen achieved a modern version of the ancient tragedy; more restricted in its vision, perhaps, but no less rich in dramatic power.

This is one explanation for the continued relevance of Ibsen's work, and why, whilst many of his most popular contemporaries are neglected, if not forgotten altogether, interest in him and his work is ever on the increase.

Ibsen once used the image of the miner in talking of his own contribution as a writer; cutting a path «hammer-blow by hammer-blow», towards the «hidden corner of the heart». The hammer is imprinted upon his grave. In his poem to the composer Edvard Grieg, he used a similar image.

«Orpheus struck, with pure tones,
the spirit into beasts, the fire into stones

Norway has enough of stones and rock
Wild beasts, by the herd and flock

Play! so beasts burst their skin
Play! so stones spark from within.»

Ibsen and Grieg were never close friends. It is doubtful whether the maverick Ibsen ever had any really close friends at all. But their collaborations yielded rich fruit; Grieg's series of ballad-settings of Ibsen's poems, and above all his much-loved incidental music to 'Peer Gynt'.

Edvard Munch's art is characterised by a search for the symbolism of the soul and melancholy introvertedness. This is not apparent, though, from his photos as a young man or later as a mature man. A nervous breakdown resulted in a marked change in his art, both in content and form. The colouring became more distinct and lighter, and the brushwork freer, as seen on the picture, centre, «The Sun» from 1912.

SCANFOTO/Arkiv

SCANFOTO/Arkiv

KNUDSENS FOTOSENTER

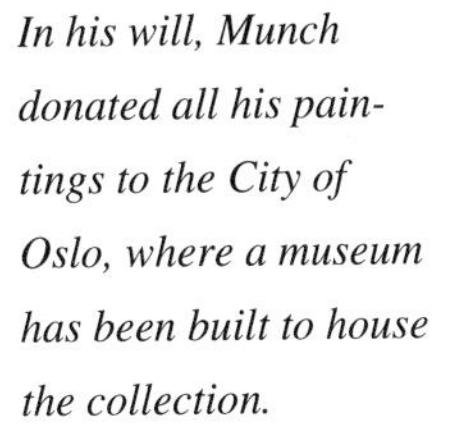

In his will, Munch donated all his paintings to the City of Oslo, where a museum has been built to house the collection.

KNUDSENS FOTOSENTER

Edvard Munch was deeply influenced by Ibsen's writing and made a series of illustrations for Ibsen's plays. He was particularly fascinated by the final scene in John Gabriel Borkman, a scene that often recurs in his works.

KNUDSENS FOTOSENTER

Henrik Ibsen won international acclaim before his death. His portrait was also reproduced in glass, as here from Bonanzaville Museum in Fargo, North Dakota.

MUNCH-MUSEET

SCANFOTO/Arkiv

MUNCH-MUSEET

Munch made many stage-sketches for Ibsen's plays, this one being for Hedda Gabler in 1907.

Henrik Ibsen's study in Arbinsgate is on display in the Folkemuseum in Oslo. Its return to Arbinsgate is called for by the Ibsen interpreter, the actor Knut Wigert, who has made an Ibsen museum of the apartment.

NORSK FOLKEMUSEUM

Edvard Munch painting Grieg surrounded by the nature that marked so many of his compositions.

KNUDSENS FOTOSENTER

KNUDSENS FOTOSENTER

SCAN-FOTO/Arkiv

KNUDSENS FOTOSENTER

Edvard Grieg by Erik Werenskiold.

They were never close friends, but Grieg composed the music for much of what the great author Bjørnstjerne Bjørnson wrote.

KNUDSENS FOTOSENTER

KNUDSENS FOTOSENTER

Nina and Edvard Grieg at Troldhaugen.

KNUDSENS FOTOSENTER

KNUDSENS FOTOSENTER

KNUDSENS FOTOSENTER

Troldhaugen, outside Bergen, has been turned into a museum, and small concerts are sometimes held in the sitting-room.

The Grieg Hall is, however, where the works of this great son of Bergen are mostly performed.

As Ibsen is to drama, so Edvard Grieg (1843–1907) is to music; his international reputation is unrivalled by any other Norwegian composer. As much respected by music experts as he is loved by audiences everywhere, the melodious accessibility of much of his music has made him one of the most popular composers in the world.

Fifteen years ago, I received a surprising reminder of Grieg's international appeal – as well as the power of the mass-media – when, climbing to the top of the Great Wall of China, I was suddenly aware of familiar tones wafting through the air towards me. It was Grieg's ballad, 'A Dream', and for one moment I feared it really was a dream; that the rigours of the climb had provoked an attack of nationalistic hallucinations! But, looking round, I saw the source of the music – a transistor radio in the hand of a soldier of the People's Army. Grieg himself would surely never have dreamt that his music would one day issue forth in such exotic circumstances!

Edvard Grieg hailed from Bergen, Norway's most urbane community, with a rich musical tradition, and was drawn into a musical career by another famous Bergen-ite, the legendary violinist Ole Bull. His musical education, however, was received abroad, where he mixed with many of the greatest composers of the period – Franz Liszt amongst them – and toured throughout Europe as a concert pianist and conductor. His most important publisher was based in Germany. Grieg, too, had strong connections with Europe and the international artistic community.

It is not difficult to place Grieg in the context of European musical history. He belongs firmly to the romantic tradition typified by Robert Schumann, though his style included impressionistic elements that anticipated Debussy.

His particular characteristic as a composer, however, arose undoubtedly from his intense engagement with Norwegian folk music, which provided him with an inexhaustable source of inspiration.

In a letter to a German biographer, he wrote (1905): «Ever since my youth, Norwegian (folkesang) folklore, the tales and sagas, but above all Norwegian nature, have exerted a huge influence on my work. It was only later that I had the opportunity to study Norwegian folk-song in any real depth. . . My ancestors were Scottish, and (what remains for me) the mysterious popularity of my music cannot be explained by its national elements alone, but rather a blending of cosmopolitan and national factors. History has shown us that all art which stands the test of time has been national art. Like any other artist, consciously or unconsciously, I stand on a national fundament, and of course I am acutely aware of my own national feelings, especially when working with material of a national nature. . . On the other hand, when Norwegian poets do not portray nature, folklore or the sagas, but simply take up ordinary themes, it has never occurred to me add a particularly national quality. In fact, I have never sought this sort of colouring. It has come of its own accord. I don't believe for one minute that a national quality can be successfully contrived. Unless the national element lies in the blood, it has no legitimacy as 'creative' art, only as 'photographic' art.»

Grieg undoubtedly had an abundance of this 'national element' in his own blood. But he transposed it, moulded it in the crucible of his own sensitivity and temperament, into a deeply personal statement, which nonetheless sat effortlessly with the musical sensibility of the time. Grieg's oeuvre is remarkably comprehensive, but it emerged from short, hectic bursts of creativity, between which he suffered long, nerve-wracking periods when his creativity deserted him completely. His compositions mostly consist of chamber pieces, pieces for the piano, ballads and choral works. His larger orchestral work caused him much agony, though the most important of these is one of the great 'evergreens' of the genre, the Piano Concerto in A-minor (1868, revised just before his death), and the 'Peer Gynt Suite' also belongs amongst his most performed orchestral pieces. Other big projects, however, such as an opera with a libretto by Bjørnson, never reached fruition, and he himself judged his only symphony (the C-minor, 1864), as an immature work of his youth, condemning it to the drawer with instructions that it should never be performed. These instructions were finally betrayed only a few years ago – a composer of Grieg's dimension cannot force oblivion upon posterity. But, despite some fine sections and a definite Grieg-like ring

SCAN-FOTO

The Nobel laureate, Knut Hamsun, sympathised with the wrong side during the German occupation, and had to pay the consequences of his choice. Almost deaf, he sat by the flickering light of a paraffin lamp, trying to grasp the meaning of the charges. At his side, the first female lawyer to the high court in Norway, Sigrid Stray.

OSLO BYMUSEUM/Sverre Heiberg

SCAN-FOTO

Knut Hamsun bought Nørholm, a large farm outside Grimstad, and made it into a model farm.

to piece, it is not hard for us to agree with Grieg's own judgment: Johan Svendsen was a greater symphonic composer.

Grieg's oeuvre has been condemned by some as truncated, rendered tragically incomplete by the composer's poor health and spasmodic creativeness, and profound psychological explanations are put forward for his failure to fulfill his potential. But this is superfluous surmise. A composer who leaves behind him such a large and varied oeuvre as Edvard Grieg, so full of life and energy, has no need to excuse himself for not having created more of something else! Grieg's lyrical temperament is present in all his music in a striking variety of shades, from poetic sensitivity to high-voltage pathos, from quiet elegy to unrestrained attack or cheer. Norwegian poets are indeed fortunate to have had as sensitive and congenial an interpreter, one who created almost complete unity between music and text, and often elevated his collaborators into famous names throughout the world.

Grieg remained faithful to the examples set him by his German teachers, but in his use of timbre – and especially the specifically Norwegian colouration which was closely related to the phrasing and rhythmns of Norwegian folk music – we see that he was a pioneer in his own right. Thus, he helped to integrate a Norwegian musical heritage into the European context, to broaden its register and establish yardsticks for other composers who sought similar inspiration in their own national folk music. Through Grieg's work, Norway's voice was heard and identified throughout the world, and became a more discenible element in European culture.

The same can be said with some justification of Edvard Munch (1863–1944), though his contribution was made in a completely different art form, in a different social context and intellectual climate, and with entirely different aspirations for his art than Grieg.

In fact, it is easier to draw parallels between Munch and Henrik Ibsen. Munch was deeply effected by Ibsen's work; he made a number of empathic lithographic portraits of the poet's visionary face, and large number of illustrations for the plays, especially 'Peer Gynt' and the later plays, which he also designed for the stage. Munch's seminal lanscape painting, 'White Night', has a similar power and frozen vision of Fate as his picturesque 'version' of the closing scene of 'John Gabriel Borkman'. Typically, it was the increasing symbolic dimension of Ibsen's later plays which most stimulated Munch's imagination. Whilst there have been numerous exhibitions dealing with Munch's work as Ibsen's illustrator, the artistic kinship implied by this work has yet to be subjected to the scrutiny it perhaps deserves.

Though Ibsen was slow to express such things, it seems the respect was at least partially mutual. The playwright's taste in visual art (he had long nurtured ambitions to be a painter) were presumably too conventional, or at least too influenced by an older aesthetic, for him to easily tune into Munch's 'rebellious' wavelength. But he had attended one of Munch's exhibitions, studied the pictures with polite interest and pleased the young artist with the comment, «You will have the same struggle with your art as I had with mine.»

In this, Ibsen proved prophetic. And I refer not merely to the resistance both men met from their contemporaries, the incomprehension and ridicule they both endured. The fiercest struggle, for Munch as for Ibsen, was that which raged within – «the war with the trolls deep in the vaults of the heart and mind». Both were soul-searchers – Munch under the yolk of the growth of psychology and the increasing obsession of art with the labyrinths of consciousness. Munch was to dissect the soul as thoroughly as Leonardo had dissected the body. And, in common with all great artists, he had to perform this dissection by cutting deep into his own self, to offer his own blood. «Art is one's lifeblood», he once wrote.

As with Ibsen, so with Munch: any brief characterisation must be false, because of his versatility, the many different phases he went through during his development, and the fact that he was continuously growing as an artist. The same applies to any attempt one might make to place his work in relation to contempory developments in the visual arts.

Munch began painting already towards the end of the 1870s, and during the next decade was clearly influenced by contempory naturalistic painting and later by the Impressionists. In the 1890s he entered his symbolist period, dominated by his work on the famous 'Frieze of Life' – a series of expressive visual-poems on the themes of Love, Hate, Jealousy, Despair and Death. These paintings are characterised by melancholy and nature-mysticism, as well as a ponderous religiosity, which has almost certainly contributed greatly to the general notion of 'Scandinavian Gloom', running as a dark stream through time from Søren Kierkegaard to Ingmar Bergmann. «The joy of life, Mother», says Osvald, in Ibsens's 'Ghosts', «We don't know much about that, up here».

In the years around 1908, when Munch suffered his nervous breakdown, one notices a clear development in his art, in both form and content. The colours become clearer and lighter, the brushwork freer. The pictures unfold into great sun-drenched landscapes (e.g. the monumental Aula-murals at the University of Oslo) Or scenes of explosive energy – men bathing, a horse pulling logs, a man in a cabbage field, road-menders. He acknowledged the breakneck development towards pure abstraction of his contemporaries, whilst stubbornly keeping to his own path, never once abandoning his own figurative impulses. It was a long path – but he remained productive the whole way, with striking self-portraits of his death-marked face amongst the very last of his paintings.

Even so, we may define Munch's enormous output of paintings, graphics, even sculpture, as Poetic Expressionism, in which the psychical content is paramount – also in landscapes or interiors – without too much fear of contradiction.

He provides an insight into his preoccupations as an artist in some of his own written statements.

In 1889, he was famously quoted in an exhibition catalogue as saying, «No more paintings of interiors, people reading, women knitting. What we need now are living beings, who breath and feel, who suffer and love. The viewer must be able to feel the holy, terrible truth in a picture, and remove his hat, as in a church».

After he had painted 'A Sick Girl', and had been reminded that this was a popular motif in visual art, he wrote, «I'm quite sure that no painter has lived the life of his motif, even unto the last cry of pain, as I have with this sick child. It is not just myself sitting there, it is all my loved ones».

On another occasion, he stated quite definitely that a chair was quite as interesting a motif as a person. «But the chair must be percieved by a person. Somehow or another, it must have moved him, and one must make the viewer moved in the same way. It isn't the chair we must paint, but what the person felt upon seeing it».

It is not as easy to define the specifically Norwegian substance of Edvard Munch's art as with either Grieg or Ibsen. People born beneath other skies might be able to discern something typically Norwegian, or at any rate Scandinavian, in his melancholy introvertedness and symbolic soul-searching. Or perhaps in the experience of nature, and the clear Nordic light, which simplifies the solid contours of landscapes, laden with mystical and magical energy.

A similar poetic mysticism is to be found in the work of Munch's great contempory, the poet and novelist Knut Hamsun (1859–1952).

Hamsun's artistic development bears a striking resemblance to that of Munch.

His first novels, 'Hunger' (1890) and 'Mysteries' (1892), are intensely poetic studies of a mental life on the verge of obsession or breakdown, with an extraordinary empathy for the nuances between the rational and the irrational, the sudden impulses and changes of mood. 'Pan' (1894) and 'Victoria' (1898), had a similarly intense, poetic blend of erotica and nature-mystery. But around 1910 Hamsun also left behind this introverted soul-searching – the desolate 'Wanderers', with its ecstatic-erotic portrayal of life «under the Autumn stars» – and turned outward, embarking on a series of epic social-satires, his lyrical sensitivity present only as undertones to his bitter attack on industrialism and commercialism. This becomes the main thrust of his later works – even though, especially the August-books are so in love with their exuberant central character that the ideological tendency of them is effectively undermined. Then, in 1917, came a novel of a totally different character: 'Harvest', which earned Hamsun the Nobel Prize for Literature, and served a glowing celebration of rural life, a hymn to the simple meaning of the cycle of sowing, cultivation and harvest, to a war-weary world. But it also describes the snake in this paradise: the evil in people and the modern world's breathless pursuit of progress.

The previous year, Edvard Munch had painted his monumental 'Man in a Cabbage Field', with his broad legs straddling his bulging harvest, which could well have been a portrait of Hamsun's Isak Sellanraa, the hero of 'Harvest'.

Early in his career, Hamsun had declared his programme as a writer in words that remind us of the extreme demands Munch made upon painting; Poets must seek a way into «the secret movements, which occur unseen in the hidden corners of the soul. . . those thoughts and feelings wandering in blue, untraceable journeys in the heart and the mind, strange activities of the nerves, whisperings of the blood, prayers of the bones, the whole unconscious life of the soul. . . It may be a totally inexplicable state of the senses; a mute, groundless, rapture; a breath of psychic pain, a feeling of being spoken to from afar, from the air, the sea; a cruel, delicate sensitivity, that allows one to sense even the buzzing of ancient atoms; a sudden, unnatural glimpse of closed kingdoms; the sense of approaching danger in a careless moment. . .» (1890)

This was a new and exiting approach to writing in Norway at the time. The only other writer to come close to perceiving such dimensions was perhaps Ibsen, whom Hamsun, paradoxically, despised for false profundity (perhaps due to his lifelong love-hate relationship with the theatre). Certainly not Bjørnson, though Hamsun worshipped him beyond all reason. His real role-models were Dostoyevski, Strindberg and Nietzsche.

The most creative element of Hamsun's work is perhaps his deeply personal, almost eccentrically subjective prose style, at once so poetic, melodious, capricious and baroque that it remains unsurpassed. Although a whole generation of young writers became so entranced by it, it had to fight its way out of the master's grip in order to find its own voice. Despite a strong undertone of the northern Norwegian dialect, Hamsun's language was always completely his own. He wrote barely a single line in which his tone, his voiceprint, is not immediately discernable.

It is this linguistic magic, so unique in Norwegian literature, Hamsun's ability to draw the reader into his own world of feelings and atmospheres, that best explains his ability to exert such a strong and immediate grip on successive generations of readers. Literary style has a tendency to lose its appeal for successive generations, to become a barrier and a hindrance to those coming to it from a different context. Not so with Hamsun. Even today, the meeting with his work is, for most readers, spontaneous and unreserved, like a sudden love affair.

LILLEHAMMER FOTO OG BILLEDARKIV/Jarle Kjetil Rolseth

Knut Hamsun was born in Garmo, in Lom, and lived there his first three years. A monument was erected to his memory, and later a little museum was built.

This love cooled considerably both during and after the war, due to Hamsun's attitude to the German Occupation. No one can explain away the fact that he stood on the 'wrong' side, with a stubbornness which culminated with his obituary for Hitler. His aristocratic contempt for modern civilisation, and a lifelong love for Germany (where he first achieved his breakthrough), rendered him uncritically susceptible to ideas of German revival. His almost perverse need to always go against the stream also played its part. But the fact is that the worst excrescences of Nazism, especially anti-Semitism, are barely be found anywhere in Hamsun's work. Hamsun was never a full-blown Nazi.

His final years were beset by misery. Hamsun was shamefully treated by his countrymen, not least by former friends who had basked in his generousity. His response was «Along Overgrown Paths», a triumph of art over old age and degradation.

Today, the tragic final phase no longer overshadows Hamsun's greatness as a writer. His best work has a freshness to it that time cannot erase.

Four great artists – whose greatness has not faded. Have they, on the other hand, overshadowed the artistic development of modern Norway, by setting examples that can seem oppressive to a new generation of artists?

This is a question so huge that I can merely hint at the beginnings of an answer. The most obvious case is Edvard Grieg. His artistic genius, with Norwegian folk music as his great energy-source, created a precedent which dominated Norwegian composition at least until the war, and which still has consequences even today. But it cannot be said to have inhibited the individuality of Grieg's successors, nor hinder the growth of other musical forms.

Edvard Munch also exerted a strong influence over recent Norwegian visual art. His use of colour, his bold, expressive style, and graphic mastery, set an example which no artist could pass by, nonchalantly. But he never established any school of art, and by the time of his death, younger artists had long since began developing formal languages in line with international developments.

Henrik Ibsen and Knut Hamsun can be seen as more isolated figures in this repect. Literary critics can of course write huge tomes on their genuine influence on modern Norwegian literature. The evidence is there, at least in echoes and resonances. But the fact is, Norway has not produced a first class playwright after Ibsen, and Hamsun's subjectivity was too unique to set its stamp on subsequent novelists. Great writers such as Sigrid Undset, Johan Falkberget and Tarjei Vesaas found their own forms, their own material.

But influences should perhaps not be measured thus.

Most importantly, the heritage of these great artists has entered into the bloodstream of the Norwegian people, as inalienable expressions of what it means to be Norwegian, and as anchors for our sense of cultural identitiy.

For each of them we must be allowed to feel the same childish pride that Bjørnson expressed in his poem about Niels Henrik Abel:

Now the world owns him
But first he was ours!

ESPEN BRATLIE

Hamsun was attached to Hamarøy, in Nordland County, the fabulous nature had an important impact on him and gave inspiration to many of his novels. A bust of him has been placed in Hamarøy.

A Thousand Years of Norwegian Food

Henry Notaker:

SCAN-FOTO/Knut Falch

Henry Notaker (b. 1941) M.A. in Norwegian literature, has been working as a journalist since 1967, at first with Aftenposten, and later with the NRK. He was NRK's permanent correspondent in Paris for four years. He frequently hosts television programs on matters of culture, society, and arts, and has done so for many years. He is the author of numerous books, amongst others on gastronomy and Norwegian culinary traditions.

According to a book about the common diet written in 1848, Norwegians are drinkers of aquavit, eaters of brown whey cheese, and guzzlers of fermented fish. As examples of Norwegian peasant culinary tradition, these dishes are well chosen, believes the author of the following article, who takes us through a thousand years of Norwegian food. If the Viking sagas are to be believed, our ancestors were importing foodstuffs over a thousand years ago, yet, right up until this century, everyday life was characterised by simple, peasant food such as fish – especially herring -, milk and corn products, and a certain amount of meat. But habits have changed.

The kitchen has, through the ages, become the natural place to stay when one ate, weaved, rested, or received guests.

KNUDSENS FOTOSENTER

NORSK FOLKEMUSEUM

NORSK FOLKEMUSEUM

In most areas, the brewing of ale has long traditions. On the larger farms, the recipes are passed from one generation to another, and in certain areas, competitions as to who can brew the best beer, are organized at Christmas time.

«. . . one evening Harald and Svein talked over drinks.» Then, as now, much mead was drunk, and drinking horns have been found at many of the Viking excavation sites. (Illustration from Snorri's Saga.)

Various tools were developed for the grinding of cereals. Solid tubs were needed to preserve milk and other liquids. The boxes used for storing and carrying food were often rose-painted or otherwise decorated. Kitchen appliances were generally made of wood and lasted for generations.

NORSK FOLKEMUSEUM

NORSK FOLKEMUSEUM

NORSK FOLKEMUSEUM

NORSK FOLKEMUSEUM/Bjørg Disington

Goblets, cups, and bottles were among the first glass-works. They were made by crafts-men with a great sense of style, and many of the older styles are copied today, with considerable success.

KNUDSENS FOTOSENTER

BENGT WILSON

Iron baking appliances were often decorated with the strangest of motives. As seen here, the apostles circling a lion that has caught Satan in its claws.

NORSK FOLKEMUSEUM

NORSK FOLKEMUSEUM

Cream porridge is more than mere everyday food, and was also served to guests. «Whatever else one might serve of delicacies, there's always someone demanding to be served cream porridge,» wrote one vicar's wife from the county of Telemark.

NORSK FOLKEMUSEUM

Cream porridge
(Rømmegrøt)

3/4 liter sour cream
150 gr. flour
1/2 liter milk, heated
1/4 tsp. salt

Over medium heat, cook the sour cream for 10 minutes in covered kettle. Sprinkle about 1/3 of the flour on top, mix in and let the sour cream bubble until the butter separates, about 15–20 min. On low heat, stir carefully now and then to keep from sticking. Remove as much butter as desired.
Add the rest of the flour, mix well. Pour in hot milk, a little at a time, mixing well after each time. Scrape the edges so that all the porridge is stirred.
Salt to taste.
Serve with sugar and cinnamon.

BENGT WILSON

Obviously, there are some foods one immediately thinks of as 'Norwegian': *lutefisk* (fish in lye), *rakfisk* (half-fermented fish), *rømmegrøt* (sour cream porridge), *spekemat* (cured meats), *geitost* (goat cheese), and *gammelost* (literally, 'old' cheese), perhaps also *fårikål* (mutton and cabbage stew) and *kjøttkaker* (meat cakes). But why not include pizza and hamburgers, taco and chips? Surely, 'Nowegian food' refers to that food which Norwegians eat, and they certainly consume more pizzas than *fenalår* (cured lamb). But, if we're to let the 'road to Lillehammer' begin one thousand years prior to the Winter Olympics, it's probably wise to emphasise historical tradition rather than nutritional statistics.

A thousand years ago puts us in the middle of the Viking period – 994 – when, if we are to believe the sagas, Norwegians had long since begun importing foreign foodstuffs. In 'Egil's Saga', we learn of a man who travelled to England to buy wine and honey for Harald Hårfagre. With him he took some typically Norwegian food, *skrei* (winter cod), to sell to the English.

'Sverre's Saga' gives us a more vivid picture of trade between Norway and Europe. We are told of King Sverre's speech, in Bergen towards the end of the 10th century, thanking some Englishmen who have brought wheat, white flour, honey and fine cloth to Norway. In the same breath, he berates some Germans who have traded rather too much wine for butter and winter cod, which the Norwegians needed for themselves.

The Norwegian word *skrei* is associated with the notion of gliding, describing as it does the cod which come into land in great shoals, to spawn during the spring. Similarly, the word for cod – *torsk* – derives from another word meaning 'to dry'. Drying on *stokker*, or sticks, was the most common form of preserving this important fish, and gave rise to another term, *stokkfisk*, which is known variously throughout Europe as *stokvisch*, *stoccafisso*, *estocafix*, or, in English, *stockfish*. In this context, it might be interesting to note that the word *bacalao* derives from the Latin word for stick.

Legal documents from the Middle Ages, make it clear that the tradition of organised cod-fishing goes back many hundreds of years. A trade in cod was well established already before the year 1000. Later on, the demand for the fish in European countries increased, not least with the introduction of new religious fast-days, when the eating of meat was banned by the church. England ceased to be the principal market, being replaced by those German cities trading regularly with Bergen, the main port distribution point for fish products from along the coast.

We know that stockfish was as much a common local food as a trade commodity. But what else were people eating during the age of the Vikings and sagas?

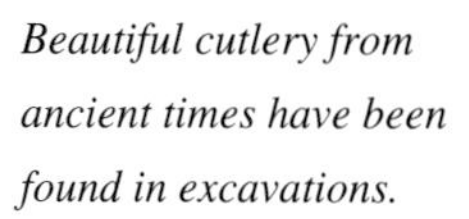
Beautiful cutlery from ancient times have been found in excavations.

NORSK FOLKEMUSEUM

Corn and milk

At the beginning of our era, a Roman writer recorded that, «The Germanic peoples grow only oats and eat only porridge». Whilst porridge was undoubtedly an important element in the Norwegian diet, the most commonly used grain at the time was barley, which, because of its use in beer production, later became a very valuable commodity. Eventually, oats did replace barley as the staple corn product, though a mixture of oats and barley continued to be used.

The Middle Ages also saw great developments in baking techniques. The most primative form of bread was made from flour mixed with water, baked on flat stones or hot cinders. In the High Middle Ages Norwegians began using sourdough, already popular in Europe for centuries, though not the form of leavened rye bread used in Denmark and Sweden.

Dairy products have always figured prominently in the Norwegian diet. Mediaeval sources make several mentions of cheese, presumably a precursor of *gammelost*, a highly pungent cheese made from fermented curdled milk. More recent types of cheese, made from fresh milk and rennet, almost certainly originated in countries further to the south.

Milk, the most common drink in the Middle Ages, was also taken curdled, or soured. In societies without access to pasturisation or refrigeration facilities, milk was seldom drunk fresh. Most sheep or goat-rearing cultures have tended to store their milk either boiled or soured, and *rømme* (soured cream) is one of the most traditional of all Norwegian foods.

Another ancient dairy drink which has survived to the present is *syra* (soured whey), the thin liquid that separates from curds when milk is curdled.

A simpler drink, belonging firmly to the lower orders, was called simply *blanda* (literally, the blend), made by mixing either soured milk or whey with water. Its lowly status if evidenced by a law from 1273, which obliged priests to ensure that people formalised their married relationships. Weddings were to take place, the law states, even if the parties could afford nothing but *blanda*; no one should incur greater costs than they could afford. The normal practice at such events was to serve beer.

Food and status

If beer was preferable to milk, there were many forms of drink considered superior to beer, for example mead and wine. 'Sverre's Saga' relates an episode from 1181 when King Magnus celebrated Christmas in Bergen. «The King's-men were allowed to drink in the main hall, whilst the guests were put in the Sunniva room. The guests were not pleased that, whilst the King's-men drank mead, they were given just beer. On the fifth day of Christmas, when the guests were drunk, they took up their weapons and made their way to the main hall to hack down the doors. The episode ended in a terrible fight which left many dead and wounded.

The word used for beer in this saga is *mungåt* (literally, good-in-the-mouth). This was considered the most common form of beer, a form of home-brew. The finest was *bjorr*: «Ale, it is called amongst people – whilst to the gods it is Bjorr», as one of the Eddaic poems puts it. The word *bjorr* is, of course, closely related to the European terms – beer, Bier, biere – and the *bjorr* itself was mainly imported from European countries, principally Germany.

For most people, both wine and mead were rare commodities. Though some honey-based meads began, eventually, to be produced in Norway, most of it had to be imported and was therefore very expensive. Wine was in such short supply that a Norwegian bishop had to write to Pope requesting permission to use beer for communion – though this was not granted. It is indicative that, in 'Edda', Odin is described as a wine drinker, whilst the more junior gods such as Heimdall must satisfy themselves with mead.

The correlation between food and social status is something we see quite clearly, very early on. In a poem called 'Rigstula', we hear of the foods in three different households. In the simplest hovel, this consists of a bowl of soup and a piece of bread, lumpy and thick with bran. Meanwhile, the well-to-do farmer feasts on boiled veal (though, owing to a hole in the manuscript, there is a degree of speculation here), and the aristocrat, a sophisticated gastronome, begins his meal with thin slices of white bread, followed by roast fowl, pork and other delicacies. Finally, he downs a jug of wine.

Norwegians diet under Danish rule

During the 1300s, Norway went into decline, entering the so-called 'Four Hundred Year Night'. But the connections with Europe did not cease altogether. Whilst Norwegians, we read, existed largely on a diet of rye bread and beer, the flow of products out of the country was prolific. Butter and fish were exported as never before, also cod and halibut, the latter becoming famous for a number of exclusive dry-fish products derived from it, which became popular snacks in the restauraunts of Northern Germany. To whit:

«The great halibut is sliced into long strands along both its sides, which are left then to dry. These dried strips are known as 'reckling'. But let the bones, fins and the fattest flesh of the fish remain together; this, when it is dried, is known as 'rav', and is considered the best of fish».

Around 1500, the word *flatbrød* (flat bread) pops up, and Peder Claussøn Friis describes baking techniques in the Hardanger region of Western Norway. The actual baking, it seems, occurred on large stone slabs, arranged such that fires could be lit beneath them. First, however, the dough is rolled out into large round cakes no thicker than a cabbage leaf. These are then lifted with thin wooden sticks onto the slabs, sprinkled with water and turned several times in the course of baking. The *flatbrød* wafers are then placed in piles up to 4 alen – 8 feet – in height and stored in the *stabbur*, or raised storehouses.

Contemporary dictionaries provide a surprising source of information on current foods and eating habits. Two hundred years prior to Ivar Aasen's tour of the rural areas, collecting and recording local dialects, one Christian Jenssøn did something similar in his own village of Askvoll, in Sunnfjord. In 1646, Jennsøn published a collection of almost one thousand local words, under the title, 'The Norwegian Dictionarium or Glossary'. This dictionary is every bit as much a goldmine for culinary historians as it is for those concerned with the history of language, because of the many detailed descriptions of local recipes it contains. In the absence of any satisfactory Danish parallel, Jennsøn defined the dishes by simply writing out the whole recipe.

The dictionary does not give us a comprehensive overview of what Norwegians ate; it was, after all, the specifically Norwegian words that Jennsøn was concerned with. Yet, we learn that in Askvoll they prepared a number of different kinds of sausage, spread flatbread with butter and cheese, used mustard, and that wood-grouse was considered the «most distinguished of game». Most popular, however, were milk-based recipes, such as:

«*Rørost*, or *skjørost*, is a cheese made from soured milk in the following manner: One takes one or more barrels of milk, and, before lighting the fire, stirs this frequently in a pan with the handle of a broom until it becomes as thin as fresh milk. The pan is then placed on a low fire, and heated until it is warmer than tepid, but not so warm that a hand cannot be emmersed in it. When curdling occurs, one removes the curds, places a cloth of coarse, clean linen into a bowl, and places the curd into the cloth. A heavy object is then placed on top of the curds, such that all the whey is pressed out».

One of the strangest words in Jennsøn's dictionary is *comperpøse*. «*Comperpøse* is the name given to a stuffing, made of fish-liver, flour, onion, grains, currents and herbs, inserted into the stomache, or head, of the cod». Fredrik Grøn discusses this dish in his book, which has become a standard text, 'On Nutrition in Norway', published in 1942. Grøn refers to dictionaries and other documents, but was not familiar with a few extremely interesting glossaries which languished in manuscript form in the Royal Danish Library, in Copenhagen. These were first printed and published by the Norwegian Language Archive in 1956–7. The most important of these, in culinary terms, was a collection made in 1698 by Jacob Laugesen Bork, the priest at Bø in Vesterålen. Regarding fish offal, he recorded the following recipes:

1. «*Rut* or *komperut*; a form of dumpling made from fish roe, liver and flour, boiled together».
2. «*Kams-hou*; fresh fish heads filled with a stuffing prepared from grain, fish-liver, herbs and spices, and then boiled».
3. «*Lever-unge* (literally, liver-children); fish livers cooked in its own stomach with salt and pepper».
4. «*Rogn-kake* (fish-roe cake); a thin cake made of fish liver, roe and flour, fried in a pan».

Many of these recipes have survived into our own time, although the contents are subject to regional variation. Laugesen Bork also gives us the oldest Norwegian recipe I know of for *kalvedans* (literally, calf dance). Whilst many Norwegians know this as a kind of milk pudding, in a number of regional dialects the same word is used to describe a form of veal brawn. In Vesterålen, it meant:

«. . .the head and hooves of the calf are boiled. All meat is then pared away from the bone, finely chopped and boiled in milk containing a little barley. When it has cooled, carve into slices and serve on a plate».

SCAN-FOTO/Arkiv

The versatile clergyman, Petter Dass (1647–1707) was someone who knew how to appreciate a good meal. This has found its expression particularly in «The trumpet of Nordland» where he in a humorous way describes the differences in northern Norwegian and foreign culinary traditions.

Petter Dass and Bishop Pontoppidan

From Northern Norway we have one of the best descriptions of food in Norwegian literature. 'Nordland's Trumpet', by the poet-priest Petter Dass, is a positively mouth-watering work, a fascinating documentation of historic foods which, amongst other things, describes in detail the difference between Northern Norwegian and foreign dishes. Dass had gone to school in Bergen

Lærebog

i de forskjellige Grene af

Husholdningen

af

Hanna Winsnes.

Christiania 1845.

Trykt og forlagt af C. A. Wulfsberg.

No one has taught Norwegians more about how to prepare food than Hanna Winsnes. «Lærebok i de forskjellige grene av husholdningen» was first published in 1843, and reprinted 13 times before 1880.

and studied for three years in Copenhagen, where he no doubt developed an extensive knowledge of foreign cookery. In his poem, he mentions turkey, capons, pheasant, cloves, cucumbers, candied peel, and much else besides. But this is not what he himself has to offer. Instead, he reaches into his childhood and early adulthood spent on the Helgeland coast; stockfish and marinated herring, flat bread and *lefse* (a thin dough-pancake, served rolled with butter and sugar), sausage and ham, turnip porridge, cabbage, egg pancakes and *gomme* – a type of cheese made from fresh milk.

This represents, by anyone's standards, a varied diet, but it was food for a festive occasion, not the everyday diet of Northern Norwegians. Neither could everybody afford to serve up such a splendid feast as the poem's Master of Alstadhaug. Still, it is interesting to note the pride with which Petter Dass presents the national cuisine.

The difference between Norwegian and foreign food is made most clear by the Bishop Erik Pontoppidan of Bergen (a man best known for his explanation of the Lutheran catechism) in his 'Account of Norway'. Pontoppidan pointed out the tendency of the urban population to prepare their food in the Danish manner, relating, of course, to the fact that large sections of the urban middle class consisted of immigrants from other North Sea countries, not least Denmark. The rural population, on the other hand, still tended to rely on the dishes we already know from earlier centuries: flatbread, porridge, fish and dairy foods. Pontippidan, who was himself Danish, claims that Norwegians highly valued sour-salted fish, such as mackerel and salmon. «If it should be to his satisfaction, no fish shall be salted but that it is not also soured».

But the Bishop was painfully aware of just how hard life could be in Norway, and he refers to the tradition of so-called *barkebrød*, a type of crude bread, baked from a mixture of flour and ground tree bark. Towards the end of the 16th century, not least during the Napoleonic Wars, a string of catastrophic famines led to the publication of a number of pamphlets outlining alternative sources of nourishment. Besides the ubiquitous *barkebrød*, these included Icelandic moss and ground animal bones, but the most important, and most fervently recommended, was the potato. The Norwegian term *potetprester* (potato-priests) recalls all those priests and other officials who, through their sermons, pamphlets and practical experiments, encouraged the peasants to invest in the potato crop. The real breakthrough here occurred in the 19th century, – due largely, one suspects, to the fact that 'necessity teaches the naked to spin' – but the public information campaigns of the 1700s should not be underestimated.

If the end of the 18th century was a tough period for the poorest members of society, it also marked the peak of upper class opulence. The rich nobles built themselves large houses, dressed in the latest fashions and gave sumptuous banquets, at which they served not only local game and fish, but also a great number of delicacies imported from Europe. We have, for example, a list of provisions purchased for a feast at the Gyldenløve's Estate, near Larvik, south of Christiania. It includes beef, lamb, veal, black and tawney grouse, hare, chicken, pigeon, duck, turkey, pike, carp, raisins, prunes, peel, olives, capers and much else besides.

NORSK FOLKEMUSEUM

Farm life was hard, especially for the milkmaids, who had to carry water, tend the herds, and make cheese and butter.

But changes, as a result of the Napoleonic Wars, were also on their way to Norway. In 1834, Jacob Aall, a nobleman, wrote: «Amongst the bourgeois, who have until now indulged in the good things of life, there is less ostentation since the war. A certain sobriety, a simpler way of life, has established itself. At banquets, the tables are not laden with so many dishes as before, nor does the wine flow quite so freely».

On the other hand, he remarks that, «Those classes previously rationed to the strictest austerity, have expanded their pleasures, considerably».

Class differences in the new Norway

What was certainly about to expand in Norway was the urban middle class, though, whilst they acquired more money and power, they never imitated the old nobility with private chefs, or foreign cookery books! What they needed, therefore, was special guidance in the art of exhibiting their newly won status, not least in matters culinary. Hence, a series of new cookery books, in Norwegian. Sweden and Denmark had had their cookery books since 1600; at last, in 1831, Norway had them, too. A contemporary subscription-invitation, asks: «How often do we not hear, in Norway, complaints about the lack of cookery books appropriate to the middle classes? Many households might wish to have the use of such an important guide. But, whilst certain so-called Cookery Books are available, so often they are not prepared with the middle class home in mind, and are too extensive in their coverage.» The books published in subsequent years were characterised by an attempt to popularise the dishes of the upper class for a broader audience. They were not concerned with traditional Norwegian food, such as one might have expected in a time of unprecedented interest in Norwegian folk tales and songs. However, in 1843, Maren Elisabet Bang published her 'Everyman's Book of Housekeeping', which included many popular, simple dishes such as fried herring, stew, porridge and gruel, potato dishes, and *prim* – a soft, sweet whey cheese – which almost certainly provides a more accurate picture of the average diet of the time. Similarly, Hanna Winsnes' pamphlet 'For Poor Housewives' – written at the instigation of social reformer Eilert Sundt, in 1857 – affords us a glimpse at the eating-habits of the poor. She has advice, for example, for those who had only a single pig or sheep, on how they might utilize the whole animal, down to the last bone and sinew; or on how best to organise a small garden. But her introduction indicates the extent of the poverty at the time. «My instructions», she writes, «As to the preparation of food are not directed at the very poorest members of our society. The shame is that there are only too many whose only food consists of a thin flour-and-water gruel, often taken without salt, or potatoes without *sul* (soured meat)».

It is hard to know how much of the food described in the cookery books actually found its way to the table, though contemporary letters, diaries and memoirs afford us a reasonable impression of the eating habits of the official and upper classes from the end of the 16th century to the middle of the 17th. Despite certain developments, the main ingredients remain the same throughout.

Conrdaine Dunker mentions 'Sago soup and grouse', 'Lobster patties and Roast Lamb'; Camilla Collett, 'Roast Lamb and Fruit Soup'; Elisabeth Welhaven, 'Veal, Fowl and Fish'; Gustava Kielland, 'Roast Meat, Wine Soup and Sponge Cake'; Hanna Winsnes, 'Smoked Pike, Roast Mutton and Pork, Princess Pudding'. Elise Aubert describes a number of meals, once of roast fowl and gooseberry porridge, another time of oyster patties, turtle soup, cod, roast reindeer and fowl. Lorentz Dietrichson recalls from his childhood in Bergen, having roast meat and sweet soup for dinner on Sundays, eg 'Roast Beef and Saffron Soup, whilst on weekdays they often had fish-in-lye. If we wish to include a whiff of opulence, we could do worse than list the ingredients of a wedding-feast organised by Hans Christian Petersen – later to be head of government – in 1840:

«Cold Lobster, Soup, Pheasant pate, Fish pudding with Oysters, Chicken with Mushrooms, Cold Liver pate, Macaroni, Pidgeon Pie, Trout, Stewed Fruit, Roast Veal, Jelly, Cake, Ice Cream, Fruit».

Basically, these menues consist of three courses – soup, meat, desert – the common combination throughout Western Europe; only on special occasions were patés and other delicacies added. Though we may note the use of imported luxury items such as spices, fruit and wine. The recipes for all these dishes were to be found in the cookery books of the time, which, on the other hand, contained not a word as to the preparation of *rakfisk* (half-fermented fish) and other Norwegian peasant dishes.

From 'Pictures of Life in the Lion-Salon', published in 1848, we get a fascinating insight into the attitudes of the upper classes towards the diet of the peasantry. The book studies Christiania society's increasing admiration for all things foreign and remarks, ironically, that «Nowadays, everything truly Norwegian, and therefore simple, lacks all resonance for us. . . We are still encumbered by so many barbaric, Norwegian traditions. True, we are not cannibals – even our worst enemies could not accuse us of so being. But we are drinkers of *Aquavit* (schnapps), eaters of Brown Whey-Cheese, and guzzlers of Fermented Fish!».

Aquavit, whey-cheese and fermented fish are not arbitrary examples of Norwegian peasant food-culture; they define it very precisely. All that is missing from this 'typical' list, is some

The teaching of home economics started on a voluntary basis at the end of the last century. The textbook was written by Hanna Winsnes.

NORSK FOLKEMUSEUM

O. VÆRING

representative of the grain-based foods, which formed another of the basic elements of the Norwegian folk diet. In official reports published around the turn of the century, in 'The Topographical Journal', we read that in Rakkestad, the staple diet was oatmeal porridge and gruel; in Sunnfjord, oatmeal bread with cured fish and soured milk, oatmeal porridge, porridge of oats and whey-cheese; Hallingdal, bread-and-beer, gruel, milk and cheese; whilst in Mandal they managed on flatbread, cheese, porridge and soured milk.

Typically, the Norwegian peasantry would seldom eat fresh meat, preferring it to be salted or dried. Cured and smoked meats were not only more economical, they were also considered to have more taste, though on the larger farms venison gradually became more popular towards the end of the 19th century.

The porridge war

During the 1860s, the country became involved in a great nutritional debate, the so-called *Grøtstriden*, or Porridge War! It began with the publication of a cookery book, 'Sensible Cooking', by P. Chr. Asbjørnsen – better known for his association with Jørgen Moe and their collections of Norwegian folk tales. His book was based, in part, on the recent findings of German chemists and nutritionists, and was critical of Norwegian cookery writers – mostly women – and aspects of traditional Norwegian cooking techniques. Among other things, he attacked the traditional habit of adding extra oatmeal to porridge at the end of the cooking process, claiming it made the porridge less digestible. Asbjørnsen was severely reprimanded by Eilert Sundt, the father of Norwegian social research, who thought that Norwegian women had probably gained all the expertise they needed, through a thousand years in the kitchen! In the end, it was Sundt – and Norwegian tradition – that was proved right, but Asbjørnsen's book also made an important contribution. Amongst other things, he emphasised the use of vegetables, and, in the second edition, introduced us to idea of eating mushrooms, with the first recipes involving mushrooms ever to appear in Norwegian.

The folk story teller Per Chr. Asbjørnsen wrote a cookery book in which he claimed Norwegian housewives couldn't make porridge properly. Eilert Sundt protested, and the ensuing public discussion has later been referred to as the «porridge war».

Asbjørnsen's cookery book was not popular with the public, losing out to one of those women he most criticised, Hanna Winsnes. Her cookery book was reprinted into eighteen editions and dominated the market completely until 1880. But many of Asbjørnsen's opinions were taken up by subsequent authors, giving rise to an increased understanding of nutrition, hygiene and the requirements of a broader social spectrum.

When, in 1890, the first school kitchens arrived, in 1890, these were important considerations, and the first recipe books prepared specifically for schools catering consist largely of dishes offering the highest nutritional value for the lowest price, not least «the commonest of our national dishes». The list includes porridge and gruel, an extensive use of offal, horsemeat, fishmeal, fish cakes, flatbread and stewed fish.

The emphasis on Norwegian rural food was even more pronounced in Hulda Garborg's 1899 collection of recipes, «Housework», written in New Norwegian, the language based on the rural dialects of Western Norway. Her spirited defence of traditional foods, such as flatbread and dairy products, was a reaction to what she saw as its decline. Urbanisation, and the ascendency of urban culture, had had an effect on the country's eating habits, though surveys from the turn of the century suggest that rural people still kept to a traditional diet, despite the replacement of milk and beer by coffee as the most popular beverage. But a development was certainly under way, as we see from Hulda Garborg's column in the journal URD, ten years later. In her diary, she writes, «I still receive letters about my articles on our national diet in URD. Many now admit we must return to much of the traditional diet, especially flatbread, oatmeal porridge, curdled milk and whey products».

The 20th century

One of the many young women active from the start of the school catering and domestic science movements was Henriette Schønberg Erken. Later, she founded her own school of domestic science in Hamar, north of Christiania, but was best known in her time as the authoress of a constant stream of recipe and cookery books. Her famous 'Stor kokebok' – 'Big Cookery Book' – published in 1914, dominated the first half of this century, especially in terms of festive food. The book is largely based on the work of contemporary foreign cooks and chefs, for example the Frenchman Escoffier, who, around the turn of the century, revolutionised international cookery. Henriette Schønberg Erken presented a modern, professional book, which included many foreign recipes, but also recipes for various types of porridge, *rakfisk*, meat cakes, *fårikål*, home brewed beer, plus an extensive supplement about food for the sick. She constantly revised the book in accordance with various developments in kitchen technology, not least the electric cooker, which made its grand entrance in the inter-war years.

Our own century is characterised by increased prosperity for large sections of the population, upset by periodic bouts of international crisis and war. Poverty and hunger during the Nazi Occupation of Norway made great demands on our ingenuity which resulted in an altogether simpler, and healthier, diet. This simplicity continued long after the end of the war, and even the grandest feast was a relatively uncomplicated affair, usually consisting of no more than three coarses – soup, meat and desert. Moreover, another custom which gained extensive popularity, was the coffee-table spread, with cakes and open sandwiches.

From the 1960s onward, the increase of imported foodstuffs and the introduction of many Norwegians to foreign culinary traditions through the rise of the charter tour, brought about a steady broadening of variety. Today, it is possible to buy exotic spices, fruits and vegetables, together with specialist recipe books and kitchen equipement, in most of the larger Norwgian towns and cities. At the same time, the old hot-dog stands, a great Norwegian institution, have largely been replaced by American-style burger and fast food restaurants. In reply to this, food stores and supermarkets stock an increasing range of convenience and micro-wave food. Research has shown that more and more people are turning to pre-prepared food, and the number of Norwegians that do without a main meal altogether is also rising.

When that is said, *mors kjøttkaker* – mother's (homemade) meatcakes – are still the most popular main meal, according to recent surveys. Moreover, sausages, which used to come a close number two, have recently been displaced in the popularity charts by fish fillets. Rice-porridge is still the habitual Saturday meal for well over half the country's population!

We must not forget the position of restaurants. These first began to make their mark in Norway around 1840, and their development parallels that of cookery literature, in other words, as a symptom of the growth of the middle class.

We began by talking about the imports and exports of the Vikings, and we have seen how the introduction of foreign foodstuffs have influenced the modern diet. But we should not forget that today Norway also exports different kinds of food to many other countries. Fish continues to head the list, with 85 % of food-related income based on the sale of this harvest of the sea. *Klippfisk* is still popular in the bacalao-land of Spain, but Norwegian salmon has won itself a firm foothold on the Iberian market, also. In fact salmon is responsible for a quarter of Norway's total food-export value today.

Another popular feature on the foreign table is Jarlsberg cheese, the most important of our dairy product exports. It may not come as any great surprise to hear that neither curdled milk nor *blanda* are exactly flowing out of the country; on the other hand Norwegian beer holds its own on the international market. And as we referred to King Sverre's attack on the import of German wine, which still occurs, we ought also to remind ourselves that Germany, in return, work their way through large quantities of Norwegian aquavit. In fact as much as 500,000 litres of the stuff per year. The Viking ships may not be operating any longer, but the trading routes are busier than ever.

BENGT WILSON

In recent years, natural and un-processed Norwegian products have become an important part of the Norwegian Cuisine. A specialty, grouse breast with mushrooms and wild berries.

BENGT WILSON

BENGT WILSON

Typical Norwegian baked goods – brown bread and flatbread made of oat flour.

NORSK FOLKEMUSEUM

Baking was hard labour in the old days. The grains would have to be ground, and the bread cooked in a narrow oven, often next to the open stove. Cheese-making was very time consuming, and large pots were needed.

SCAN-FOTO/Jan Greve

SCAN-FOTO/Jan Greve

NORSK FOLKEMUSEUM

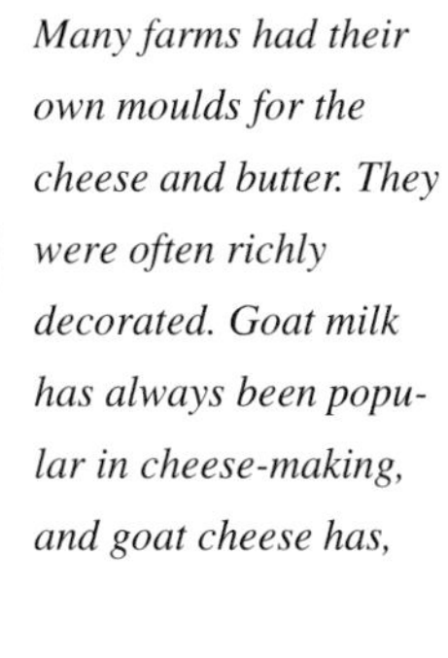

Many farms had their own moulds for the cheese and butter. They were often richly decorated. Goat milk has always been popular in cheese-making, and goat cheese has, through generations, been the cheese mostly eaten in Norway. The production used to take place on the local farms, whereas today all cheese is made by dairies.

KNUDSENS FOTOSENTER

One of the most popular Christmas cookies, goro.

BENGT WILSON

In the country as in the cities, lots of coffee is drunk. Coffee drinking is a natural part of social gatherings. If it's too warm, one could drink it out of the saucer.

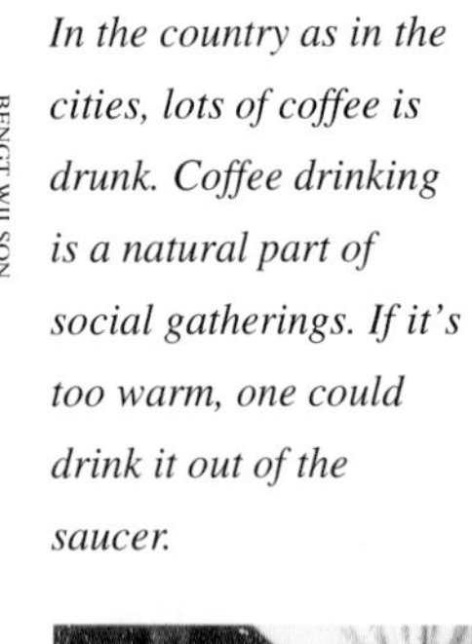

BENGT WILSON

BENGT WILSON

«Tynnkaker» and Sognelefse – lefse from Sogn – are popular baked goods on many farms.

NORSK FOLKEMUSEUM

SCAN-FOTO/Jan Greve

SCAN-FOTO/Jan Greve

NORSK FOLKEMUSEUM/F. Köhn

Even today, coffee parties are the commonest type of gathering. Various cookies and cakes are served, or perhaps wafers with cream and cloudberry jam.

KNUDSENS FOTOSENTER

Salted trout, ready for smoking. Mackerel (opposite) is also suited for smoking.

Fermented trout, ready to be served.

BENGT WILSON

BENGT WILSON

KNUDSENS FOTOSENTER

BENGT WILSON

Stavanger herring is, to many, a delicacy. Others prefer fish heads dried outside on racks.

A common dish, beef soup and meatballs, with parsley and potatoes.

KNUDSENS FOTOSENTER

KNUDSENS FOTOSENTER

BENGT WILSON

Meat cured in salt and smoked has been eaten in this country for centuries. Salt-cured ham, mutton and sausages served with flatbread, sour cream and butter is considered a feast. Drying of the ham close to the fjord apparently gives an extra taste to it.

BENGT WILSON

KNUDSENS FOTOSENTER

Sausages, or hot dogs, are sold on every street corner but are also a popular dish at home. Sandwiches are often served at night or to luncheon guests. Hashed-meat cakes (right) are the most popular of all dishes.

NORSK FOLKEMUSEUM/Wilse

KNUDSENS FOTOSENTER

How long this male moose will be left alone, is uncertain. In all likelihood, he is going to end up at someone's table, possibly as a roulade. A typical sidedish is Brussels sprouts, which go well with all types of game.

SAMFOTO/J. B. Olsen/Sørensen

BENGT WILSON

Weidemann 92

Great Feats in The Frozen Wastes

SCAN-FOTO/Jan Greve

Thor S. Winsnes (b. 1922), M.Sc., has devoted his entire professional career to working with polar geology. For more than 40 years, he has been connected with the Norwegian polar insitute, Norsk Polarinstiutt. Since 1939 he has taken part in 43 polar expeditions. Most of them have taken place in the Arctic, but seven have been to Antarctica.

Thor S. Winsnes:

Norwegians have always been drawn to desolate, white expanses, and the great ski and sleigh treks of the polar expeditions have served as an inspiration for generations of skiers. Three men in particular command a central position in Norwegian polar exploration; Fridtjof Nansen, Otto Sverdrup and Roald Amundsen. Thanks to their pioneering efforts, world science gained a unique body of material, a young nation gained great confidence, and large tracts of the polar regions were brought under Norwegian jurisdiction.

Fridtjof Nansen also had artistic talents, and the sketchbook was always a part of his expeditions. One of his most famous drawings, of the flaming northern light, which he so often saw.

FRAMMUSEET

Norway has produced many polar explorers and the great frozen wastes, both to the north and south, would seem to hold a perculiar fascination for Norwegians. The great feats of endurance at the poles, the endless treks across the white deserts, have given rise to their own kind of glory and inspired generations of skiers right up to, and including, our own time.

Three men in particular stand in the front row of polar explorers, both nationally and internationally; they are Fridtjof Nansen, Otto Sverdrup and Roald Amundsen.

Fridtjof Nansen

Nansen was born in 1861 at *Store Frøen,* a farm just outside Christiania, with the forests and mountains of *Nordmarka* on his doorstep. Already in his boyhood, *'Marka'*, as it's known, was his natural arena. He became a keen outdoorsperson, an expert hunter and skier, and fierce competitor. He participated in the Husebybakken ski jumping competition, a national competition and precursor of the Holmenkoll event, where he proved himself to be the best ski-jumper from the Norwegian capital.

SCAN-FOTO/Jan Greve

At 21, he moved to Bergen where he studied marine-biology, and in the same year undertook his first Arctic Ocean voyage, with a seal-hunting ship. Whilst carrying out research in the Greenland Sea, the glittering plains and coastal mountains entranced him, awakening a serious desire to become aquainted with this austere and inhospitable land.

In 1888, at 27 years of age, Nansen took his doctorate in biology, at the same time as preparing a large-scale exhibition to Greenland. He planned the trip down to the smallest detail, not least to the construction of the sledges, which needed to be a light and practical as possible. His design is still the most widely used, even today.

Fram, Nansen's polar vessel, was constructed by Colin Archer, according to Nansen's specifications. Archer built several rescue boats, and on the occasion of the 50th anniversary of the rescue service, Redningsselskapet, three stamps, including the two above, were issued in his honour.

Nansen's First Exhibition

No less than 40 people applied to take part in the Greenland expedition, and Nansen was very thorough in his selection. The five that were chosen were ship captain Otto Sverdrup, lieutenant Oluf Christian Ditrichson, farmer and seaman Kristian Kristiansen and the two Lapps Samuel Balto and Ole Ravna. They travelled north with the seal-hunting ship 'Jason', arriving at Nansen's chosen starting point in June.

The men and their equipment were put onto a large rowing boat which was to take them onto land, but the boat was damaged by ice and had to be hauled out for repair. In relatively bad weather, they drifted southwards with the ice for ten days, from 65.5 degrees north to below 62 degrees. They rowed northwards again, hugging the land, and 24 days after they left the 'Jason', arrived at Umivilksfjord, more than 500 kilometres to the north. This was to be the starting point for their great trek across Greenland.

In those days, there was great public interest in voyages of discovery, and Nansen's daring expedition was described in his great book, 'Skiing Over Greenland'. Over 700 pages long, the book provides a lively insight into the importance of preparation, and the numerous hardships the team had to endure, as well as defining, in an accessible form, the objects of this extremely dangerous exercise. Later, he published 'The Life of the Eskimos', based on the studies he had made of the indigenous people of Greenland.

Nansen married the year after his return. His wife, Eva, was the daughter of one of the greatest explorers of the time, zoologist Michael Sars. Nansen was subsequently appointed assistent curator at the Department of Zoology at the University, but his real interest lay in other areas. He wanted to carry out an expedition to the North Pole, to drive through the pack-ice, by boat, straight across the Arctic Ocean.

In 1884, on the south west coast of Greenland, the remains were found of an expedition which had floundered, three years previously, to the north of the New Siberian Islands. The ship equipment must have drifted across the Arctic Ocean, down the east coast of Greenland to the point where they were discovered. This amounted to a distance of 2,900 nautical miles in three years, giving an average speed across the Arctic Ocean of 2.6 nautical miles per day. It was well known that logs from Siberia had found their way to the Greenland coast, indicating a constant stream running from Siberia to Greenland; now, it's flow-rate was mapped.

To the North Pole by Ship

Nansen understood that this information could be utilised in his exploration of the unknown regions of the Arctic Ocean, and he presented his theories in Norway and England, but to little avail. His theories went against the principles of polar exploration, and won him little support.

He did not give up. His aim was to build a ship that would withstand the pressure of the Arctic pack-ice, which had wrecked so many ships. To the ship's architect, Colin Archer, Fridtjof Nansen suggested a form of hull which would allow the ice to push it upwards instead of crushing it. Nansen calculated the entire expedition could be achieved for 450,000 kroner. Norwegian parliament granted him 280,000 and the rest he raised privately.

The ship, which Eva Nansen named *'Fram'* ('Forward') weighed 400 tons. It had a short, wide hull, which would be easier to manoeuvre in the ice, and the form of the hull was rounded such that the ice would not grip it. In addition, the propeller and shafts could be winched up out of the water. The reinforced frame and hull of the ship were constructed of solid oak and the crow's-nest on the forward mast stood 32 metres above sea level.

The rudder and propellers were made so that they, if needed, could be hoisted. Its chances of being wrecked by the drift-ice, were in fact, great. Below: Fram's logo.

SCAN-FOTO/Rune Baashus

SCAN-FOTO/Rune Baashus

21st July, 1893: The ship sails from Vardø, in the extreme north of Norway. There is a crew of eleven on board, in addition to Nansen himself and Otto Sverdrup, as captain. They have provisions enough for five years. On their way eastwards, they take on board 34 dogs, besides the five they already have with them from Norway. During the voyage they discover a number of previously unknown islands and, after great difficulties, round the northernmost tip of Siberia, Cape Chelyushin. The journey continues eastwards until they reach the New Siberian Islands, from where the *'Fram'* pushes out into the open sea. For a number of days, they are able to proceed northwards, but on 20th September, at 78 degrees north, they come to the edge of the pack-ice. It soon becomes apparent that, from now on, the ice flow will decide their direction and speed. A sounding shows a depth of 1,500 metres and with that the theory of a shallow ocean basin collapses.

At first they drift eastwards, but then the ice changes direction southwards and they reach a southernmost point of 77 degrees 43', one and a half months after entering the ice. This does not please Nansen, but he can only trust the evidence of the Siberian logs. Again, they begin to drift northwards. They sustain several onslaughts from the ice, but the hull of the *'Fram'* performs as planned. On Christmas Eve, they are 79 degrees 11' north.

Research on the Arctic Ocean

The moral and health of the crew is good. 2nd February, they pass 80 degrees. They take continuous soundings, but a line of 3,475 metres proves too short. They extend it with an ordinary rope and the depth is indicated at between 3,300 and 3,900 metres, thus putting paid to all theories about a landmass in the Arctic Ocean.

Temperature measurements also give surprising reults, showing warmer water beneath the layers of ice. The Gulf Stream clearly finds a way into the Arctic Basin and compensates for the cold waters which bring the ice out of the Basin and into the East Greenland Stream.

Progress is slow, the wind does not give the ice the speed they had hoped, and an impatient Nansen begins to toy with the idea of abandoning the *'Fram'* and making an attempt on the pole by dog sledge, as soon as the daylight arrives in February or March.

In November, he announces his plan to the crew, and choses Hjalmar Johansen as companion. In addition to the sledges, they build canoes which will make it possible to cross any sea lanes in the ice. The canoes are 3.70 metres long by 0.7 metres wide, shorter but much wider than those used by the Innuit, and can take provisions and equipment for three months. Otherwise, they are constructed according to the Innuit model, so that, with sealskins tied round the hole in the deck, they are completely watertight. Nansen must reckon on having to cross open sea on his way back to Spitzbergen, Frans Josephs' Land or Novaya Zemlya. Consequently, special sledges are built and experiments carried out with cooking methods, clothes and other equipment.

Christmas 1894 is celebrated with great cheer and, just after New Year, the ship withstands the worst of the pressure from the ice, which is so powerful that all provisions and equipment are unloaded onto the ice as a precaution.

By the end of January, they're at 83 degrees 45' north, and on 14th March the great push forward begins, following the failure of two attempts the previous month, due to overloading of the sledges. With three reinforced sledges, each bearing a load of some 250 kgs, plus two cannoes, drawn by nine dogs, Nansens reckons to be able to travel for 100 days, 80 of them with the aid of the dogs. The equipment is extremely lightwieght. One tent weighs 1.4 kgs, and a special primus stove, which utilizes over 90 % of its heat, means that cooking twice a day for 120 days will only require 20 litres of paraffin. They arm themselves with two guns, each fitted with both rifle and shotgun barrels, and 180 rifle and 150 shotgun cartriges.

Halted by Extreme Cold

They set off northwards in extremely low temperatures, around –40 degrees C. It is heavy going through areas of skrugarder, which exhausts the dogs. Little by little, these are slaughtered individually to provide food for the others. Every time they stop for rest or sleep, the unpredictable drift-ice takes them southwards, slowing their progress terribly. 7th April: they decide to turn south and make for Franz Joseph's Land. This is at 86 degrees 4' (they discover in retrospect). The journey begins well, but after a week, their clocks suddenly stop, which hinders their calculations of latitudinal position. Conditions worsen, the snow begins to melt and great sea lanes open up in the ice.

June 1st: they find themselves at the edge of a large sea lane and have to take to the canoes. Provisions begin to run low, but they are soon able to hunt. June 22nd: they shoot a seal, but the going has become so bad they are confined to camp – 'Camp Yearning' – for a month.

The day after they eventually set off again, what they at first take to be cloud formations turns out to be land in the distance. By 7th August all that separates them from three small islands is a short stretch of water. They kill the last two dogs.

15th August: in his diary, Nansen records his joy at seeing moss and small flowers between the rocks. They continue southwards, unsure of their location.

27th August: decide to set up camp for the winter – there are large numbers of walrus and ice bears and they lay down a store of meat and blubber. They build a small hut – a length of driftwood provides the ridgepole, with walrus skins forming the roof. In this 'cave', they spend the winter.

By the end of February, animal life has returned, providing fresh meat, and they prepare to continue south. First, they must improvise new equipement, and it is 19th May before they make a start, paddling the canoes in the water and hauling their equipment after them.

Three weeks later they arrive at the south coast of the island. Whilst they are scanning the horizon, the canoes come loose and drift away from the land. Nansen strips off, throws himself into the icey water and, with superhuman effort, is able to reach the canoes and climb on board.

An Unexpected Meeting on the Ice

17th June: a miracle occurs. Nansen is trying to work out a route forward when he suddenly hears dogs barking. He follows the sound and comes face to face with a man, Jackson, who is leading a British expedition to Franz Joseph's Land. He invites Nansen and Johansen to travel back on his ship, which subsequently arrives on 7th August.

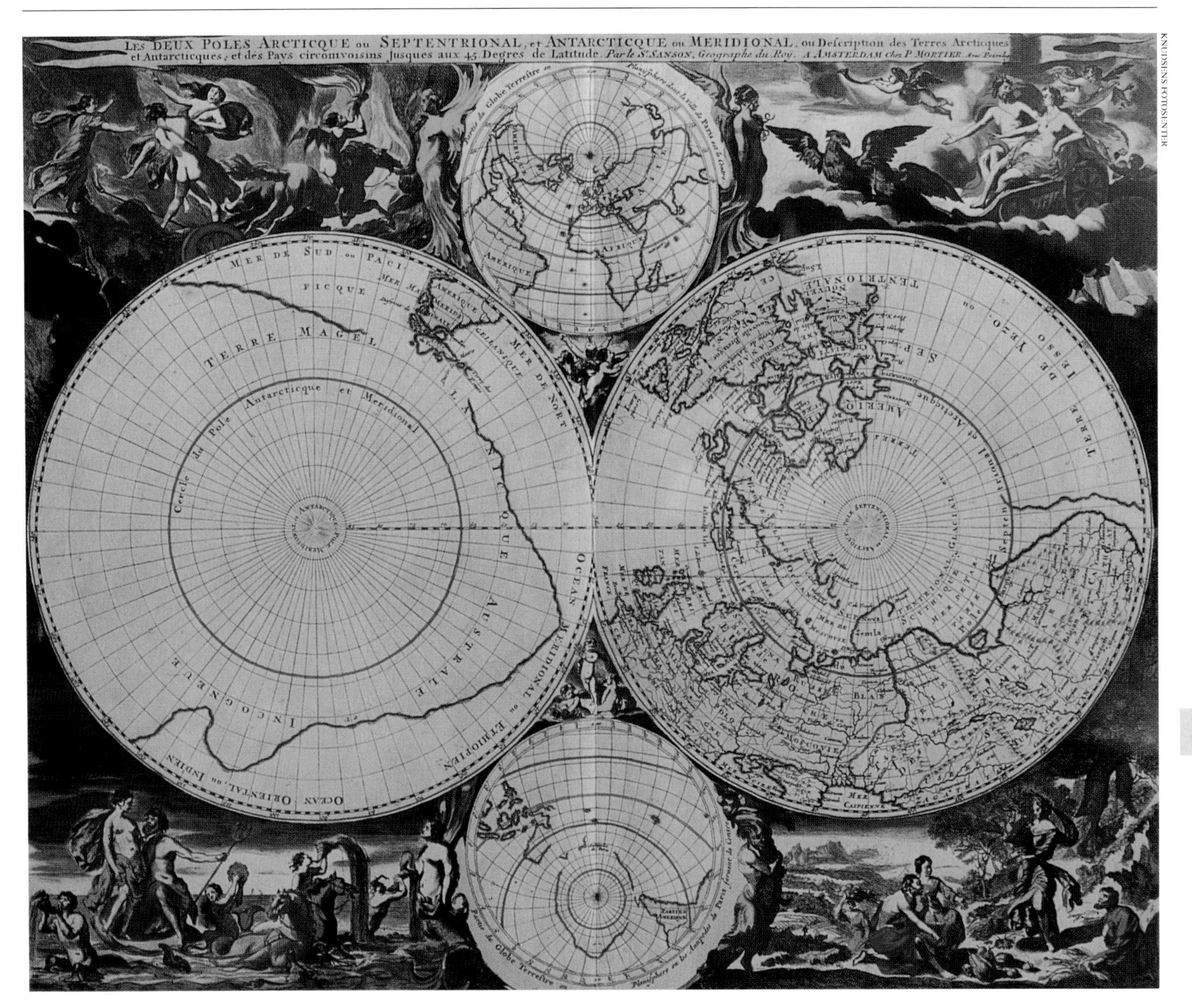

KNUDSENS FOTOSENTER

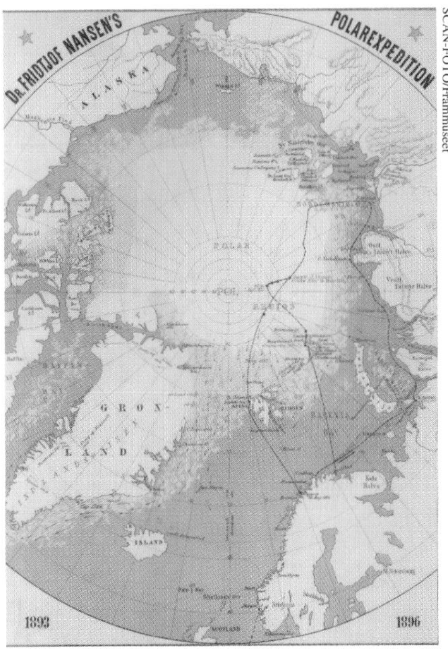

SCAN-FOTO/Frammuseet

Maps of the polar areas were virtually non-existent. The Dutch map above showing the Arctic and Antarctic areas is one of the oldest known.
Left: A map of the Fram expedition of 1893–96, drawn by Knud Bergslien.

Fridtjof Nansen and Hjalmar Johansen wave goodbye to the crew of the Fram as they set off on skis on their great trek across Greenland.

Even the dogs bore ribbons when the Fram crew celebrated the 17th of May.

Far right: An unexpected meeting of Nansen and Jackson in the frozen wasteland.

UB's NANSENSAMLING

THE ILLUSTRATED LONDON NEWS.

SCAN-FOTO/Frammuseet

SCAN-FOTO/Frammuséet

A well-known photo of Fridtjof Nansen, used in publications throughout the world.

Following his exploits in the polar deserts, new tasks awaited Nansen, as a diplomat and humanitarian. He became envoy to London and later played an important part in the League of Nations, in Geneva. At the end of the First World War, he organized the repatriation of prisoners of war, and in the Ukraine and Volga regions he carried out relief operations, saving millions from starvation. Through his efforts, refugees were given official papers, which still today carry his name, namely the Nansen passports. In 1922, he was awarded the Nobel Peace Prize.

SCAN-FOTO/Frammuséet

UB's NANSENSAMLING

UB's NANSENSAMLING

SCAN-FOTO/Arkiv

Up until his death, Fridtjof Nansen was a popular subject of the press. As seen here, conversing with a British journalist.

NORSK FOLKEMUSEUM/Olav Bjaaland

The target reached, the Norwegian flag was planted on the South Pole on 14th December 1911. Roald Amundsen had his name engraved forever in history as one of the great explorers.

A proud Roald Amundsen, on the deck of Fram, before the departure of the great expedition from Oslo. The crew was hand-picked, and Amundsen knew they could all be trusted.

NORSK FOLKEMUSEUM/Wilse

SCAN-FOTO/Frammuséet

NORSK FOLKEMUSEUM

At an early stage, Amundsen discovered the advantages of exploring the hostile regions by plane. In 1926, with the Italian Umberto Nobile as his pilot, he crossed the North Pole on his way from Spitsbergen to Alaska, on board the airship Norge. Two years later Nobile went down in an airship, and Amundsen flew out to his rescue. His plane vanished, and Amundsen went to his grave in the frozen deserts.

NORSK FOLKEMUSEUM/Wilse

NORSK FOLKEMUSEUM/Wilse

SCAN-FOTO/Edmund Shea

Amundsen's ship, Gjøa, lay nearly forgotten in Golden Gate Park in San Fransisco before she was brought back to Norway and placed beside the Fram museum.

Otto Sverdrup led Fram on the great journey from 1893–96, and later led the polar expedition of 1898–1902, to the Arctic, where huge areas were mapped, and annexed in the name of the Norwegian King. He is considered one of the truly great polar explorers.
Right: Sverdrup and Nansen on board Fram.

UB's NANSENSAMLING

NORSK FOLKEMUSEUM

13th August: they arrive back in Vardø.

In Hammerfest, a week later, a telegram comes from Skjærvøy announcing the arrival of the *'Fram'* with all in good health. Thus, the happy ending to the expedition, prior to the triumphant coastal procession to Christiania.

This was to be Nansen's last great expedition. The scientific results were published in six, huge volumes, and the whole project, led and carried out with such exemplary style, remains one of the classic Polar expeditions of all time.

Society now had other tasks for Nansen. In 1905, he served an important role in the dissolution of the Union with Sweden, and later he was appointed to a leading position in the League of Nations. In the wake of World War One he led the organisation for the repatrisation of prisoners of war, and in the Ukraine and Volga districts, millions were saved from starvation thanks to his great humanitarian efforts. «Charity is realpolitik», claimed Nansen, and in 1922 he was awarded the Nobel Peace Prize. He became the first High Commissioner for Refugees, and the highest award for work amongst refugees is known as the Nansen Medal. Nansen died at his home, *'Polhogda',* in May, 1930.

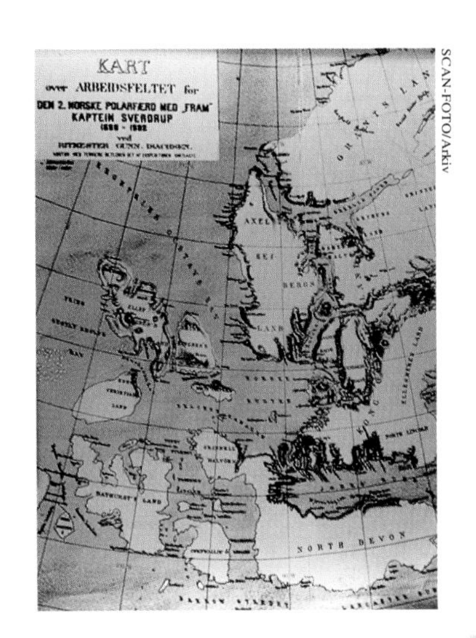

SCAN-FOTO/Arkiv

The map showing the route of Sverdrup's expedition, where a number of a scientific measurements were carried out, e.g. of the width of the ice and the depth of the ocean.

Otto Sverdrup

Already as a 17-year-old, Otto Sverdrup had crewed on long-haul ships, acquired his mate's certificate and, in 1877, his master's certificate.

When Fridtjof Nansen announced his plans to ski across Greenland, Sverdrup applied for inclusion in the team.

Sverdrup subsequently proved himself a master of polar conditions. Having captained the *'Fram'* on Nansen's 1893–99 Arctic Ocean expedition, his reputation as a polar explorer was such that when Axel Heiberg and the brothers Amund and Ellef Ringnes declared their willingness to fit a new polar expedition, it was Sverdrup they chose to lead it after advice of Nansen.

The expedition was planned in consultation with Nansen and the sponsers, the plan being to explore the unknown northerly areas of Greenland, using the *'Fram'* as base. If conditions rendered this impossible, Sverdrup was free to sail to other Arctic areas.

Nothing was spared in the preparations. Provisions for five years were loaded on board the 'Fram', which had meanwhile been fitted with an upper stern-deck, giving considerably more room on board. The members of the expeditions were selected from a large number of applicants; a cartographer and a doctor were joined by a botanist, a zoologist and a geologist. The total crew numbered 16 men. 27th June, 1898: the *'Fram'* leaves Norway for Greenland. After three weeks on a stormy sea, she enters the pack ice off Southern Greenland. Further up the west coast, the ice diminishes, and they put in to several places to take on water and 70 sleigh-dogs.

In Melville Bay, they again meet the pack ice, and are forced to abandon attempts to cross Smith Sound. They harbour for the winter in a sheltered bay on the west coast, behind Prince of Wales Island.

The sea provides plenty of walrus-meat, excellent food for the dogs, whilst the land gives them musk and hare. From this base, they concentrate on mapping previously unexplored areas of Ellesmere Isand, together with routine scientific exploration. The many Norwegian names on modern maps of the area bear witness to these activities.

16th October: They see the sun for the last time of the year. Sverdrup ensures there is always something to be getting on with; in addition to the continuous recording of scientific tests, there is great industry on board.

Christmas and New Year are ostentatiously celebrated, prior to preparations for the summer's sledging expeditions. These begin in early spring from the *'Fram',* which receives a visit from local Innuits.

Charting a New Land

Plans to push through to the north coast of Greenland again prove impossible, and Sverdrup decides instead to move the *'Fram'* to a new position further west, where there are large areas to explore. They find a new winter harbour in a small fjord on the north side of Jones Sound. They have not managed to get as far west as they had hoped, but the conditions are favourable for an expedition westwards, using small rowing-cum-sailing boats for the sea lanes. They take with them dog food, to establish depots for the winter sledging expeditions, and wait nearly a month for the ice to be strong enough for their return trip, using a sledge built with materials cannibalised from the boat.

Later in the autumn a number of sledging expeditions are carried out, and the area along the Jones Sound is mapped. There is plentiful game in the area and they hunt musk ox and polar bear for fresh meat. The winter is spent much the same as last year, but on 20th March the big sledging expedition sets off. After many adventures, all are back on the *'Fram'* by 19th June.

There are still great areas to be explored, and the men are full of energy. Sverdrup decides to continue into the Jones Sound as far as possible and seek a new winter harbour there. Furthest westwards in the sound, in the Gåsfjord, the *'Fram'* remains throughout the winters 1900–01 and 1901–02. The latter is not planned but impossible ice conditions frustrate all attempts to get free. First in the spring it is possible for methodical exploration to continue.

The large islands are named Amund Rignes Island, Ellef Rignes Island and Isachsen Land. The largest of the islands to the east of these is named Axel Heibergs' Land. A whole collection of smaller islands and fjords are also given Norwegian names.

The sledging expeditions happen in various stages. One of the sledging parties reach 81 degrees 40' on the north west side of Ellesmere Island, after a 77-day journey. Another chart an area further to the west, covering 550 km in 67 days.

SCAN-FOTO/Keystone

Roald Amundsen. He always dreamt of conquering the North Pole, but ended up going to the South Pole.

Triumphant Return

The second season is spent in sledging expeditions to the west and south, but at last on 6th August, 1902, the *'Fram'* breaks free of the ice and can head homewards. On 18th September, she returns in triumph to Christiania.

An area equal of 200–300 000 sq.km. had been charted and mapped, and the scientific findings of the expedition were published in four thick tomes with sections on astrology, cartography, botany, geology, zoology, meteorology and terrestial magnatism.

The areas charted were claimed in the name of the Norwegian King, but the foreign minister failed to secure the annexation in accordance with international law, and Canada later asserted her claim under the sector principle. Thus, the territories discovered by the Sverdrup Expedition came under Canadian jurisdiction. In 1930, the Canadian Government purchased all of Sverdrup's original journals and maps for the sum of 67,000 dollars.

Otto Sverdrup died in 1930, at the age of 76. Following the second *'Fram'* Expedition, he was reckoned one of the greatest polar explorers of all time and his advice was sought by many subsequent explorers. He led various search expeditions in the polar area when he was well over 60 years of age and, as many of his obituaries stated, as a practitioner Otto Sverdrup was unrivalled.

Roald Amundsen

Roald Amundsen is remembered first and foremost for his great powers of organisation and leadership. Though no scientist himself, his expeditions included specialists who brought back from his expeditions important scientific data.

Amundsen was born on 16th July, 1872, in Borge, near Sarpsborg in the south east of Norway, the son of sea captain and shipowner Jens Amundsen. When Roald was still young, the family moved to Christiania, and it was there he began to study medicine.

His first polar expedition, following a trip with seal hunters in 1894, was as mate in the Belgian Antarctic expedition, led by de Garlachek. This included an unplanned for winter which taught him a great deal about Antarctic conditions. Upon his return he acquired his master's certificate and began to plan his own polar expedition. In his youth, Amundsen had been fascinated by Franklin's attempt to discover the so-called North West Passage, and he decided now to complete Franklin's task.

With his own money, he purchased a 70-foot arctic schooner, equipped it with a motor and, in the summer of 1901, embarked on a voyage in the Arctic Ocean to try out the little ship, which he named the *'Gjøa'*.

Spring, 1903: the *'Gjøa'* stands ready, with a crew of 6. The plan is to explore the magnetic north pole, in addition to the usual cartographic assignments and studies of plant and animal life. The crew has been chosen accordingly. Amundsen leaves behind him extensive debts, sailing before his creditors manage to seize his vessel.

NORSK FOLKEMUSEUM/Wilse

Roald Amundsen wearing the trademark wolf-skin coat he used on his expeditions.

A Struggle Against Cold and Ice

In Greenland, they take on board 10 sleigh-dogs. Conditions are good and they reach the Lancaster Sound and Beechey Island, which has served as a winter harbour for some previous expedition, without difficulty. Magnetic readings suggest that they must search further to the south for the magnetic north pole. Amundsen is also convinced that this route offers them the best chance of coming west, through the narrow, shallow sounds, where the pack ice is less formidable. They experience several groundings and storms together with a dangerous on-board fire, but make their way steadily westwards. At the south east extreme of King William's Land they find a good site for the winter, calling it Gjøahavn.

This proves an ideal site for magnetic tests and offers good hunting, also. They build a house on land and before long receive their first visit from the Innuits. A major sledging expedition, to determine the exact location of the magnetic north pole, is planned. In the middle of March, Amundsen and Helmer Hansen set off with two sledges, each pulled by five dogs, but temperatures measuring a steady -50 degrees centigrade force them to turn back. Another attempt is made on 6th April, and by their return on 27th May, they have successfully passed over the magnetic north pole. The summer is dedicated to further studies. Amundsen himself carries out ethnographic investigations into the local Innuit people. 2nd April: Godfred Hansen and Ristvedt leave on a mapping expedition to Victoria Island and return on 26th June with excellent results.

Mid-August: the *'Gjøa'* leaves her winter harbour after almost two years and moves slowly west. The tendency of the *'Gjøa'* to ground hinders their progress, but eventually the waters deepen and clear, and on 26th August they meet their first ship coming from the west. Unfortunately, it turns out to be a bad year for the ice and together with various other ships, the *'Gjøa'* is forced into another period of 'hibernation'. Amundsen undertakes further sledging expeditions, and crosses the mountains to the south to the nearest telegraph station, 40 days away, to announce to the world the discovery of the North West Passage. It is March before he returns, with post and news. The ice continues to hold them prisoner, and it is the end of August before they round Point Barrow.

After a triumphant arrival in Seattle and San Francisco, Amundsen and his men travel home to Norway where their enthusiastic countrymen honour the new polar explorers. The *'Gjøa'* is brought from San Francisco Golden Gate Park back to Norway and installed next to the *'Fram House'* on Bygdøy, near Christiania.

The scientific data is so extensive it takes many years to process. A lack of funds hinders publication, which does not occur until 1933, in three large volumes.

SCAN-FOTO/Novosty

Many years after Roald Amundsen's death in the polar sea, his watch was recovered by a Russian expedition.

The Desire for Conquest of the North Pole

Amundsen's next goal is to explore the North Polar Basin and, as the jewel in the crown, to conquer the North Pole itself. He wishes to repeat Nansen's voyage with *'Fram'*, entering the pack ice through the Bering Straits. The further to the west he can enter the greater his chances of reaching the Pole. He approaches Nansen for the loan of the *'Fram'*.

But in the meantime, the North Pole is reached – first by Cook in 1908 and later by Peary. Amundsen has staked everything on this expedition, but now interest in it begins to cool. In order to save his reputation and future as a polar explorer, Amundsen alters his plans, setting his sights on the South Pole, instead. August 1909: the *'Fram'* sails south, and everyone believes she will round Cape Horn on her approach to the Bering Straits. In Madeira the crew and the rest of the world are told that the North Pole must wait – the goal of the expedition is the South Pole. A British expedition under the leadership of Robert Scott is already on its way south with the same intention. This is Scott's second attempt. He receives a telegram from Amundsen announcing the Norwegian plan just as he leaves Australia on his way south. The news is not well received by the British, but Amundsen thinks it fair enough. The British exhibition has great advantages; they have knowledge of both local conditions and the route to the pole from earlier British attempts.

Amundsen manoeuvres the *'Fram'* through the Antarctic ice to The Bay of Whales, on the Ross Barrier, which he believes will provide them with the best starting point. By 12th August, the *'Fram'* arrives and equipment can be unloaded onto the ice shelf. They move into a prefabricated hut and hollow out a series of rooms in the surrounding snowfield to house the various activities (a method adopted by many subsequent polar expeditions.)

One day, Scott's ship *'Terra Nova'* suddenly turns up and the British are able to assess the competition. They note the Norwegian dog teams, and observe their preparations. The *'Fram'* sets out on a long oceanographic project whilst Amundsen plans the attempt on the Pole. Provision depots are established at 80, 81 and 82 degrees south. During the winter, the experiences from these depot-trips are analysed. Everything can be simplified, rationalised – sledges and their loads are rebuilt and reduced to less than half their weight. Boots, tents and sleeping bags are redesigned.

The South Pole

All are anxious to get going, and already on 7th September they set out. But improvements in the weather do not hold; temperatures drop to under –50 degrees centigrade. Neither dogs nor men are able to function and they turn back. Amundsen revises his plan. The Pole team will now consist of five men, whilst the other three will explore Edward VII Land, to the east.

19th October; the journey to the Pole begins. They have four sledges, each pulled by 13 dogs. They keep the pace down to save the dogs – the loads are very heavy. They manage about 28 km a day. On 3rd November, the pedometer indicates arrival at the 82 degree depot, but thick fog makes it impossible to find. Next day, they see the marker flags to the east and west of the depot itself.

After this, they are in unknown territory, and after some days they spy mountains to the south west, a whole range, through which Amundsen must find a way up to the Polar Plateau. 16th November: they reach the foot of the mountains and lay down provisions for 30 days. All that is not strictly necessary is left behind. After a short reconnaissance, a route is chosen. This follows a line up the mountain, dropping down onto the snow fields, then on, but in the event they meet the great glacier coming down from the plateau itself, the Axel Heiberg Glacier. The snow is loose and the glacier riddled with crevices. But the dogs achieve the impossible and on 20th November, after 12 exhausting hours on a slope of some 1,500 metres, they reach the top.

Here they slaughter 24 of the dogs for food. A storm delays their departure, but soon they are on their way again, with three sledges, each pulled by six dogs, carrying provisions for 60 days. In the poor weather they almost careen into a ravine, managing to stop only at the last moment. With an improvement in the weather they continue through undulating, crevice-filled areas. By 5th December they are finally up on the plateau and establish a camp at more than 3,200 metres.

From here, they head south. 8th December: they pass 88 degrees 23' south, the previous record set by Ernest Shakleton.

14th December: at 15.00 hours, the instruments indicate that they are over the Pole, and five hands hold aloft the Norwegian flag, planting it firmly in the snow to the words; 'Thus we plant you, dear flag, at the South Pole and name this plain whereupon it flies, King Haakon VII's Plateau'.

For the next few days, they fan out in different directions, undertaking a number of scientific tests. 17th December: they raise a small reserve tent, with the Norwegian flag and a pennant of the *'Fram'* flying on top. In the tent they leave excess equipment and two letters, one to King Haakon and one to Robert Scott.

The First Norwegian to Gain a Flying Certificate

The return journey goes quickly; conditions are good and the sledges light. It takes just three weeks to cross back over the plateau and descend to the depot at the foot of the mountains. The journey across the barrier also proceeds well. They arrive in Framheim on 26th January. Behind them, a journey of some 3,000 km, which they have completed in 99 days. The next day, the *'Fram'* arrives and they prepare to leave. From Tasmania, Amundsen sends a telegram home announcing the conquest of the South Pole. Amundsen's interest for polar exploration continued, unabated. He realised the potential of flying as a method of exploration and became the first Norwegian to acquire a civil flying certificate.

The First World War caused the suspension of his plans, but in 1918 he left Oslo on board the *'Maud',* to seek the North East Passage. The expedition was to take three years. In America he ordered two aeroplanes, one of which had the capacity for long range flights, planning to let the *'Maud'* freeze fast in the pack-ice and use the planes to explore areas to the north. In the event, the planes crashed almost immediately; aerial exploration thus rendered impossible, Amundsen abandoned the expedition. The *'Maud'* remained in the ice for three years, under the command of Captain Wisting.

Amundsen did not give up. He worked hard to fund a new flying expedition, this time using Spitsbergen as his point of departure. The American, Lincoln Ellsworth came to his aid; two flying boats were ordered and, in 1925, Amundsen took off from New Ålesund, on Spitzbergen, for the Pole. Engine trouble forced him to land on the ice at 87 degrees 44' north. After a dramatic 24 days, during which they managed to prepare a runway with the aid of a small axe, they took off in one of the planes and returned to North East Land, on Spitzbergen. Here they were sighted by a fishing trawler and brought back to New Ålesund, in one piece.

Upon his return, Amundsen set off on a series of long lecture tours to raise funds for another attempt. This time, he used an Italian made airship, called the 'Norway'. On 22nd May, this passed over the North Pole on its way from Spitzbergen to Teller, in Alaska.

Amundsen's final polar expedition was in 1928. On 18th June, he flew north from Tromsø with a flying boat to rescue Nobile, whose airship had crashed on the ice. On his way, Amundsen's own plane crashed and thus the Arctic Ocean, to which he had dedicated so much of his life, became his grave.

The Philately of the Olympic Games

Fredrik C. Schreuder:

SCAN-FOTO/Rune Baashus

Fredrik C. Schreuder (b. 1937), industrialist and businessman from Oslo, began as a philatelist in his schooldays. He had his first exhibition of stamps, with sporting motives, in 1951. Ever since, he has concentrated his collection on Olympic stamps, and is the owner of an important private collection. Olympic philatelists have grown sizeably in numbers, and many countries now have separate organisations for this activity.

The field of Olympic Philately is comprehensive. The first Olympic Games of our modern times, hosted by Athens, Greece, in 1896, were partly financed by means of an issue of 12 postage stamps. These stamps, particularly when cancelled during the Games, are considered most interesting by Olympic philatelists. Since the Antwerp Olympic Games in 1920 special postage stamps and cancellations have been issued by the host country of all Olympic Games. From the Tokyo Games in 1964 onwards the number of stamp issues and cancellations in connection with the Olympic Games has virtually exploded. This article presents a survey of the development of Olympic Philately.

ΟΛΥΜΠ. ΑΓΩΝΕΣ
ΕΛΛΑΣ
18
96
ΑΘΗΝΑΙ
10
ΛΕΠΤΑ
ΛΕΠΤΑ
10

Themes from the ancient games often feature on the postage stamps published in connection with our modern Olympic Games. Naturally, it is Greece which has most extensively utilised this philatelic connection with the original games, but France and Belgium have also used classical motifs, during the 1920 and 1924 games.

From the ancient games, we have the images of the Olympic Torch, the victory laural wreath and the Olympic oath, all traditions which are represented in modern philatelic design.

During the ancient games, all hostility and war had to be put aside for a month, and any regional power attempting to break this cease-fire could expect to be severely punished. Unfortunately, this convention has proved impossible to transfer to the modern games.

The actual events from ancient Greece, far fewer in number than in the modern games, have been widely represented on postage stamps. Athletics provided the backbone of the arrangement with a range of track and field events including running, long jump, discus and javelin. Other events included horse-racing, boxing and wrestling.

Both the Greek gods and Greek mythology played a central role in the original Olympic Games, with sacrifices offered to the former that they might protect the games and their participants from harm.

1968
ΕΛΛΑΣ
ΔΡΑΧ
HELLAS
5

ΔΙΕΘΝΗΣ ΟΛΥΜΠΙΑΚΗ ΑΚΑΔΗΜΙΑ
ΕΛΛΑΣ - HELLAS ΔΡ. 6

1984
14
HELLAS
ΕΛΛΗΝΙΚΗ ΔΗΜΟΚΡΑΤΙΑ

1980
8
ΕΛΛΑΣ HELLAS

Λ 80
ΕΛΛΑΣ

ΕΛΛΑΣ
ΔΡ. 4.50
XVII ΟΛΥΜΠΙΑΣ : 1960

ΕΛΛΑΣ
ΔΡ.
2.50

ΕΛΛΑΣ
ΔΡ. 5

ΕΛΛΑΣ
ΔΡ. 12.50

10
10

60
ΑΘΗΝΑΙ
60

ΟΛΥΜΠΙΑΚΟΙ ΑΓΩΝΕΣ
3
ΔΡΑΧΜΑΙ ΔΡΑΧΜΑΙ
3

ΟΛΥΜΠ. ΑΓΩΝΕΣ
5 ΛΕΠΤΑ 5

30 ΛΕΠΤΑ 30

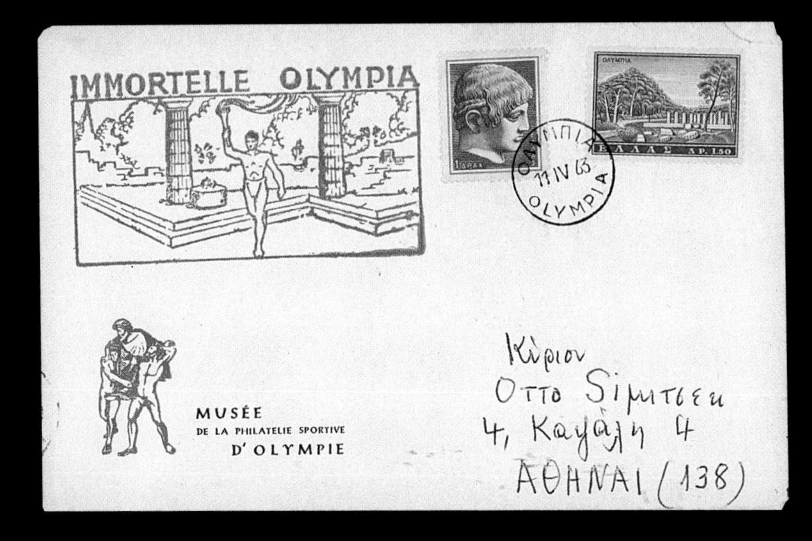
IMMORTELLE OLYMPIA
ΕΛΛΑΣ ΔΡ. 1.50
OLYMPIA
MUSÉE
DE LA PHILATELIE SPORTIVE
D'OLYMPIE
Κύριον
ΑΘΗΝΑΙ (138)

Pierre de Coubertin and the International Olympic Committee

The father of the modern Olympic Games was the Frenchman Pierre de Coubertin (1863–1937). Already in his mid-20s he had begun to play with the idea of reviving the games, and having discussed the notion with leading public figures in both France and England, he presented his plans at an official meeting in Paris, in 1892. The response was more positive than he had dared hope, although few at the time understood the implications of de Coubertin's vision.

He continued to develop his plans, and travelled widely to canvas support, including a trip to the U.S.A in 1894. He succeeded in convening an international congress in Paris in June of the same year, where it was unanimously decided to revive the ancient tradition of the Olympic Games. Furthermore, it was decided that the first modern Games should be held in Athens, in 1896.

At the Paris Congress, the International Olympic Committee (IOC) was established with the Greek Vikelas as its first president. He was replaced in 1896 by Coubertin himself, who continued in the post until the Prague IOC Congress, in 1925.

Pierre de Coubertin died in Geneva in 1937, and his heart is buried in the park of the Olympic Academy, in Olympia.

Coubertin has also secured his place in the Olympic philately, with Haiti as the first country to honour him, with a series of three stamps in 1939. San Marino has published two series of stamps depicting the presidents of the IOC, and France marked the Centenary of Coubertin's birth with a special postmark. A special postmark was also issued in Olympia to celebrate this event.

The most important philatelic acknowledgements of the IOC are connected to the Swiss issues in 1944, to celebrate the 50 Year Jubilee of the Committee, and in 1984 for the 90 Year Jubilee. The latter commemorates the use of Lausanne the IOC base since 1915, and the Olympic Museum in Lausanne is well worth a visit. Three stamps and two special postmarks were issued to coincide with the 1925 Prague Congress of the IOC, and the commemorative postmark for the 1930 Congress in Berlin is, today, quite rare.

Atelier de Fabrication des Timbres-Poste, PARIS.

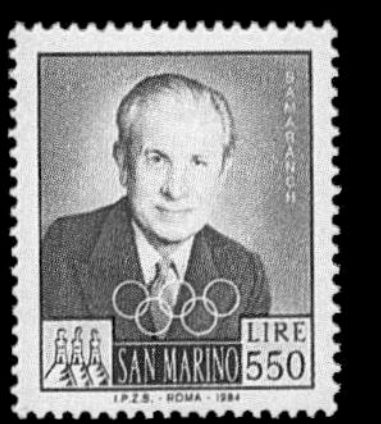

01842

ΚΥΡΙΑΝ
Μ. ΛΟΓΟΔΟΣΙΔΗ
ΕΥΦΡΑΝΟΡΟΣ 16
ΑΘΗΝΑΙ - ΠΑΓΚΡΑΤΙ

T 502

The First Modern Olympic Games – Athens 1896

To organise the first modern games in less than two years was an ambitious project indeed. Financial problems arose, and there was strong opposition from elements within the Greek Government to the prioritising of such an event. In fact, the prime minister of the time chose to resign his post in protest, and it was only thanks to the Greek Crown Prince Konstantin, chairman of the Organising Committee, that it was possible to mobilise enough support to ensure the progress of the arrangement.

The most expensive aspect of the first modern games was, without doubt, the construction of a new stadium in Athens. Had it not been for George Averoff, a wealthy Greek exile and an enthusiastic supporter of the Organising Committee, the stadium would probably not have been completed in time, if at all. Averoff has also been honoured with his own stamp.

The issue of a series of 12 postage stamps, proved an important element in the financing of the first games. A law was passed securing 50 % of the income from the sale of the stamps for the organising of the Games. Of the 12 stamps, 8 bear separate individual designs, and this marks the first use anywhere of sports motifs on postage stamps.

The first modern games were held between March 25th and April 3rd 1896, and stamps and letters bearing postmarks from this period are of particular interest to the philatelist.

Indeed, the stamps and postal history of the 1896 games constitute, without doubt, the most interesting elements of Olympic philately.

COMITÉ HELLÈNE

DES JEUX OLYMPIQUES

SOUS LA PRÉSIDENCE DE

S. A. R.

MONSEIGNEUR LE PRINCE ROYAL DE GRECE

Monsieur

Imprimerie de la Hestia

The Decennial Games-Athens 1906

Philatelists also have a particular interest in the series of 14 stamps issued in connection with the Decennial Games, held in Athens in 1906. Although not officially recognised as Olympic Games as such, this event received the full support of the IOC. They also proved particularly successful, and helped establish the position of the games, following less than successful arrangements in Paris (1900), and St Louis (1904).

Unfortunately, there are a number of forgeries of stamps commemorating the 1896 Olympic Games, and, similarly, stamps and postal cancellations issued during the 1906 Decennial arrangement.

ΕΛΛΑΣ — GRÈCE
ΕΠΙΣΤΟΛΙΚΟΝ ΔΕΛΤΑΡΙΟΝ
ΠΑΓΚΟΣΜΙΟΣ ΤΑΧΥΔΡΟΜΙΚΟΣ ΣΥΝΔΕΣΜΟΣ
CARTE POSTALE
Union universelle des Postes

Monsieur
Pasq: Sperco
Banquier
Smyrne

108 P & C. Athènes

The Olympic Games 1900–1902

There were no stamps issued in connection with the games in Paris in 1900, nor those in St Louis in 1904, or London in 1908, all of which were arranged in conjunction with World Fairs. The Olympics were confined to the shadows of these huge events, and suffered as a consequence.

The Stockholm Games, in 1912, however, were considerably more successful and the Organizing Committee could justly pride themselves on the arrangement. The position of the Olympic Games was thus consolidated, such that it was able to survive the traumatic years of the First World War. Although no postage stamps were issued in connection with the Stockholm Games, a few interesting cancellations were used, which today are in great demand amongst collectors. Two of these relate to the Olympic Stadium in Stockholm.

Since the games in Antwerp, in 1920, it has been the custom to issue commemorative stamps in connection with the Olympic Games, and special cancellations have also often been used. Promotional postmarks have also been used in connection with the Games on a number of occasions, particularly in Germany for the 1936 Berlin Games, and the Melbourne Games in Australia in 1956.

The first country to finance its participation in the Olympic Games through income derived from the sale of postage stamps was Portugal, for the Amsterdam Games in 1928, when the host nation also derived some income to cover the cost of the games from an issue of postal stationery.

Uruguay was the first country to issue stamps commemorating its own success in the Olympic Games, when the national team won the gold medal for football both in 1924 and 1928. A series of 3 stamps was issued to mark the achievement on each occasion.

Since the 1964 Tokyo Games, there has been a veritable explosion of philatelic activity in connection with the Summer Olympics, with the various host nations issuing so many postage stamps, miniature sheets, postal stationery, and cancellations that it has become difficult to maintain the overview. The postal program has become «big business», and the various postal services as well as the Olympic Organising Committees have derived financial advantage from the increase in interest from collectors.

From a purely philatelic point of view, the years prior to 1960 are certainly the most interesting. The relative primitiveness of printing techniques gave rise to numerous essays, proofs and printing varieties which offer the philatelist considerable challenges.

On the other hand, more recent stamps have a greater aesthetic appeal, with an increasing beauty in their design.

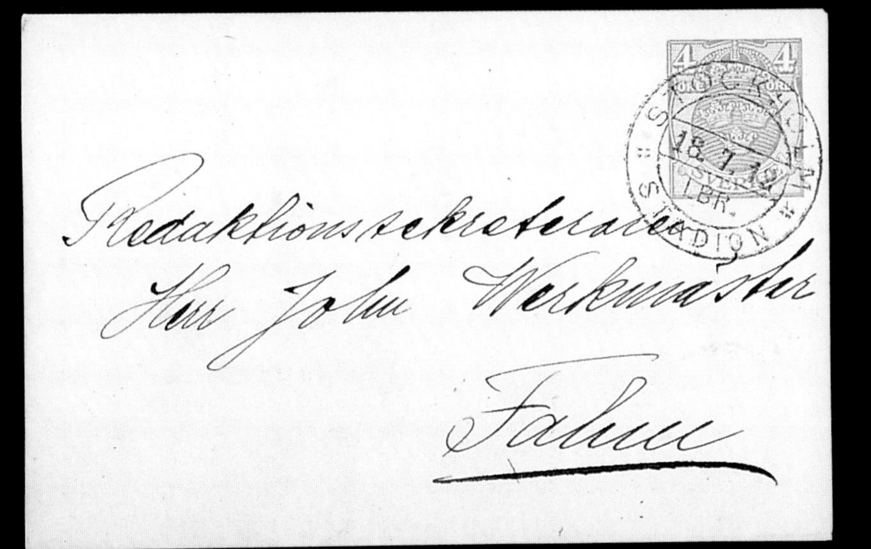

VII OLYMPIADE 1920
ANVERS · ANTWERPEN
BELGIQUE · BELGIE
5c 5c
POUR LES MUTILÉS + 5c
VOOR DE VERMINKTEN

VII OLYMPIADE 1920
ANVERS · ANTWERPEN
BELGIQUE BELGIE
15c 15c
POUR LES MUTILÉS + 5c VOOR DE VERMINKTEN

VII OLYMPIADE 1920
ANVERS · ANTWERPEN
10c
BELGIQUE BELGIE
POUR LES MUTILÉS + 5c VOOR DE VERMINKTEN

COLOMBES-VILLAGE OLYMPIQUE
POSTES FRANCE
VIIIe OLYMPIADE
PARIS 30 1924
FRANCE
OLYMPIADE 1924
25
VIIIe OLYMPIADE
PARIS-1924
POSTES FRANCE
50 PARIS 1924
COLOMBES
OLYMPIQUE

OLYMPIADE
STEUNT HET NEDERLANDSCH
OLYMPISCH COMITÉ
SALUS POPULI SUPREMA LEX
HET HEIL DES VOLKS ZY DE HOOGSTE WET
Als daar straks de wereldgasten
juichend door de straten gaan –
moet HEEL Neerland kunnen zeggen
daar heb IK aan meegedaan! –
COPYRIGHT DAGBLAD DE TELEGRAAF. AMSTERDAM
Tien cents
SERIE A. 1-1000. O. E. H. B. A. H.
BRIEFKAART
POSTZEGELS RECHTS
BOVEN IN DEN HOEK!
VLUGGER VERZENDING
10-11V
19 · III
1928

J.O. 1928
CORREIO
CORREIO
15c
AMSTERDAO
PORTUGAL

CORREIOS
MULTA
30c
PORTUGAL

The Olympic Flag and the Olympic Flame

Pierre de Coubertin was most concerned with the importance of Olympic symbols, and he initiated the design of an Olympic flag, presenting it to the 1914 IOC Congress in Paris. The flag, depicting a white field with interlocking rings of blue, green, yellow, black and red, symbolises the five continents united by the Olympic ideal. The colours also represent those contained in the flags of all countries of the world. This Olympic Flag was first flown over the 1920 Antwerp Games. Since then, the hoisting of the flag has been an important feature of the opening ceremony of each games, and its presentation to the successor host-nation an important feature of the closing ceremony.

The use of a torch to transport a flame from place to place, and to mark important occasions, has its roots in Greek history. The carrying of the Olympic flame was introduced into the symbolism of the modern games in Berlin, in 1936. The flame was ignited on the altar of Zeus, in Olympia, and relayed through seven countries to the Olympic Stadium in Berlin.

After 1936, this practice entered into the permanent ritual of the Games. The torch is brought to the Olympic Stadium during the Opening Ceremony; the Olympic Beacon is lit and continues burning throughout the games.

The Olympic flag and the journey of the Olympic flame have been commemorated on stamps and cancellations in many countries. A series of postal cancellations tracing the journey of the flame from Olympia to Patras, on the Pellopones peninsula, prior to the London Games in 1948, is of special interest. Owing to the state of war existing between different regions of Greece, the procession was not without risk.

Lillehammer took over the Olympic flag in Albertville. Up until the 17th Olympic Winter Games in February 1994, the flag will be kept in a case decorated with brass plates engraved with the names of every city that has hosted the Games since 1952.

SCAN-FOTO

ΕΛΛΑΣ
Λ.50

ΕΛΛΑΣ HELLAS ΔΡ.7

0,10
JUGOSLAVIJA

1976
ΕΛΛΑΣ·HELLAS ΔΡ 25

ΕΟΡΤΑΙ ΔΑΔΑΣ
XIV ΟΛΥΜΠΙΑΔΟΣ
ΟΛΥΜΠΙΑ - ΛΟΝΔΙΝΟΝ
HOLYDAYS OF FLAM
XIV OLYMPIADAS
OLYMPIA - LONDON
1948
ΠΥΡΓΟΣ
18 VII 48 17
ΑΦΙΞΙΣ
ΕΛΛΑΣ

AUSTRALIA
XVIth OLYMPIAD
MELBOURNE—1956

Deutsches Reich
12 +6
OLYMPISCHE SPIELE 1936

1S + 50g
REPUBLIK
ÖSTERREICH

Olympia-Fackel-Lauf 1936
Athen - Hellendorf - Berlin
Postkarte
HELLENDORF
31.7.36-12
über
PIRNA

The Effect of Politics and War on the Games

Whilst the ancient games effectively precipitated a cease-fire between warring factions, such an arrangement has not been possible in connection with the modern games.

In 1916, during the First World War, the Olympic Games should have been held in Berlin. The Games had to be cancelled, and Germany was excluded from the 1920 Antwerp Games, as punishment.

During the Second World War, both the 1940 and 1944 games were also cancelled. In 1940, the winter games had been planned for Sapporo, in Japan, and the summer games for Tokyo. Owing to the Sino-Japanese War, the decision was made to move the winter games to Garmisch Partenkirchen, in Germany, and the summer games to Helsinki, but, in the event, neither arrangement proved possible.

Throughout the post-war period there has been a steady stream of boycotts of the games by individual nations, in protest against military or other aggression, by various nations. The Soviet invasions of Hungary and Afghanistan led to boycotts by other countries in 1956 and 1980 respectively, and the Soviet Union operated a reciprocal boycott of the Los Angeles Games, in 1984. The worst disturbance of any Olympic Games, however, was the slaughter of 11 members of the Israeli Olympic team by Palestinian terrorists in 1972, in Munich. Despite the subsequent decision to continue with the Games, many participants could not face competing after what had happened.

Notwithstanding these incidents, there is no doubt that organized sport has helped to strengthen the ties between countries. Difficult as it might be to measure, the Olympic Games have themselves contributed to the cause of peace, friendship and reconcilliation.

They have also been abused by regimes wishing to promote the supposed excellence of their political system or ideology. Hitler's aim in the 1936 games was not simply to exhibit the effectiveness of the Third Reich, he also wanted to support his theory of the superiority of the Aryan race. In the post-war period, the communist regimes of Eastern Europe invested hugely in their leading athletes, whose success was to prove to the world the superiority of the Communist System. Unfortunately, these regimes have shown no qualms about the use of illegal and dangerous practices, not least the use of anabolic steroids, to achieve their goals.

Even those games cancelled by war have been to some extent commemorated by the issue of stamps and postal cancellations. The theme of the Olympic Games as a promoter of peace and reconcilliation has also received philatelic support.

MEINEN FREUNDEN ZUR ERINNERUNG AN DIE
OLYMPISCHEN SPIELE 1936 UND 1948 GEWIDMET,
MÖGE DIE UNSEELIGE, DAZWISCHEN LIEGENDE
ZEIT DREIER OLYMPIADEN, DIE IN BERLIN VON
EINEM TÖNENDEN ERZ, EINER KLINGENDEN SCHELLE
EINGELÄUTET WURDE, DIE MENSCHEN ZUR BESINNUNG
ZWINGEN UND DIE JUGEND DER WELT ZU AUFGABEN
RUFEN, DIE NICHT IN DER GEISTESAKROBATIK DER
ATOMBOMBEN IHR ENDE FINDEN WERDEN,

256 /300

The Winter Olympics 1924–1936

Pierre de Coubertin was a keen advocate of the inclusion of winter and alpine sports into the Olympic programme. There were obvious impediments – meteorological and topographic – to the winter and summer games sharing venue and timetable, though the 1908 London Games included a figure skating competition, and in 1920, Antwerp organised both figure skating and ice-hockey. In his memoirs, Coubertin records thinking, in 1921, that the development of winter sports in various countries, and their dedication to the ideals of amateurism and sportmanship, made their non-inclusion in the Olympic programme a great loss to the movement.

An advisory conference on winter sports was held prior to the 1921 IOC Congress in Paris. Paradoxically, it was the Nordic countries who most vehemently opposed the organisation of a Winter Olympics, presumably for fear that this would detract from their own winter sports arrangements. But this opposition was quickly reduced, and the Congress was able to announce a Winter Sports Week, to be held in 1924, in Chamonix, under the protective wing of the IOC. Though this was not referred to as the Winter Olympics.

The Chamonix Sports Week proved a great success, and the Nordic opposition to the notion of a winter olympics was considerably reduced by both Norwegian and Finnish success. The Norwegians dominated the skiing events, with strong performances by Thorleif Haug, Johan Grøttumsbraaten and J. Tullin Thams, whilst the Finns, Claes Thunberg and Julius Skutnabb, took the honours in speed skating.

ČESKOSLOVENSKÁ
PRAHA
-5.VI.25 12
1925
MEZINÁRODNÍ KONGRES OLYMPIJSKÝ
CONGRÈS OLYMPIQUE INTERNATIONAL

ČESKOSLOVENSKÁ
PRAHA
-5.VI.25 12
1925
MEZINÁRODNÍ KONGRES OLYMPIJSKÝ
CONGRÈS OLYMPIQUE INTERNATIONAL

ČESKOSLOVENSKÁ
24.V.25 16
1925
MEZINÁRODNÍ KONGRES OLYMPIJSKÝ
CONGRÈS OLYMPIQUE INTERNATIONAL

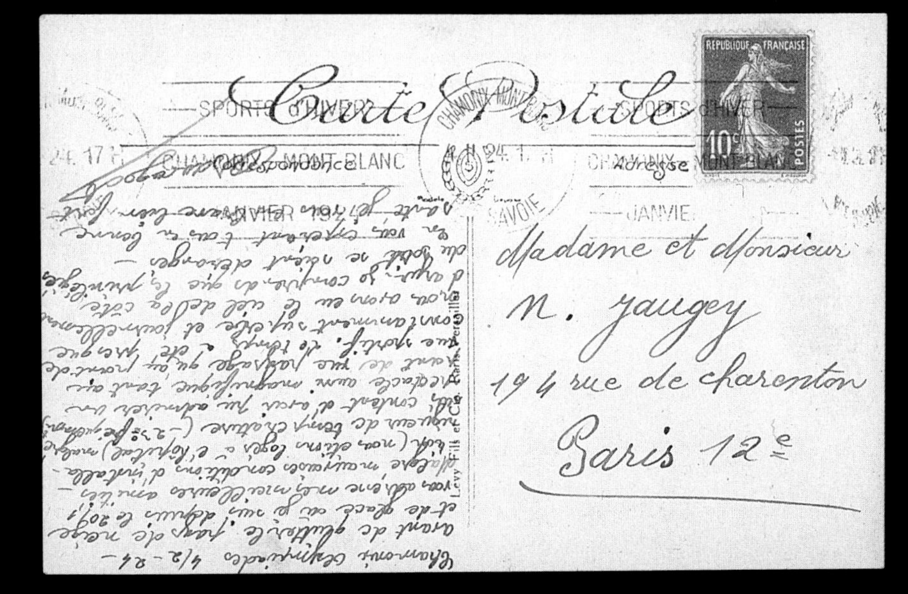
Carte Postale
Correspondance
Adresse
SPORTS D'HIVER
CHAMONIX-MONT-BLANC
JANVIER 1924
RÉPUBLIQUE FRANÇAISE
POSTES
Madame et Monsieur
N. Jaugey
194 rue de Charenton
Paris 12e

IIMES JEUX OLYMPIQUES
ST-MORITZ 1928
COMITÉ OLYMPIQUE SUISSE
Comité d'organisation St-Moritz
HELVETIA
Herrn
J. Rössler- Orovsky. Generalsekretär
des Tschechosl. Olymp. Komitees
Prag. II.
Palack Nabrezi 4
IIMES JEUX OLYMPIQUES D'HIVER
St Moritz 11-19 Févr. 1928
R St. Moritz-Dorf № 719
Eilsendung
Exprès - Espresso

The Winter Olympic Games 1924–1936

At the IOC's Congress in Prague, in 1925, it was formally agreed to arrange Winter Olympic Games, now with the full support of the Nordic representatives. Though there is nothing explicit in the minutes of the meeting concerning the 'promotion' of the Chamonix 1924 arrangement to the status of official Winter Games, this was implied by the decision to hold the 'second' Winter Olympic Games in St Moritz, Switzerland, in 1928. Thus, in all literature concerning the winter olympics, Chamonix 1924 is taken to constitute the First Winter Olympic Games. There were no special stamps issued either for the Chamonix Games, or the 1928 St Moritz Games, though a special postal cancellation was employed during the 1924 Chamonix event, to commemorate the Winter Sports Week. It is noticeable that this cancellation, which today is highly valued, makes no reference to the Olympic Games, nor makes any use of the Olympic symbols.

The first postage stamp to be issued in connection with the Winter Olympics was in 1932, at Lake Placid in the United States. The opening ceremony, on February 4th, was also commemorated with its own special postal cancellation.

Garmisch Partenkirchen, in Germany, hosted the 1936 games, which were commemorated by an issue of 3 postage stamps and two cards of postal stationery. A number of cancellations were in use during the games, and various towns had their own promotional cancellations for the games.

Certain gold medalists from the period 1924–1936 were honoured with their own postage stamps, including Thorleif Haug, Johan Grøttumsbraaten, Ivar Ballangud, Birger Ruud and Sonja Henie. She was even awarded her own special postal cancellation in Germany, which she earned by taking the gold medal in figure skating in 1928, 1932 and 1936.

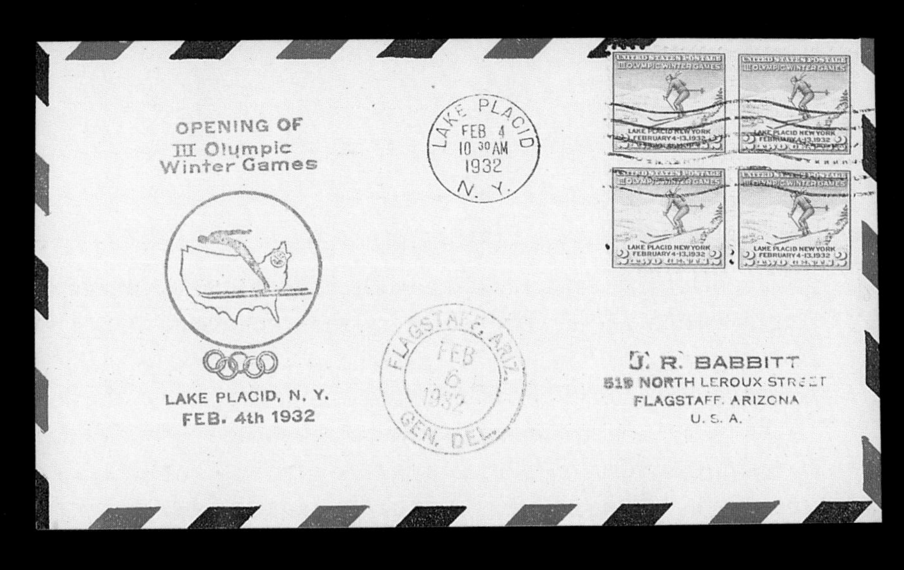
OPENING OF
III Olympic
Winter Games
LAKE PLACID, N. Y.
FEB. 4th 1932
LAKE PLACID
FEB 4
10 30 AM
1932
N. Y.
FLAGSTAFF, ARIZ.
FEB
6
1932
GEN. DEL.
J. R. BABBITT
519 NORTH LEROUX STREET
FLAGSTAFF, ARIZONA
U. S. A.

80
Deutsches Reich
6+4
OLYMPISCHE SPIELE 1936

Deutsches Reich
12+6
OLYMPISCHE SPIELE 1936

Deutsches Reich
25+15
OLYMPISCHE SPIELE 1936

NORGE
4KR
THORLEIF HAUG

NORGE
4KR
JOHAN GRØTTUMSBRÅTEN

NORGE
4KR
BIRGER RUUD

NORGE
4KR
IVAR BALLANGRUD

BERLIN SW 68
13 8 38
Sonja Henie
Die Eiskönigin
20th CENTURY FOX
225

012
Deutsche Reichspost

NORGE
4KR
SONJA HENIE

The Winter Olympics; St Moritz 1948 and Oslo 1952

The Swiss town of St Moritz hosted the second Winter Olympics, in 1948. Although the combination of slalom and downhill skiing had been included in the programme at the Garmish Partenkirchen games in 1936, it was in 1948 that alpine events really became a part of the winter olympics. The Giant Slalom was introduced in 1952 and the Super G event in 1988.

In 1948, cross-country skiing was dominated by the Swedes, whilst the Finns dominated the Nordic combination. Norwegians took all the medals for ski-jumping and three distances of speed skating. None of these victories is commemorated philatelically.

Switzerland issued a series of four postage stamps for the games, and a special postmark was used in St Moritz throughout the duration of the games. In addition, there were promotional cancellations used in Basel, Lausanne and Zurich, but otherwise the philatelic programme was modest.

Oslo hosted the 1952 Winter Olympics, and this marked the first time the games were held in a major city. The games took on the character of a national holiday; schools were closed for two weeks and the public flocked to the events. The giant slalom and downhill races were held at Norefjell, to the north of the city, but all other events took place in Oslo itself. Japan and Germany participated for the first time since the war, having been excluded from the 1948 games. Also for the first time, the cross-country skiing event for women was included in the programme, and the Finns swept the board.

Both in terms of organisation and personal performance, the Oslo Games proved a huge success. At Bislet, Hjalmar Andersen took gold in the 1500, 500 and 10,000 metre speed skating; at Holmenkollen, Arnfinn Bergmann won the ski-jumping, Stein Eriksen the giant slalom, Simon Stallvik the Nordic combination, and, most unexpectedly, Hallgeir Brenden won the 18 km cross-country event. He repeated this achievement in Cortina, 1956, where the distance was reduced to 15 km. All the 1952 Norwegian gold medalists are represented on stamp issues released in connection with the 1994 games in Lillehammer. The Norwegian Post Office issued a series of three postage stamps for the 1952 games, and the essays of these are of great philatelic interest. In addition to a hand cancellation used for the duration of the games, from 14th to 25th February, the games were advertised beforehand by a machine cancellation of the endless roller type. A number of post offices in Oslo also had their own Olympic machine cancellations, some of which are today quite valuable. Those which we know of are from the following post offices; Oslo Br., Holmenkollen, Skøyen and Vika (type 1), Elisenberg, Gamlebyen, Grunerløkka, Homansbyen, Majorstua, Moløkken, Solli and St Hanshaugen (type 2).

Scandinavian Airlines Systems (SAS) used a promotional cancellation in connection with the winter games in Oslo and the summer games the same year in Helsinki. We know of such cancellations from the SAS offices in Frankfurt, Copenhagen, New York and Stockholm.

OLYMPIA 1948
ST. MORITZ
HELVETIA 5

OLYMPIA 1948
ST. MORITZ
HELVETIA 10
+10

OLYMPIA 1948
ST. MORITZ
HELVETIA 20
+10

OLYMPIA 1948
ST. MORITZ
HELVETIA 30
+10

OSLO
1952
15+5
POST
NORGE

OSLO
1952
30
+
10
POST NORGE

OSLO 1952
55
+
20
POST NORGE

NORGE
4KR
HJALMAR "HJALLIS" ANDERSEN

Norske OL-vinnere
NORGE
4KR
HALLGEIR BRENDEN
ARNFINN BERGMANN
STEIN ERIKSEN
SIMON SLÅTTVIK
1994
N·O·K
Kr.20

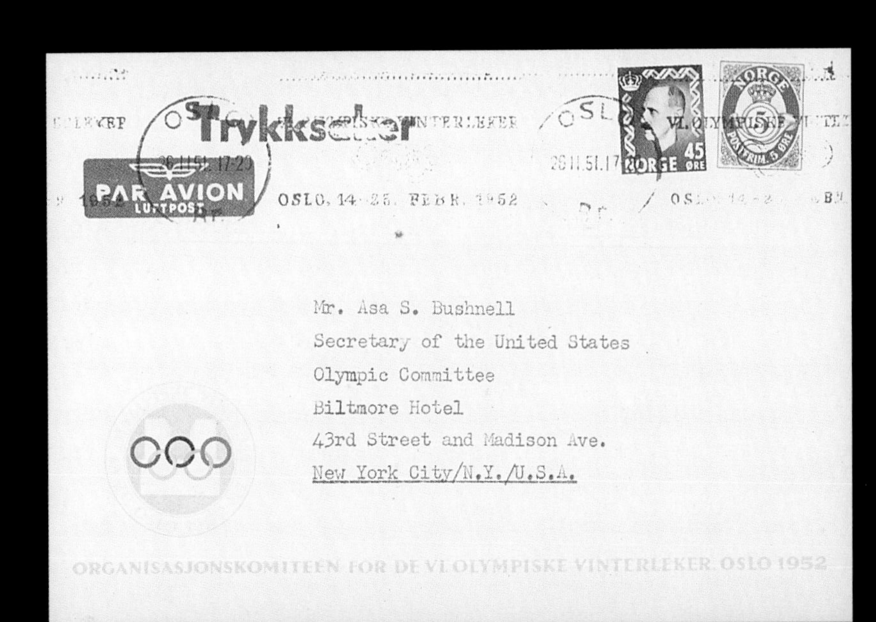
Trykksaker
PAR AVION
LUFTPOST
OSLO, 14.-25. FEBR. 1952
NORGE
45
ØRE
Mr. Asa S. Bushnell
Secretary of the United States
Olympic Committee
Biltmore Hotel
43rd Street and Madison Ave.
New York City/N.Y./U.S.A.
ORGANISASJONSKOMITEEN FOR DE VI OLYMPISKE VINTERLEKER OSLO 1952

Recent Winter Games

Until now, the Winter Olympic Games have been held in the same year as their summer counterpart, but from the 1994 Lillehammer Games, this has been changed, such that the two arrangements are held alternatively every second year.

The number of events at the winter games has steadily increased, from 13 in 1924, to 22 in 1952, and 57 in Albertville, in 1992. Probably the most significant change is the huge increase in women's events, from 1 in 1924 – figure skating –, to 4 in 1952, and 24 in 1992. This increase is mostly accounted for by the increase in cross-country skiing and speed skating events. The biathlon and tobogganing were added to the programme in, 1960 and 1964, respectively, whilst ice dancing was introduced in 1976 and short-track skating in 1992.

There has been a similar expansion in the Olympic philatelic programme, with the volume of postage stamp issues greatly increased, though not to the same extent as those connected with the summer games. In the period from 1956 to 1984, no host nation released more than two issues. For the 1988 games, the Canadian Post Office issued five series comprising eleven postage stamps, the French issued fourteen stamps and one miniature block in connection with the Albertville Games, and the Norwegian Post Office is planning five miniature blocks and three stamp series related to the Lillehammer Olympic Games.

The number of issues by participating countries has also increased tremendously in the post war years. In so far as these represent a country's own Olympic winners, or other special occasions or symbols, they can be of philatelic interest, but generally speaking the olympic issues from the more exotic nations are ignored by philatelists.

There has been a similar development in the number of postal cancellations connected to the winter Olympics. This process began in Cortina, 1956, when the Italian Post Office issued a series of special cancellations depicting the individual olympic events. This was followed up in Grenoble in 1968, Sapporo 1972, Sarajevo 1984, Calgary 1988 and Albertville in 1992. In the years since the Sarajevo games, it has also become the practice to issue special cancellations related to the procession of the olympic torch. The torch's procession for the Albertville games was sponsored by the French Post Office, and this will be repeated by the Norwegian Post Office for the Lillehammer Games in 1994. This event is likely to be commemorated in a way that will give much pleasure to olympic philatelists.

Olympic philately is an interesting hobby for anyone with a collector's mentality who is also fond of sport, and Olympic philately is as international a movement as the Olympic Movement itself. Olympic philatelists are to be found in virtually every country in the world, and some years ago, on the initiative of the IOC president, Juan Antonio Samaranch – himself a keen keen collector of Olympic philately – the Federation Internationale de Philatelie Olympique (FIPO) was founded. This organisation is supported by the IOC and the International Philatelic Organisation, FIP. There are also separate organisations for sport philatelists in Great Britain, Germany and the USA.

SCAN-FOTO/Rune Baashus

From Albertville to Lillehammer

Arne Bonde:

Arne Bonde (b. 1924), the chief editor of this book, is a senior member of the Norwegian press. He started his career with the news agency, NTB, has been chief editor of VG, and director of the publishing house, Ernst G. Mortensens Forlag. He was appointed the first director of NRK's P2 radio in Trondheim, and works today as a senior adviser to the director of the Norwegian Broacasting Corporation, NRK. For many years he was a correspondent for the American news magazines Time and LIFE.

Norway's greatest Olympic triumph in the history of the games occurred in Albertville, two years prior to the Lillehammer arrangement. Nine gold medals bring with them certain obligations, and the expectations for the 17th Winter Games are truly formidable. There are grounds for these expectations. Never before have Norwegian participants been better prepared, and on «homeground», the whole nation will be behind the country's sportsmen and women, demanding that they, once again, «show the world what's what»!

SCAN-FOTO/Jan Greve

SCAN-FOTO/Jan Greve

The national teams enter the full stadium after the Olympic flame is lit (previous page). Cameras, large and small click continuously.

SCAN-FOTO/Tor Richardsen

«Flight SK 1994 from Geneva has just landed», announced a voice over the public address system at Fornebu Airport, outside Oslo, and cheers rang round the packed arrivals hall. The glistening white Scandinavian Airlines Systems plane taxiing towards the air terminal bore the name Vegard Viking, and had only a few hours earlier been named by Prime Minister Gro Harlem Brundtland. She landed in Oslo, together with much of the Norwegian party returning from Albertville with Norway's largest harvest of medals in the history of the Olympic Games.

The party entered the terminal building, to be greeted by great public rejoicing, with music, flowers, trumpets and flags, as the enthusiastic crowds welcomed home our sports heroes and heroins.

Four years earlier, it had been an entirely different story; there was no such welcome for the returning team from the Canadian town of Calgary. Then the Olympic «first» involved no single Norwegian competitor gaining the highest position on the medal-winners podium, despite previous Norwegian gold medal-winners having been picked as favourites by the media for the skating events and, most certainly, for ski jumping.

SCAN-FOTO/Jan Greve

Would you like a souvenir programme . . . ?

Neither, must it be said, was such optimism unreasonable. Prior to Calgary, many Norwegians had produced fine performances, and all had organised their seasons such that their form should peak in Calgary. Perhaps, in the event, the pressure of expectation became too great; in any case, it all ended in tears. «A National Catastrophe», declared the banner-headlines in one of our largest national newspapers.

But if the pressure of expectation was great before Calgary, it was nothing compared with that which developed during the 1991/92 winter season, culminating in the igniting of the Olympic Flame in Albertville on 8th February, 1992. Our cross-country skiers, led by Vegard Ulvang and Bjørn Dæhli, had with only one exception won every race of the seasons' World Cup events. The womens' form was on a steadily rising curve, as was that of both men and women biathlonists. After many years, we had rediscovered our form in the skating events, and at the European Championships in Holland, shortly before Albertville, both Johan Koss and Geir Karlstad proved themselves capable of a place on the Olympic winners podium in three of the classic events. We weren't quite so strong in our old hunting grounds of ski-jumping and the Nordic Combination, and not even the most optimistic sports commentator reckoned on Norway taking the most precious of metals away from these events. But this should be balanced by our chances on the alpine courses. In the World Cup cross-country events, Norwegians had moved steadily up the field; if actual gold was out of reach, we were certain to pick up a respectable number of points. True, one of our best hopes, the down-hill expert Atle Skårdal, was excluded from the games by a severe injury shortly before the games, and a similar fate had befallen one of our very best women, Julie Lunde Hansen, but this had no dampening effect on the general optimism.

The newspaper's increasing panegyric portrayal of the Norwegian performance curve, and the enthusiasm and determination of the participants, infected the whole Norwegian people – known, anyway, as the most chauvenistic in the world, not least in anything relating to winter sports.

A Bad Start

A few critical voices attempted to dampen the assumptions of victory, but they fell largely on deaf ears. Already on day one, however, following the magnificent opening ceremony at Albertville, the sombre premonitions of the critics received credence by the ignominous 11–1 defeat of Norway's ice-hockey team at the hands of Czechoslovakia. And the following day, on the first full day of competition, the pessimists were «told-you-soing» for all they were worth!

Our cross-country women were nowhere near the medals in the 15 kilometre race, and the best a Norwegian could manage in the 90 metre ski jump was 35th!

More positive things were happening, however, on the demanding men's downhill run, in Val d'Isere. Jan Einar Thorsen finished fifth, and Lasse Arnesen eighth, proving the pedigree of our alpine team. Atle Skårdal, nursing his injured leg at home in Norway, was more than satisfied with his colleagues performance, and next day, in the downhill section of the Nordic Combination event, Thorsen hit the jackpot. Amongst exclusive international circles in the chic alpine town, talk again turned to the Norwegians, who for the last two seasons had tended to assume a place for themselves amongst the alpine elite.

There would be more talk, later in the games.

In the meantime, our women cross-country skiers failed to fullfill our expectations, and doubts began to creep into the collective Norwegian mind: were we heading for disappointment again? Such doubts were put aside on the Monday morning, as Terje Langli, Erling Jevne, Bjørn Dæhli and Vegard Ulvang lined up for the start of the 30 kilometre race in Les Saises. About a hundred Norwegian spectators, enthusiastically waving the national flag, had found their way to the pleasent alpine town in the middle of this massive mountainous area dominated by the magestic Mont Blanc. Nervous Norwegian trainers, oilers, doctors and masseurs gathered around the starting area, all conscious that this would be a decisive effort. For years, the 30 kilometre event has been a problem for Norwegian competitors, resulting so often in ignominous defeat. As one of the oilers was heard to mumble, «There's a curse on us, at this distance».

But the curse was tranformed into a blessing on this occassion, one which will always stand out as one of the greatest events in Norwegian skiing history. Early in the race, all four Norwegians confirmed the upward thrust of their form-curve. «This is going well!», cried radio-journalist Håkon Brusveen, perhaps the most experienced and sober-minded ski commentator ever. Himself a gold medal winner thirty two years earlier at Squaw Valley, Brusveen monitored the skiers from four different places along the route, and became increasingly certain that they would manage to see off their most dangerous rivals.

SCAN-FOTO/Olav Olsen

All the world could see during the cross-country skiing competitions, were the backs of the Norwegian skiers. This one belongs to Bjørn Dæhli, as he crosses the finish line backwards, winning the 4 × 10 km relay for Norway.

An Explosion of Olympic Happiness

Which, subsequently, they did, quite brilliantly! Ulvang, Dæhli of Langli took all three medals, and Erling Jevne came in at number five. The victory fever on the stands was indescribable, and at home in Norway there was an explosion of Olympic joy as almost three quarters of the population sat glued to their television screens, or followed Brusveens commentary on the radio.

For the rest of the day, talk was of nothing else amongst the many Norwegians at the various Olympic arenas in Savoi. In Norway, recordings of the race were repeated more or less continuously throughout the day, both on television and radio. In schools and the workplace, on buses and trains, all people could talk about was the triple victory. At the victory ceremony that evening, as the three Norwegian flags were run up their poles and the national anthem rang out across Les Saisies, the eyes of the president of the Norwegian Skiing Association Johan Baumann, and all the other dignitaries from the Norwegian olympic and sport mileau, filled with tears, whilst the close-ups of the three faces on the podium disclosed the true joy of sport.

This proved to be only the introduction to Norway's strongest ever showing in cross-country skiing events. Norwegian men took gold in all five distances. Both Ulvang and Dæhli returned home with three golds and a silver medal each. Ulvang won the 10 and 30 kilometre races, in addition to his part in the victorious relay team, and took the silver in the 15 km Pursuit Start. Dæhli took the gold in the 15 km Hunting Start, 50 km and relay, in addition to taking silver in 30 km. They positioned themselves at the head of the peerage of Norwegian Olympic winners, surpassing the achievements of ski-king Thorleif Haug, skating-ace Hjalmar Andersen and ice-queen Sonja Henie, all of whom in their time managed three Olympic gold medals. Ivar Ballangrud still occupies the throne itself, with four golds, two silvers and a bronze, but this state of affairs is unlikely to survive Lillehammer 1994, where both Ulvang and Dæhli will be found amongst the competitors.

Of course, there was some dissapointment over the failure of our women to stay amongst the leaders on the cross-country course, as well as the poor showing by our biathlon team. Our

Nordic Combination skiers did well across country, but sadly less well on the ski jump. However, there can be no doubt that an astonishing performance by the Frenchman Guy Fabrie, one the most popular of all Olympic winners, greatly increased French interest in this event.

Cross-country skiing has always been principally a Scandinavian affair, a national sport in Sweden, Finland and Norway. Despite the gradual increased participation by other countries, and the fact that the Eastern Europeans, French, Italians and Japanese are often to be found amongst the front runners, international interest in the event is slight compared with that for alpine-events. It is the hair-raising downhill race and balletic slalåm which most of the world tends to associate with ski-sports.

Thus, the achievements of the Norwegian cross-country team were somewhat overshadowerd, internationallly at least, by the performance of our men's alpine team who, with two golds and two bronzes, were the best team overall. A young team, characterised by keenness, comradeship, and a strong will to win, had been put togther in record time. Team-veterans Atle Skårdal and Ole Kristian Furuseth, were proved correct in their contention that Norway had ample talent and that all of those chosen for the team were capable of taking a gold medal. Skårdal was injured, Furuseth's form deserted him, but Kjetil Andre Aamot and Finn Chr. Jagge grabbed themselves first place in respectively the Super G and slalåm.

SCAN-FOTO/Olav Olsen

There were Norwegian flags in abundance in Albertville, the largest of them displayed in front of the Norwegian stand in Les Saisies, after the victory in the 30 kilometre race.

The Fantastic Final Day

Their success created two days which the Norwegian people are unlikely to forget in a hurry. At 12.15 hours on Sunday, 16th February, the stadium at Val d'Isere could as well have been Holmenkollen, in Oslo. The Super G-run was lined by an expert audience of Frenchmen, Germans, Austrians and Americans waited to cheer on their favourites; even the best orientated of them couldn't help but be surprised by the fact that the best time was recorded by a little-known Norwegian, Kjetil Andre Aamot. And, as if this wasn't enough, third place was taken by Jan Eril Thorsen, with Ole Kristian Furuseth directly behind. With his eighth place, the last Norwegian in, Tom Stiansen, secured what was the best performance by a Norwegian team in international alpine-competition of all time. The Norwegian public was being treated to many great moments, and as the medals rolled in so the nation became increasingly sports-mad. Together with the achievements in the 30 kilometre race, the most memorable day was the last, February 22nd. As the clock approched ten in the morning, there was a palpable exitement amongst Norwegians at Val d'Isere and Les Saisies, not to mention those sat glued to their radios and television sets at home. Open-mouthed, the entire nation followed Finn Chr. Jagge's dancing descent of the slalåm slope to the best time of the round.

Simultaneously, the first intermediate times began coming through from the 50 kilometre cross-country race, where our boys were all amongst the leaders. As they approached the finish, the tension was unbearable. An impudent 40-year old Italian, Maurilio de Zolt, was maintaining a furious pace. Leadership of the dense, energetic knot of front-runners changed again and again, but finally, Bjørn Dæhli forged ahead, his own pulse-rate matched by every single one of his countrymen following every second of his progress via t.v. and radio. Dæhli kept hold of his lead to the end, securing an eighth gold medal for Norway, with Maurillio de Zolt coming in impressively for the silver. «A miracle-man», Håkon Bresveen described him, and bid the Italian welcome to Lillehammer.

An hour later, the exitement was scarcely less for the second round of the slalåm. Would the young Finn Chr. Jagge be able to cope with the pressure of being in first position at this stage of the competition? True, he had a good lead over his challengers, but amongst them was none other than Alberto Tomba, who had shown so many times before what a marvelous competitor he was. Adding to the pressure on Jagge at Vald'Isrere was «half of Italy», gathered to cheer Tomba, who during the course of the season had acquired nothing less than superstar status. But 'Finken' Jagge proved equal to the task, Whilst we held our collective breadth, he sped down the slope, every bit as supple and elegant as the great Tomba, and crossed the finishing line with a full half

Thorleif Haug used to be the regent of cross-country, with three Olympic gold medals from Chamonix in 1924, but in Albertville his record was bested by two men, Vegard Ulvang and Bjørn Dæhli.

SCAN-FOTO/Knut Snare

Bjørn Dæhli also won the gold medal in the 50 kilometre cross-country race, whereas the incredibly fast Italian, Maurilio de Zolt, secured himself a silver medal.

SCAN-FOTO/Skimuseet

SCAN-FOTO/Knut Snare

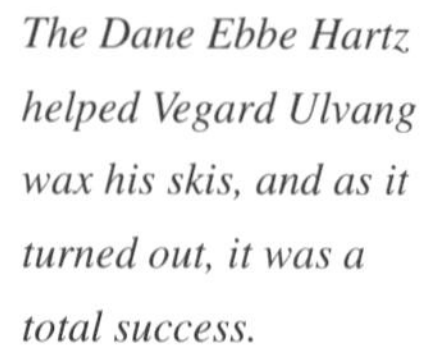

The Dane Ebbe Hartz helped Vegard Ulvang wax his skis, and as it turned out, it was a total success.

Triumphant cheers as it became clear Dæhlie had secured the victory in the pursuit race. Right: The relay team receiving their medals. Far right: Dæhli, Ulvang and Terje Langli appearing together on Norwegian radio and television.

SCAN-FOTO/POOL/Jan Greve

SCAN-FOTO/Skimuseet

SCAN-FOTO/Knut Snare

Vegard Ulvang secured the victory in the 10 km classical cross-country race (left), and below, a triumphant Bjørn Dæhli after the 50-kilometre victory.

SCAN-FOTO/Olav Olsen

SCAN-FOTO/Knut Snare

SCAN-FOTO/Pressens Bild/Jan Collsjöö

There was no shortage of Norwegian flags in Les Saisies, just like at ski championships at home.

SCAN-FOTO/Tor Richarsen

Two medals obtained in the same discipline. Kjetil André Aamodt and Jan Erik Thorsen won the gold and bronze medals in the Super G downhill races. Below: Kjetil Aamodt on the slalom tracks, he ended with a bronze medal.

SCAN-FOTO/Tor Richardsen

SCAN-FOTO/Tor Richardsen

Finn Chr. Jagge was leading after the first round of the slalom competition. He didn't give in to the pressure and came away with a gold medal. For once, the all-time favourite, Alberto Tomba, congratulating Jagge, had to do with the silver medal.

SCAN-FOTO/Tor Richardsen

SCAN-FOTO/Knut Falch

SCAN-FOTO/Helge Mikalsen

The gold medal is secured, and Geir Karlstad is ready to receive the honours after the 5000 meter race. Top: enthusiastic spectators: Queen Sonja, King Harald and Johann Koss.

SCAN-FOTO/Morten Uglem

SCAN-FOTO/Jan Greve

SCAN-FOTO/Magnar Kirkenes

SCAN-FOTO/Knut E. Holen

SCAN-FOTO/Jan Greve

Johann Koss (above, top) and Ådne Søndrål also received medals. In the picture above, they display the fruits of their work, 5 medals in all. It was no match to the all-time champion Hjalmar (Hjallis) Andersen's numbers of distinctions, though.

The young Finn, Toni Nieminen, fulfilled all expectations of him. Norway left empty-handed in the ski-jump competitions, as well as in the bobsleigh events.

SCAN-FOTO/Jan Greve

SCAN-FOTO/Tor Richardsen

SCAN-FOTO/Jan Greve

Fabrice Guy secured one of the most popular victories for the host country, France. He won the gold medal in the combined classic Nordic style competition. In the team competition, Trond Einar Elden, Knut Tore Apeland and Fred Børre Lindberg won the silver medal, and were congratulated by Queen Sonja.

Stine Lise Hattestad won a bronze medal in mogul racing, one of the new freestyle events.

SCAN-FOTO/Jan Greve

SCAN-FOTO/Tor Richardsen

second's advantage over the Italian star. In a competition where hundredths of seconds can decide a result, this was an astonishing victory.

It would be an understatement to describe Norway's reaction to all this as ecstatic. As it became clear that the ninth gold medal was in the bag, the entire nation erupted. Virtually the whole population followed the thriller, whether at home, at work or even in shops and stores. Indeed, in a large electrical store in Oslo, one customer celebrated the victory by tucking an expensive television set under his arm and marching swiftly out of the shop. He didn't look back. The other excited customers and sales assistants merely registered that he put the set in a car and drove off.

A Sports-mad Nation

Norway fairly flowed with champagne throughout the two weeks of the Games. Not least in Vegard Ulvang's hometown of Kirkenes, in the far North of Norway. As his first gold medal was secured, the corks popped not merely in people's homes; in the freezing winter snow, the whole town gathered for a spontaneous celebration in the town square, with the suggestion that it be immediately renamed Vegard Ulvang Square! His second gold medal saw the Kirkenes State Wine and Spirits Monopoly emptied of both real champagne and all other sparkling beverages, new supplies of which were barely on the shelves in time for the rush following the golden-boy's third, great triumph.

The Norwegian Broadcasting Corporation (NRK) confirmed the unique sports-madness that infected us during the Albertville games, as daily surveys of viewing and listening figures indicated formidable new records. The average Norwegian spent three hours and twenty minutes in front of the television daily. NRK broadcast a total of 137 hours of Olympic coverage, and other channels available in the country made their contribution also. NRK's radio service, not to be intimidated by the massive television coverage, put out over 70 hours of its own coverage, live from the various Olympic arenas, and on individual days more than 800,000 Norwegians tuned in. Some of the television broadcasts achieved an 80 % audience, which is more than the most popular of NRK's Saturday evening entertainment programmes, including the despised Eurovision Song Contest (which over the years has been so heavily criticised that *everyone* has to watch it.)

How will the Lillehammer Games compare to Albertville?

If the expectations prior to Albertville were high, one can safely say that the pressure on Norwegian competitors in Lillehammer will be in a different league altogether. Few sports-mad Norwegians, still less sports-reporters, will be satisfied with less than the nine gold medals brought back from Albertville. This time we shall be competing on home -ground, and everyone remembers the advantages this brought in 1952, when our sportsmen and women fulfilled all our expectations, winning seven gold medals, three silvers and six bronze.

Even the more cautious observer has ample grounds for optimism. Not because of the so-called home advantage, but rather because the whole country is investing so heavily in the 1994 games. The success in Albertville was the result of a conscious, systematic programme of preparation, which our leading sports personalities campaigned hard to help finance, largely through sponsorship. The competitors were given certain economic guarantees, which allowed them to devote themselves completely to their task. The best trainers available in different events were brought in. Thorough scientific tests were carried out at the Olympic athletics centre at Sognsvann, in Oslo, and most of the Olympic team undertook intensive training programmes at specially selected training sites.

Money had much to do with the Norwegian triumphs in Albertville, though to say so is not in any way to disparage the many sportsmen and women we have developed into winners. As early as 1984 *Norges Idrettsforbund* (the Norwegian Sports Federation) and the Norwegian Olympic Committee, presented «Project 88», intended to prepare the way for top performances by Norwegian athletes in Seoul and Calgary in 1988. Sections of the business community, which had just begun to experience the positive public-image aspects of sponsorship, declared their willingness to support the project financially. The awarding, in Seoul, of the 1994 Winter Games to Lillehammer, provided momentum for this work. A project was initiated – *«Olympiatoppen»* (the «Olympic Success» project) – in which large companies committed themselves to sponsorship in return for the right to use the Olympic symbols in marketing and promotion.

There can be no doubt that the achievements of the Norwegian team in Albertville rendered the task of fund-raising in the run-up to 1994 considerably easier that it might otherwise have been. Which is just as well, because a few years previously, the budgets presented by the top sports-managers would have been unthinkable.

In Albertville, the Norwegian support system, especially for our cross-country skiers, was most impressive. Quite apart from trainers, Norway fielded a pool of experts who systematically tested the conditions from early in the morning on every day of competition. Some Norwegian experts found it a little hard to take that a Danish colleague provided Vegard Ulvang with decisive piece of advice prior to one of his gold medal performances. (What do the Danes know about snow?!) In addition, seconds lined the course, keeping our competitors orientated about their position in relation to the rest of the field. Before and after the race all were attended to by doctors, masseurs and physiotherapists. Only psychiatrists and psychologists were missing.

SCAN-FOTO/Olav Olsen

Throngs of flag-waving Norwegian supporters filled the arenas at the Albertville Games.

Scepticism Soon Forgotten

The organisation of Albertville was closely observed by those responsible for mounting the games in Lillehammer. As soon as it was known Lillehammer would host the 94 games, representatives were dispatched to Albertville to follow preparations there. Numerous Norwegians visited the various French venues, and all returned home sceptical. They predicted traffic chaos on the narrow alpine roads between the different Olympic sites, wretched conditions for the expected thousands of press people, a lack of accommodation for visiting spectators in the vicinity of the Olympic venues.

But by the time the Olympic Flame was ignited on the evening of February 8th, many observers both from Lillehammer and the Norwegian Olympic Committee admitted to being extremely impressed. Not only by the spectacular opening ceremony, but mostly by the fact that all the infrastructure was completed, that traffic progressed smoothly, and that the numerous spectators were properly accommodated. Even if the sports journalists were not particularly enamoured of their cramped, aluminium containers!

Many in Norway criticised the Lillehammer organisers for beginning their preparations too early. Three whole years prior to the Games, a large organisation had been put together and, not least, budgets presented which scared the life out of both politicians and ordinary citizens. Those responsible took the reactions in their stride. They were aware of the scale of the challenge; the fact that Lillehammer required a considerably more extensive building programme than had been the case in Albertville. To have the building programme ready, and the infrastructure in place in good time for the games – that's to say, a year in advance – would take time. Though not meant as a trial-run of the Olympics, most of the venues are to be used for the World Cup events, in 1993, and thus the Olympic organisers continued working indefatigably, and the building work reached completion without delay. The goal was perfectly clear; the 1994 Games would be the best ever in the history of the Winter Olympics.

Certainly, they will be unique in at least one aspect: the whole nation stands behind it. Sport-obsessed Norwegians will, together with sports enthusiasts from the whole world, fill the stands, halls and venues. Both short and long ski-runs throughout the Olympic town will be lined by experts and enthusiasts, whose cheers will spur on the participants and ensure they give of their ultimate best.

The Olympic Games in Lillehammer will be the greatest national celebration in Norway's history, and the aim of all Norwegians is a harvest of medals to top that from Albertville.

Once again, we shall show the world how it is possible.

The Games have come to an end. The flag is lowered, and the Olympic rings are removed from the stands. The mayor of Lillehammer, Audun Tron, was presented with the Olympic flag which will wave over Lillehammer at the 1994 Winter Games.

SCAN-FOTO/Knut Falch

SCAN-FOTO/Magnar Kirkenes

At the closing ceremony, Norway bid the world welcome to the next Olympic Winter Games. The evocative scene featuring a Viking ship and a glittering polar bear carrying Sissel Kyrkjebø, together with mascots Kristin and Håkon, and complement of Vikings, made for a beautiful and popular ending to Norway's spectacular performance in Albertville.

SCAN-FOTO

Vegard Ulvang carries the flag during the closing procession in Albertville.

SCAN-FOTO/Knut Falch

The returning athletes brought home the largest collection of medals ever won during any Olympic Games. The Prime Minister christened a SAS aircraft «Vegard Viking», and the plane, which serves the Geneva-Oslo route, was given the number SK 1994. More homage was paid in Oslo, and when the Olympic flag arrived in Lillehammer, popular celebrations were the order of the day.

SCAN-FOTO/Jan Greve

SCAN-FOTO/Knut Falch

SCAN-FOTO/Jan Greve

The Summer Games in Barcelona, in 1992, were a continuance of the powerful Norwegian performance in Albertville. There were moments of joy and disappointment, but the end result was the best summer Olympics for Norway in 40 years. Two gold medals, four silver and a bronze medal went to the Norwegian athletes. Norway was first among the Nordic countries, and also did well overall in the nations-competition ranking 21st on the list, with 51 Olympic points.

Wrestler Jon Rønningen repeated his triumph in Seoul by securing his second gold medal in the closing seconds of an extraordinarily exciting final match.

SCAN-FOTO/Ingar Johansen

The women's handball team initially did not qualify for the Olympic Games, but was allowed to take part when Yugoslavia was excluded because of its civil war. The Norwegian team started off disasterously with a soaring defeat to the South Koreans, the very team they lost to during the final in Seoul in 1988. In the following matches, however, they regained their stride and optimism ran high before the Olympic final, where they were once again to meet the speedy South Koreans. It didn't work this time, either. Norway lost 21 – 28, and had to do with silver.

SCAN-FOTO/Ingar Johansen

The kayak-paddler Knut Holman was disappointed, even though he did win a silver medal in the 1000-metre. Two days prior to this he had taken the bronze medal in the 500-metre.

SCAN-FOTO/Ingar Johansen

SCAN-FOTO/Ingar Johansen,

SCAN-FOTO/Vidar Ruud

The young Linda Andersen collected Norway's second gold medal by lively and well-planned sailing in her Olympic dinghy. She thus became the first Norwegian woman ever to win a gold medal during the Olympic Summer Games.

Veteran miniature shooting competitor Harald Stenvaag came home with a silver medal, as did double four teammates Lars Bjønnes, Rolf Thorsen, Kjetil Undseth, and Per Albert Sætersdal, only missing a gold medal by a few 100ths of a second.

SCAN-FOTO/Ingar Johansen

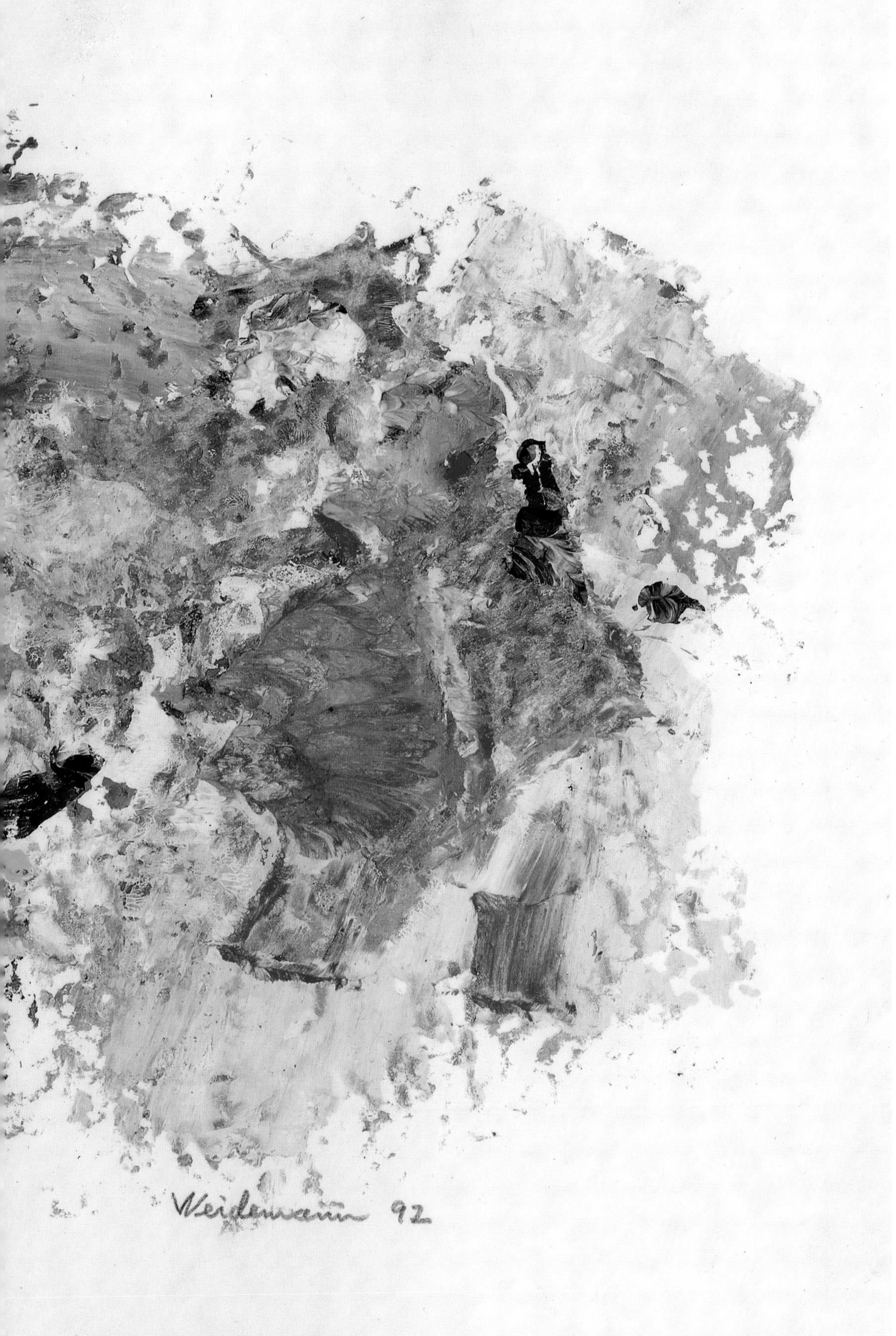

The Obstacle Race

Ola Matti Mathisen:

LILLEHAMMER TILSKUER

Ola Matti Mathisen (b. 1942), editor, has a broad journalistic background. As political editor of the Lillehammer Tilskuer for more than 20 years, he has kept close track of the efforts in his «own back yard» to bring the Winter Games to Lillehammer. He has travelled the world with various delegations and attended all the Olympics held since Norway first applied for the games.

There were very few in Norway who realised what the Olympic arrangement would demand in terms of resources. Preparations for the 17th Winter Games developed into something of a 50 km race with tripwires, with the financial side of the arrangement creating the worst headaches. The initial budget of 2 billion *kroner* has ended up as almost 10 billion*! From day one, there has been trouble across the board; about political control, the competence of the director, siting of venues and buildings – but mostly, about money.

(* Throughout the article, the term 'billion' is used in the American sense, ie where 1 billion = 1 000 millions)

The mayor of Lillehammer, Audun Tron, was met by the mayors of the other Olympic host towns, Hamar and Gjøvik.

LILLEHAMMER FOTO OG BILLEDARKIV/Jarle Kjetil Rolseth

SCAN-FOTO/John Stenersen

IOC President Juan Antonio Samaranch, at a breakfast with King Carl Gustaf and Prime Minister Gro Harlem Brundtland. It's claimed that the Swedish King arrived late for the breakfast, by which time the Norwegian premier had already convinced the all-powerful president that Lillehammer was the right choice.

SCAN-FOTO/John Stenersen

When Lillehammer was awarded the 17th Winter Olympics, on 15th September 1988, celebrations in the little valley town continued into the early hours and all opposition to the games was muffled by the intoxication of victory. But even this intoxication had its Blue Monday. Few imagined then that the process of realising this gigantic project would come to resemble a 50-kilometre race with tripwires. In a typically Norwegian manner, more or less every aspect of the process was plagued by conflict and dissent, not least with regards to the budget and the placing of sites and buildings. Leadership came and went – in true Olympic style.

During the application stage, no one questioned the accuracy of estimates of the games' eventual cost. In the last phase, the sum being bandied about was 1.8 billion kroner. Soon after the announcement of Lillehammer's selection, the leader of the Olympic committee, Sigmund Thue, was operating with a figure of 2.6 billion, which included almost half a billion kroner interest repayments. He declared, unreservedly, that the taxpayer would not have to foot any of the bill. Four years later, the reality is that Olympic-related investments in addition to those allowed for in the State budget total altogether around 10 billion kroner, against an estimated income of something like 2.5 billion. True, the official Olympic budget is still around seven billion kroner but this figure includes only the investments over the culture budget. True, also, is that many of the investments included in the Olympic budget would have to have been made sooner or later, anyway. But preferably later.

But back to Thue who, in the exultation following the award, stated: «We have income enough to cover the costs from our own purse. Only a catastrophe affecting the whole arrangement will necessitate economic participation by the State». At the time, he estimated income of 3 billion kroner, leaving a net profit for the Games of half a billion kroner. Thue, later to become director of marketing and development for the Games, can console himself with the fact that he was not the only one to miscalculate in the preparatory stages.

There was some disquiet when, a few months after the jubilant day in Seoul, reports in the press suggested that the calculated costs exceeded the original budget by some half a billion kroner. But the Olympic Committee poured oil on these fears. The astute Director General, Per Haga, who would later become the principal bookkeeper and controller of the Olympic issue, accepted the assurances. But he must have had a premonition of what was to come; he reminded us that the investment programme would not be clear until six months hence. «First then will the figures mean something and give us some idea of what the Games will cost. The figures floating around at the moment are based merely on calculations in themselves based on rough projections», he said.

Over Christmas 1988, information emerging from Calgary also somehow failed to set the alarm bells ringing. The Canadians announced that the Calgary Games were turning out to cost double the amount projected for the Lillehammer arrangement. The newly appointed head of the Lillehammer Olympic Organising Committee, Petter Rønningen, opined that «there's much there that is twice as big as here». He knew precisely why the Calgary Games had become so expensive, he assured us, and was sure Lillehammer would turn out far more cost-effective. «The way things are looking at the moment», he said, «There's every reason to believe we will have an economic success on our hands».

One expert who took a closer look at the figures for Calgary and compared them with those for Lillehammer pointed out that the running-expenses of the 1988 games came to around 600–800 million kroner, whilst they were calculated to be no higher than 100 million in Lillehammer. When the final budget was drawn up, it proved to be more than 20 times too low, and represented the worst single miscalculation of the whole preliminary budget.

First and foremost the attention in the first post-celebration period was focussed on personalities. That bank director and lawyer Ole Sjetne was more or less automatically chosen as president, came as no surprise, given his excellent leadership during the application phase. Nor was Petter Rønningen's appointment as managing director remarkable, given his role as Sjetne's right-hand-man both in their professional life and in the Olympic project. Already in 1981, Rønningen was secretary for the secret committee – also known as the «12 sworn men» – who prepared the first reports, and this officer and farmer's son from Ringebu led the Olympic syndicate which drew up the unsuccessful application for the 1992 Winter Games. He was also the only one of 30 applicants willing to publicly announce his application prior to the final decision being reached. The Olympic project was never, despite loud protests by the mass media, subjected to the Public Information Act.

The response to Rønningen's appointment was generally positive, especially locally, where his declaration that «we shall take good care of this fine town», was especially appreciated. One voice, however, raised itself in protest: the local newspaper, The Lillehammer Observer, thought the appointment smacked a little too much of «Provincialism and Olympic nepotism». The newspaper was of the opinion that a leading figure from the Norwegian business community ought to have been brought in for such a central job.

The Facilities Equation

The question of facilities has been every bit as fraught as that of personnel in the run up to the Olympics. Immediately after the awarding of the games to Lillehammer, suggestions were made about distributing the venues further afield than had been stated in the application. The Mayor of Lillehammer, Audun Tron answered thus; «There is much interest in the provision of facilities, from Oppdal in the north, to Oslo in the south. It must be made clear, however, that the Lillehammer Council has signed a contract based on the application upon which the IOC reached their decision. In other words, our hands are tied on this matter».

The indoor skating stadium was the hottest potato during this phase. This important card had been put on the table at the eleventh hour in Seoul by the chairman of the Norwegian Sports Association, Hans B. Skaset, to the despair of the rival Swedish applicants. The Mayor of Lillehammer chose his words carefully. Lillehammer would, of course, build such a facility if the town so wished, but its subsequent use would have to be carefully evaluated. Already at the beginning of December 1988, the huge concern Kværner Properties tabled plans for a project at the mouth of the River Lågen, on Lake Mjøsa. There was a flood of more or less fanciful Olympic projects; architects, consultants and others put up millions and began to form alliances and syndicates the better to be able to compete when the time came. For example, no less than 20 architects based in the Olympic town formed themselves into the Lillehammer Architects Team, and as such won the contract for planning and coordinating the most expensive single project of the games, namely the 1/2 billion kroner Radio and Television Centre, at Storhove.

Lillehammer Council commissioned a comprehensive planning process, which included, among other things, an over-all plan for the Games, and an analysis of the town and of the local natural and cultural landscape. A major aim of the process was to preserve Lillehammer's natural and environmental uniqueness, and the distinctive character of the town itself. This provided the foundation for the idea of the 1994 games being the «Environmentally-friendly Olympics», whose keen supporters included the honourary president of the games, the then Crown Prince Harald, who took a number of opportunities to state that the greatest challenge of the arrangement was the preservation of Lillehammer's character, not least during the building phases. In the spring of 1992, the now King Harald declared himself satisfied with what he had seen on a tour of inspection of the Olympic facilities.

The council engaged in an emotional internal debate about the siting of the cross-country and biathlon courses. The decision was between Jorkestad, just north of the town, which had been named in the Olympic application, or Abbortjern, to the east. Not least the tourist industry was happy with the decision in favour of the latter. The site for the ski-jump and the bob and luge runs, stated in the application as Balbergskaret, proved likewise a moveable feast. This project required the defacing, with a new road, of Lillehammer's most picturesque «town mountain», Balbergkampen, and was eventually abandoned. And with that, the only ready-made facility in Lillehammer was excluded from the equation! In fact, in the event, the Winter Olympics precipi-

SCAN-FOTO/Helge Mikalsen

As early as in 1981, Lillehammer started planning an application to host the Olympic Games. Bank manager Ole Sjetne was a major force in this, and was supported by the city, in particular after the election of Audun Tron as mayor. When Albertville got the 1992-Games, the two optimists became even more eager in their efforts.

SCAN-FOTO/Helge Mikalsen

Minister of Foreign Affairs Thorvald Stoltenberg worked quietly behind the scenes to advance Norway's bid for the Games.

SCAN-FOTO/Aage Storløkken

tated the closing down of the second largest ski-jump slope in Norway, and the Olympic ski-jump ended up situated at Kanthaugen, to the east of the town centre, where many a hard competition had been fought, over the years, on the the Lysgaard skiing slopes.

It had been suggested that the bob and luge runs should be placed to the immediate north of the ski-jump at Kanthaugen, but it was eventually considered that this 'ugly duckling' of the winter games would represent too dramatic an encroachment on an area of outstanding natural beauty, already put under great pressure. In fact, in the end, Lillehammer had to fight tenaciously to retain the bob and luge run at all, in the face of Oslo's strong claim to site it at Holmenkollåsen. An area in the vicinity of Hunderfossen, in the very north of Lillehammer's environs, offered the ideal solution. Here, the run was incorporated harmoniously into the landscape in what must be, environmentally speaking, a model facility.

The question of halls for inside events was extremely delicate and was not really solved until 1990. The application had stated that all such facilities – four in all, two of which would be temporary structures – would be situated in Lillehammer itself. Eventually, the need for three halls in addition to the skating rinks – due to the introduction of short-track skating into the Olympic programme – was recognised. But to fill Lillehammer with arenas which had no possible application after the Games were over, was a political and economic impossiblity, and the notion of the dispersal of these facilities to other Mjøsa towns was retrieved from the drawing board, where it had been abandoned during the application phase. The International Ice Hockey Association, which had previously been opposed to the dispersal of facilities, suddenly found it acceptable, thus opening up the possibility for the dispersal of the event to all three Mjøsa* towns.

SCAN-FOTO/Rune Baashus

The skating hall was sent all over the place, until it finally came to rest on a site at Åkersvika in Hamar. The building itself, in the form of an upturned Viking ship, became the symbol for the whole 1994 games.

Exploding Costs

The Lillehammer Olympic Organising Committee (LOOC) started producing pins early on in the planning process. The pins soon became collectors' items, and their sale has generated an important source of income.

1989 was the year the cost of the arrangement exploded. It began gently enough, with a contribution from the state of 160 million kroner for the first investment phase. This was, principally, to go towards the road building project. On the income side, there was positive news: the American television company CBS agreed to fork out 300 million dollars for the rights to broadcast the games to the USA. This was a remarkably high figure, in fact no more than 9 million less than ABC TV had paid for the American rights in Calgary, where, of course, the games were taking place on America's doorstep. The president of the LOOC, Ole Sjetne took this gilt-edged contract as proof of the uniqueness of the Lillehammer 'product'. The LOOC was to keep two-thirds of the fee, and CBS committed themselves to broadcasting 120 hours of the games.

During the autumn of 1989, 100 experts in 19 planning groups worked feverishly to try and determine the cost of the arrangement. What went on in the inner sanctums of these groups was the subject of many a rumour, but the great shock first emerged at the end of September. The popular tabloid daily, Verdens Gang (VG), announced that the Storting could expect a total figure of 6 to 7 billion kroner. In light of this, the newspaper asked, reasonably enough, how realistic was the original state guarantee of 1.8 billion kroner? The minister of culture, Hallvard Bakke, sent a firm letter to the LOOC and Lillehammer Council, following up a correspondence from earlier the same summer in which he had expressed his concern about the estimates, and urged moderation. In his autumn letter he again appealed to the two recipients for greater modesty in their planning. He described the sitution as alarming and suggested that costs would have to be considerably reduced before the government could justify presenting the budget to parliament. Hallvard Bakke made it quite clear that both politicians and the country at large would be critical of unnecessarily high costs. He referred particularly to the RTV centre and drew attention to the obviously substandard preliminary work; misunderstandings alone had put the calculations out by 300 million kroner.

(* Mjøsa = Norway's largest lake, situated some 200 kms north of Oslo.)

Director General Per Haga stated that the rumoured budget was totally unacceptable. This razor-sharp 'grey eminence' of the department campaigned intensely to have the figures reduced. In one of his few subsequent public statements on the matter, he remarked, «In Lillehammer, they had not calculated on my ability to calculate».

Former Chairman of the Norwegian Olympic Committee, Jan Gulbrandsen, entered the arguement. He maintained that, taking into consideration the huge investments which society would have had to make anyway, irrespective of the Games, and the implicit effect the Games would have on society, it was highly unlikely that the arrangement would end up in deficit. He backed this up by drawing attention to the Swedish calculation implying an indirect income for society of around 6 billion kroner for the projected Östersund games. Also, he reminded us, Albertville had been able to operate with a budget of only 3.6 billion only because the infrastructural investments of 4.4 billion (mostly for road and rail links) had *not* been included in the sum. On this basis, Gulbrandsen was in favour of all road, rail and telecommunication costs, including costs for the RTV centre, being excluded from the Olympic budget, because they were facilities which would serve the whole of society, whose provision was simply brought forward due to the games.

The revised figures were ready by the end of November 1989. They were closely guarded against leakage until after the LOOC had made its statement in the plenary meeting, and the shock in the Olympic organisation can be imagined when, no sooner had the figures been sent out to its members, than they appeared in the local newspaper.

The total figure which so shook many people was 7.75 billion kroner – that is, three times the original state-guarantee. The largest increase was for 'arrangement and running costs', with the committee commenting that this element of the budget «seems not to have been subject to thorough calculation». In addition, the cost of the bob and luge run and the total cost of the provision of sports facilities had tripled. In the original state-guarantee, the arts were distinguished by their absence; now, they had a budget of 250 million kroner. Once these figures had been presented, speculation as to what politicians would do about the situation was rampant. The most frequently mentioned solution was to disperse the games in order to disperse the costs. In particular, it was suggested that the men's downhill-skiing be moved from Kvitfjell in Ringebu back to Hafjell in Øyer (ie. the original suggestion), that the ski-jump go to Holmenkollen in Oslo, and that the skating events be held in the open air. With fateful irony, Lillehammer's mayor, Audun Tron, spent these dramatic days completely incapacitated by sciatica in Lillehammer County Hospital. But there was nothing wrong with his powers of speech: «It will not be cheaper to disperse the games. And, in the face of such a dispersal happening, we might as well tear up our contract with the IOC to arrange the 1994 Olympic Games!».

After another round of stiff cuts, Lillehammer Council and the LOOC presented contradictory figures, with the Council some 340 million kroner higher, at 6.7 billion. This did not include outlay for broadcasting facilities or the fund for subsequent use of facilities. The Council included costs of roads, water, sewers and electricity, which it did not think it possible to finance alone. At the same time, local politicians wanted more consideration shown for the environment, architecture, and subsequent use of Olympic facilities than the LOOC had provided. The Council also put the budget for the RTV centre at 420 million, as against the LOOC's figure of 270 million. The politicians pointed out that such 'modest' investment would not prepare the ground for long term outside-investment into research, training and media development. The project ended up with a price tag of 500 million kroner and became absolutely the largest single investment of the Games. The effect on development was formidable. The original calculation allowed Opplands District High School, which was to take over the RTV centre after the games, to increase its intake of students from 600 to 1,600. (It soon became apparent that this figure was actually very much higher still.)

A number of different explanations were put forward for this budgetary miscalculation. It was pointed out that the application for a state-guarantee submitted in January 1987, was largely based on a previous application, from February 1985, and did not take into consideration many

Lillehammer'94
©®

Birkebeiner
Lauget

ABB • IBM • PROCORDIA
SPAREBANKEN NOR
STATOIL • TELEVERKET
POSTEN • TBK • VOLVO

The main industrial sponsors of the Lillehammer Olympics make up the Birkebeiner's Guild, whose purpose is to serve as consultants to the organising committee. In return, the nine companies, or co-arrangers, have exclusive rights to the use of Lillehammer Olympic symbols and images.

ABB is a part of the ABB Asea Brown Boweri group, a leading international supplier of electronic systems to world markets. The agreement with ABB covers the planning and installation of electronic systems in Lillehammer.

IBM, established in 132 countries, is responsible for the computer systems and computer software. They supply the necessary computer systems for planning and arranging the 1994 games.

Posten, the Norwegian postal service, will supply a range of services before and after the Winter Olympics. They are responsible for organising the Olympic Flame relay through Norway and are also issuing special Olympic stamps.

Sparebanken NOR, the official bank for Games, is responsible for operating banking services in and around the Olympic sites.

Scandinavia's largest food company, Procordia, will be responsible for providing the two and a half million meals to be served during the Games. The company has exclusive rights to all food and drink sales in the arenas, and shares responsibility with LOOC for lodging and feeding the athletes in the Olympic village.

Volvo is involved in planning the transportation arrangements. Between 80,000–120,000 people will flow in and out of Lillehammer every day. Volvo supplies cars, mini-buses, trucks and vans.

TBK, the Norwegian telecom, will supply 10,000 telephones, cable-TV for 11,000 television sets, 110 km of outdoor cabling, computer communication networks for all the arenas, and the security systems. Televerket, the PTT, is responsible for the public communication networks and transmission services, national and international, through images, words, text and data.

Statoil, Norway's state-owned oil company, supplies oil products for LOOC's fleet of 1,300 vehicles. The Olympic Flame will be fuelled by gas provided by Statoil.

of the expensive changes of premise. In addition, a steady stream of new demands had subsequently emerged:
- more space for Radio, television and telecommunications
- greatly increased number of media personnel
- the requirement of an indoor skating track
- enormous expansion of the Olympic Arts Festival
- upgrading of infrastructure (roads, water-supply, sewers, electricty) needed to satisfy increased demand
- greater investment required for environmental and security considerations, sanitation and the control of drug-abuse amongst athletes.

Disquiet Amongst the Personnel

The most dramatic occurrence amongst the personnel in 1989 was the resignation of the president of the Olympic Committee, Ole Sjetne, though the behaviour of information officer Gunnar Mjell created the most turbulence. This former chief of information for the Defence Command in Northern Norway, developed a tense relationship with the media, who complained that he was inhibiting the free flow of information. Declarations and promises that the LOOC wished to be more open than the public legal organisation appeared not to be honoured in the event.

Owing to the clamp put on information by the LOOC, little if any of what was occurring in the wings was made official. The confusion therefore was great when Sjetne announced his resignation on October 3rd. Neither was it reduced by his refusal to comment on the reasons for his resignation, except to suggest it was based on personal differences. He refuted any connection between his resignation and the budgetary difficulties, though he admitted these had affected levels of cooperation. The media identified Per Haga and Hans B. Skaset as having been Sjetne's principal opponents and critics. Their idiosyncratic, uncompromising manner was reckoned to have put them on something of a collision course with the more urbane, diplomatic Sjetne. The tone he met from Haga and Skaset would have been very alien to his character and experience.

Vice-presidents Audun Tron and Arne Myrvold attemped to dissuade Sjetne from resigning, assuring him that he had the full confidence and backing of the steering committee. Hallvard Bakke took the same line, though he also made it known that Per Haga had the full backing. Haga kept silent, refusing either to confirm or deny that he and Sjetne had been in conflict.

In a flood of speculation about Sjetne's possible successor, the names most frequently mentioned were Thorvald Stoltenberg, Gerhard Heiberg and Hans B. Skaset. Stoltenberg made it clear he was not in the running, and the even money was then on Skaset, not least because Per Haga's support for him was well known. Skaset, chairman of the Norwegian Sports Association, let it be known that he was not adverse to the idea, and Haga warned of his readiness to use his right of veto, invested in him, or so he argued, by the large stake the State had in the Olympic arrangement. On the very day the new President was to take up his position, Aftenposten, the largest newspaper in the country, announced that Heiberg had turned down the post and Skaset was the man. But the truth was that Heiberg had accepted the post for a six-month period; he had remained true to his resolution not to seek to be Skaset's successor at the Norwegian Sports Association.

There was no limit to the positive words of welcome for the new president. 'The Happy Choice', and 'The Right Man in the Right Place', ran the headlines about this central figure from the Norwegian business community who now took over the captaincy of a somewhat listing Olympic ship. In Lillehammer also, the announcement was greeted with satisfaction, not least because it was thought that Heiberg would understand the project from a business perspective and thus be prepared to follow up the region's original reason for seeking to host the games.

Gerhard Heiberg launched his regime with a dose of self-criticism on behalf of the LOOC: it had not found the appropriate tone in its dealings with the media, and the internal leaks had led to an partial presentation of circumstances. Many of the negative issues could have been given a more positive angle if the media had been given different background information. He was also surprised that the LOOC had not come further in the decision-making process.

Parallel with the struggle over the budget, the project was reorganised in line with the transfer of responsibility from a local to national level. This was a logical consequence of the budgetary problems. Skaset was quite clear about the need for this. He was unequivocal that it would not be possible for the Storting to grant the levels of finance implied by the new estimates without the establishment of a more responsible and operational body to assume the running of the project. In his opinion it was impossible to 'bridle' the Olympic Games with the exisiting organisational model, in which Lillehammer Council assumed the main responsibility and the LOOC, the sports associations and the State were merely partners. Skaset demanded an ownership company, which would run the project on behalf of these three bodies, with all the power invested in it by the Storting's decision. The Storting and the business community had to have an addressee, responsible for taking decisions quickly and effectively.

The desired future management-model was first outlined in the Olympic proposition presented by the Ministry of Culture in February 1990. This suggested the requirement for a single body to coordinate a) the work of LOA (the development company, which had been under the control of the Lillehammer Council), b) the organisation of subsequent use of facilities, and c) the LOOC. The Ministry wished for a reduction of State involvement in the preparations and a system of management by resolution.

SCAN-FOTO/Arne Øverby

Mayor Erik S. Winther lost patience with the discussions on the placement of the downhill course, so he took matters into his own hands . . .

The Mayor as Lumberjack

But 1990 began with a continuation of the arguements as to what should happen where. Even the town of Gjøvik made itself unpopular with Lillehammer by suggesting that the cross-country skiing and biathlon events should be held at the Norwegian Championship course at Øverby. The mayors of the two Mjøsa towns had agreed wholeheartedly that the Olympic region should stand together against pressures to syphon off events to other parts of the country. But the incident also had elements of 'tit-for-tat': before Christmas, politicians in Lillehammer had supported the idea of Gjøvik council contributing 25 million kroner of its own money to the indoor ice rink.

Earlier in the year, a confrontation between the new Minister of Culture, Eleonore Bjartveit, and the Mayor of Ringebu, Erik S. Winther, reverberated throughout the country. The Ministry refused to allow tree felling on the downhill skiing slopes in Kvitfjell because it had not yet been formally decided that the mountain would be an Olympic site. In order that valuable time be not lost, Winther retorted by opening up a council fund and giving the green light for felling to begin. «Those that have common sense can use it,» said Winther, winning himself, through his disobedience towards a government minister, the status of a hero in Gudbrandsdalen.

First signals from the Government suggested that there would be no demands for dispersal of the games beyond the Ringebu-Hamar axis, thus securing the concept of a compact Olympics. There was uproar from local Conservatives. Local party activists resigned their membership, claiming that the party-leadership in Oslo were intending to disperse the games more or less throughout the country. Such a dispersal, they argued, would not only amount to a breach of contract, it would be highly immoral, given that it was precisely Lillehammer's compact-concept which had pipped the Swedish application from Östersund at the post. The distance between Hamar and Kvitfjell was actually longer than that between Östersund and Åre, the furthest limits of the Swedes' proposed facilities.

But despite many positive aspects, the Government's Olympic proposals in February, were something of a cold shower for Lillehammer, supporting as it did the idea of a provisional facility at Kvitfjell, to be dismantled after the games. Opplands District High School profitted most from the proposal: the RTV centre, costing 500 million kroner, was given the go-ahead, meaning an eventual increased capacity for the school from 600 students to 1600. On the other hand, the Government's plan to use 400 million of the receipts from the State football pools, sent shock-waves across the nation. Hans B. Skaset threatened to resign on the issue, but didn't.

The Olympic sites were situated more or less in accordance with the wishes of the Olympic Committee and Lillehammer Council, though Oslo was given a glimpse of hope with regards to the bob and luge events. It was suggested that Hamar should be given the skating hall, and that ice rinks should be built in Lillehammer, Hamar and Gjøvik. The cross-country and biathlon courses were to be sited in the Abbortjern/Kanthaugen area of Lillehammer.

Local Conservative leaders were not at all happy with the notion of a provisional facility at Kvitfjell, and felt the Government was forgetting Lillehammer's reasons for wanting to host the games in the first place. The Norwegian Skiing Association, the International Skiing Association (FIS) and Ringebu council joined forces in their fight for a permanent facility, with FIS making it quite clear that they could not accept a provisional arrangement. The Opposition gave the Government of Jan P. Syse a hard time in the Storting over its Olympic Proposal, the Labour Party's Olympic spokesman, Kjell Borgen, describing it is as unclear and insubstantial. The Conservative Party's own Olympic Committee also poured its own oil on the troubled waters by promising the bob and luge run to Hunderfossen. The Storting Committee's final recommendation awarded a total of 130 million kroner for the Hafjell/Kvitfjell projects and abandoned the idea of a provisional facility. It also stated unequivocally that all Olympic arenas should be sited in the Mjøsa area. Even the organisational structure was outlined, to be headed by a joint steering committee. Local satisfaction was considerable. Lillehammer's Mayor said that the recommendation showed that Olympic standards were finally being reached, and the Olympic President admitted that it conceded more than he had dared hope.

When the issue came up in the Storting at the end of April, 1990, there was no lack of strong reactions to the recommendations. The Labour Party's Berit Brørby Larsen, from Oppland, lay into what she called «the messengers of the Law of Jante»*, saying, «Every heart was lifted for a while, but it didn't take long before we were making complete idiots of ourselves in the eyes of the world with our Olympic preparations. Can there really be anything as hopeless as trying to argue with the messengers of the Law of Jante? And the Storting has more than its fair share of them. The whole thing is so Norwegian it's embarressing!».

Sigbjørn Johnsen (Labour Party, Hedmark), later to become finance minister, warned against becoming blinded by the costs of the Games, pointing out that, as in the oil industry, money needed to be spent in order for it to be earned. Marie Brenden (Labour, Oppland) was of the opinion that to do so would be dishonest to the IOC, who selected Lillehammer, and to Lillehammer rivals for the 1994 games in the application phase. On the other hand, it was emphasised that dispersing the games to Hamar and Gjøvik was advantageous in the context of subsequent exploitation of the facilities. On the whole, however, the atmosphere in the Storting during this Olympic debate was as undramatic as its predecessor had been dramatic. Whilst the two extreme parties, Socialist Left and the right-wing Progress Party, followed their own agendas, the Labour Party joined forces with the parties of the Centre Right coalition to ensure the important starting signal was issued!

Haakon's Hall and the cross-country and biathlon courses were to be built with State contributions of respectively 193 and 68 million kroner. A subsidy of 85 million kroner went to the ice rink at Gjøvik, 65 million to the rink in Hamar and 200 million for the skating centre in the same town. A financial framework of 509 million kroner was put on the Radio and Television Centre, and the Hafjell/Kvitfjell project received 130 million. The Government was given full authority to control subsidies for all other facilities, including the cultural arrangements in Lillehammer, and the infrastructural developments. The muddle over money from the State football pools was solved with a compromise allowing 30 % of all receipts from the pools to be made available to the Olympic building budget, partly financed by an extra 8 rounds of pools spread over the following 6 years. Satisfaction with the parliamentary decision was widespread. Mayor Audun Tron of Lillehammer felt that, at last, his message had been read and understood.

([1]* The Law of Jante = the Law of Conformity. *Jante* = the fear of being different.)

The people of Lillehammer rejoiced after the news broke that the town had been awarded the 1994 Winter Games.

SCAN-FOTO/Knut Falch

SCAN-FOTO/John Stenersen

SCAN-FOTO/Bo Mathisen

Many dramatic situations arose over budgets, the location of arenas and management. The protagonists were the then Minister of Cultural Affairs, Hallvard Bakke, Director General Per Haga, and Gunnar Mjell and Lillehammer Olympic Director Petter Rønningen. Mjell had to step down, at an early stage, from his position as director of information.

SCAN-FOTO/Per Svein Reed

Culture on a Par with Sport

The cultural side of the arrangement was equally dogged by conflict during the first two years after Lillehammer had been awarded the games. According to the Olympic Charter, the cultural or arts programme must be of a similar standard and be given equal weight to the sports programme. Consequently, plans were drawn up for a new concert hall-cum-theatre and exhibition facilities at Maihaugen, an extension for the Lillehammer Municipal Art Collection, and the restoration of the magnificant old Banken banquet hall. In addition, an extensive programme of arts events both at home and abroad was planned for before and during the games. A budget of around 400 million kroner was set, though this was to include any building requirements, plus costs incurred by the opening and closing ceremonies. But in Lillehammer itself, the whole issue raised an intense, sometimes bitter, argument. A majority of local polititians wanted a new arts centre based in Folket's Hus (Trade Union House) instead of the investments for Maihaugen. The conflict was so intense, that it almost delayed the delivery of the application for a state guarantee, just before Christmas 1989. The conflicting sides divided themselves along traditional lines, with the Labour and Socialist Left parties going one way and the centre right parties going the other. Finally, the Minister of Culture, Eleonore Bjartveit, was obliged to force the issue by deciding in favour of the Maihaugen development, much to the anger of local Labour Party activists.

Consequences

What the Olympics would cost Norwegian society, and what consequences it was realistic to reckon with, has been one of the main themes of discussion throughout the whole period. A socio-economic analysis carried out by Geir Asheim (Norwegian School of Economics and Business Management), Dag Bjørnland (Gøteborg University) and Arild Hervik (District High School in Molde) concluded that the net socio-economic cost of the arrangement would be approximately 3 billion kroner. Interest paid on this deficit over 10 years would result in lender-profits of 500 million kroner per year. The tourist industry is reckoned to turn out the largest beneficiary of the Games. But if this industry should underwrite the 3 billion kroner deficit alone, overseas tourism would have to increase by 40 % per year for 10 years, a most unlikely event, in order to offset the effect. If one reduces this figure to 10 % per year, there would remain a deficit of 313 million kroner. The researchers managed to track down 113 million of this margin, bringing the joint account to around 200 million kroner per year. This boils down to a sum of 350 kroner per Norwegian – for the pleasure of organising the Winter Olympics 1994! Subsequent exploitation and consequences of the arrangement was placed on the agenda in Spring 1989, with the establishment of a special 'subsequent use' committee (EBUK). This comprised of representatives from the local authorities in Lillehammer, Ringebu and Øyer and various areas of the Norwegian business community and society generally. The State limited iself to observer status, much to the disappointment of the local authorities involved. The «Olympics Minister», Hallvard Bakke, was accused of opting out of this important aspect of the arrangement. He was reminded that the Government and Parliament had stated, right from the beginning, that the work of EBUK should be afforded full weight and status as an essential aspect of the Olympic project. The committee's greatest task was to harness the 'growth-impulses' inherent in the Olympic development and to ensure that the various facilities were sensibly located, owned and managed. Towards the end of 1989, the president of the committee, Odd Arve Lien, threatened to disband it after Jan P. Syse's centre-right coalition government cut its support for the committee's work from the next budget. Eventually, EBUK was wound up and replaced, in May 1990, by Lillehammer Olympic Growth (LOV), which became the third wheel on the wagon (along with the LOOC and the development company LOA). The LOV company was to own, manage, maintain and develop the Olympic and other facilities, in partnership with the local authorities in the Olympic region.

SCAN-FOTO/Knut Falch

Åse Kleveland was appointed director of the cultural arrangements, but before she could even begin her work, she was called to a cabinet post. As Minister of Cultural Affairs, she bears the political responsibility for the Games.

A public fund was a necessary basis for this work. In the very first state-guarantee application, this fund was stipulated at 65 million kroner, but the deficit for the Olympic facilities had been put at 370 million for the 20 years following 1994. Only the alpine facilities were expected to break even. Even so, the total requirement for the Subsequent Use Fund calculated at 400 million kroner, was 50 million less than in Calgary.

Not unsurprisingly, the Syse government's decision to fix the fund at 65 million kroner – and not to release it until after the games were over – came as a great shock. If this was carried through, said Lillehammer's Mayor, then others would have to take over the responsibility of maintaining and managing the Olympic facilities. The Olympic President had announced his satisfaction with the fund, before it had actually been announced, though he accepted criticism for this, afterwards. Following intense lobbying, the new Labour Government adjusted the amount to 200 million kroner, which figure was subsequently accepted by Parliament.

There was further disquiet over the budget throughout 1990. Per Haga again demanded considerable cost cutting, with Finance Minister Arne Skauge naming a figure of several hundred million. The Olympic President found this figure so unreasonable that he threatened to resign. But, finally, the figures settled down at a level acceptable to the Olympic organisation. Not least, the leadership were satisfied at being given permission to move sums from one project to another without having to clear it first with the Ministry.

The First 'Green' Olympics

When construction work was finally begun, it soon became apparent that the sluggish state of the economy was the project's best friend. Some of the first contractors admitted openly that they would not turn a profit on the work. They had submitted low tenders merely to be able to keep their employees in work, and hopefully to increase their chances of a few bites of the Olympic cake, later on. Those that hoped the Olympics would be a gold-rush were sadly disappointed. In the first phase of developement, very few local firms managed to win contracts at all, though a summary at the beginning of 1992 showed that half of the total number of contracts had gone to local companies. In addition, outside firms have employed local manpower for their projects.

By the autumn of 1990, serious work was under way. In the beginning of September the Minister for Culture, Eleonore Bjartveit, turned the first symbolic sod on the RTV centre's site, with a enormous spade made from laminated wood produced by the Moelven company. Moelven would subsequently set their stamp on the various hall's with laminated beams of more than 100 metres in length.

Local people in the Olympic region were not least concerned about the outward appearance of the various facilities. In the event, any anxiety that the tight budgets would limit the suppleness and boldness of architectural vision proved groundless. Thanks to the special architectural committee, encouraging integrated and bold design, the results in this area are very good. The skating hall in Hamar, in the form of an upturned Viking ship, provoked particular, and justified, admiration. Great emphasis was placed on the need for the Olympic buildings to harmonise with the local architectural style and landscape. A good example, is the bob and luge run, which blended in so well with its surroundings that it ended up as something of an environmental-ornament, rather than the games' usual 'ugly duckling'. One question which had hovered for a long time between the LOOC and the Norwegian Ice Hockey Association was finally solved. This issue was so fraught, that for a while the president of the Ice Hockey Association actually boycotted meetings of the LOOC's steering committee. The LOOC leadership cut the knot by placing Haakon's Hall, in Lillehammer, and the Gjøvik Hall at the disposal of the ice hockey competition. The figure skating was moved to the rink at Hamar, also to be the venue for the short-track skating. This meant that all the skating events were gathered together in Hamar, a logical choice given the town's proud skating traditions.

The 'Green', or environmentally-friendly label became attached to the Lillehammer Games after Prime Minister and Chairperson of the United Nation Commission for the Environment and Development, Gro Harlem Brundtland, fought for the Norwegian application in Seoul. Since then, Lillehammer has been subtitled an 'environmental-political showcase', and the IOC in Lausanne has been a keen supporter of the 1994 Game's environment-friendly profile. In fact,

IOC president Juan Antonio Samaranch adopted the profile for both his organisation and himself, allying himself closely with the 'Project Green Olympics 94' and functioning as something of Green watchdog.

The green profile has permeated the development stages and will also figure highly in the Games themselves. Everyone in the Olympic organisation has been encouraged to 'Think Green', whether it concerns energy-saving, encroachment upon nature, or use of snow scooters and horses.

«As a nation, we're sitting in something of a glass-house, because we have helped create such high expectations of what Norway can achieve on the environmental issue», said the Games' environmental coordinator, Sigmund Haugsjå. On the other hand, a 'Green' profile didn't necessarily mean increased costs; in many instances, the reverse has been true.

The 'Green' profile is an important element of the total impression of Norway which it is hoped the Olympics can help broadcast to the world, thereby increasing interest in our country and encouraging people to visit it. The Olympics will present Norway as a first class winter-sports venue and a country characterised by high-quality.

The Olympics are Lillehammer's

The games in Albertville marked the beginning of the run up to the 1994 games. For the first (and only) time, only two years separate two winter games and, naturally, Lillehammer drew as much as possible on the French's expertise and experience from Albertville.

During the closing ceremony for the 1992 games, Norway and Lillehammer supplied an effective foretaste of what will happen on the 12th February 1994. At a cost of 3 million kroner, and in the course of just four minutes, more than a billion television viewers throughout the world were introduced to a country up near the North Pole with a fascinating history. Kjersti Alveberg's program also embraced folk myths and legends, underscored by Jan Garbarek's hypnotic music. Finally, the word LILLEHAMMER was written in fire across the whole world.

The Mayor of Lillehammer, Audun Tron, received the Olympic flag from his Albertville counterpart, Henry Dujol. This is the same flag which has been passed between the host nations for every winter games since Oslo in 1952, and Audun Tron bore it home. In Lillehammer's Søndre Park, 10,000 people were waiting for him, and the reception turned into a virtual repeat of the victory celebrations on 15th September 1988. At last, Lillehammer had the Olympic spotlight to itself, and could concentrate totally on making, and publicising, its own arrangement. Both Norway's huge success in France, and the fact that Lillehammer had now definitively taken over the baton, created a fresh wave of enthusiasm throughout the country. And enthusiasm was to prove a vital commodity. Over the years the project was to give rise to much frustration and despair, especially over the question of budget and the placing of facilities. This Olympic struggle was described as typically Norwegian, given that Norwegians make much better opponents than partners, according to the conclusions of those who have researched into our national psyche and manner.

On the costs front, the 'basic budget' of seven billion kroner has been constantly adhered to. If one includes 2 billion in costs born by either the councils or the State, and reckon with a private investment of roughly another 2 billion, the entire Olympic budget ends up at around 11 billion kroner, although this is almost certainly a conservative estimate.

The greatest question for the nation – and one which will almost certainly never receive a concrete answer – is whether or not the Lillehammer Olympic Games 1994 will turn out to be worth this kind of investment. If one choses to accept the researchers' figure of a cost per. head of 350 kroner, one might be tempted to ask what *else* worth having could a Norwegian buy for that sum? This is the most important point – the Olympic's plus factor can only be determined by the country itself, in what it *makes* of the games. The Olympic Games are a *possibility* which may or may not be realised. We *shall* make the games a festival of sport and national celebration which will be noted all over the world. We *can* turn the games into a tool to make something of lasting value to us all.

The hosts have been inventive when it comes to raising funds for the Olympics. Every day, a T-shirt inscribed with the number of days remaining until the opening of the Games is sold at public auction. Many shirts command four-figure sums.

SCAN-FOTO/Geir Olsen

SCAN-FOTO/Geir Olsen

It cost a pretty penny, but Ola E. Myhre is proud of his «Countdown Lillehammer» T-shirt.

Hockey and speed-skating are popular sports in Hamar, which has hosted a number of international competitions in its outdoor stadium. The Olympic Games, however, require indoor arenas.

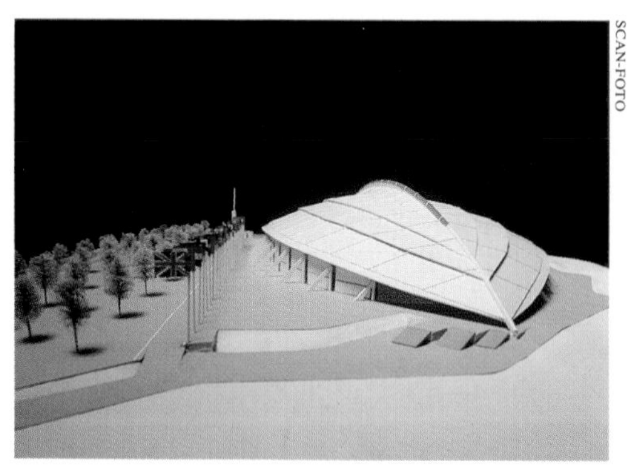

SCAN-FOTO

The biggest ice arena is shaped like a capsized Viking ship, elegant, yet daring. It will be the world's largest ice-sports hall, 100 metres wide, 240 metres long and 25 metres high, with a surface area of 26,000 square metres. Spectator capacity is 6,000.

From the air – or looking down from the motorway – the hull-shaped arena is an impressive sight.

SCAN-FOTO/Jarle Kjetil Rolseth

SCAN-FOTO/Hans Brox

SCAN-FOTO/Hans Brox

Ever since the long-ships of the Viking Era, Norwegian have had an affinity for wooden constructions. Suppor-ted by huge laminated wood beams, the arena required considerable engineering skills to build.

SCAN-FOTO

The ski-jumping facility on the outskirts of Lillehammer will serve as the main arena. This is where the Olympic Flame will be lit during the opening ceremony on February 12th 1994, casting its light over the games for 16 days. Both the opening and closing ceremonies will be held at this arena, which can hold 50,000 spectators. The free-style facility will be built to the right of the ski-jumps. Also close by are the cross-country and biathlon arenas.

SCAN-FOTO

LILLEHAMMER FOTO OG BILLEDARKIV/Jarle Kjetil Rolseth

Not far from the ski-jumps, are the two large Olympic arenas, the Håkon and Kristin Halls. The latter was completed in 1988 and has already been used for international ice hockey tournaments. The Kristin Hall arena will be used for training during the Games, with the matches held in Håkon Hall and in the mountain hall in Gjøvik. Håkon Hall covers 18,000 square metres and seats 10,000.

SCAN-FOTO

SCAN-FOTO

The alpine disciplines will be held on Hafjell and Kvitfjell, 15 and 50 km north of Lillehammer, respectively. There's room for 25,000 spectators at both places.

LILLEHAMMER FOTO OG BILLEDARKIV/Jarle Kjetil Rolseth

SCAN-FOTO/Jarle Kjetil Rolseth

Hockey players will do battle in an arena blasted out of solid rock 120 metres inside the mountain in Gjøvik. The 6,000 sq. metre arena seats 5,000 and is the largest facility of its kind in the world. Below: 250,000 cubic metres of rock were blasted out of the mountain to make room for the arena.

SCAN-FOTO

SCAN-FOTO

SCAN-FOTO

The luge and bobsleigh tracks are situated 15 kilometres north of Lillehammer, in Huseskogen, by the Hunderfossen waterfalls. Equipped with an icing system that secures equal conditions for all participants, and constructed out of solid concrete, the tracks are works of great precision. There's room for 10,000 people to safely enjoy the races.

SCAN-FOTO/Ingar Johansen

SCAN-FOTO

SCAN-FOTO/Morten Hval

In the centre of Lillehammer, a giant clock shows the number of days left before the opening of the 17th Olympic Winter Games, on 12th February 1994.

The Arts Olympics

– Prior to and during the Olympic Games 1994

Ingar Sletten Kolloen:

SCAN-FOTO/Knut Falch

Ingar Sletten Kolloen (b. 1951) spent five years with Den Norske Bokklubben, a book club run by the four major publishing houses in Norway, before becoming a journalist for Aftenposten. Eight years on, he was among the first to start work for LOOC, in Lillehammer. His primary activity has been the cultural arrangements, but he has also served in other capacities, such as spokesperson for LOOC. In 1992 he became editor of Dagningen, a daily newspaper.

Already at the turn of the century, the father of the Olympic Games, Baron Coubertin, talked of the value of a pact between sport and the arts. From the moment Norway was awarded the 17th Winter Olympics, weight was given to the notion of an Arts Festival to take place prior to, and during, the games. Meticulous preparation underlies one of the country's largest ever cultural events. The author of the following article has played a central role in the preparations. He tells of the cooperation between local, regional and national cultural interests groups, and how Lillehammer, with the assistance of the 1994 Olympic Games, once again became a proper centre for the arts.

Wooden box from Segalstad Farm.

LANDBRUKETS OL-UTVALG/Jarle Kjetil Rolseth

In February 1994, Lillehammer will be the arena for a massive cultural review, or Arts Festival, where Norway's most distinguished creative and performing artists will gather, together with leading international artists, in a cultural village costing 250 million kroner, donated from the Olympic budget.

This is also the story of the small town of Lillehammer, which after struggling for a hundred years to become a centre for the arts, finally achieved its goal, thanks to ski-jumpers, ice-hockey players and bob-sleighers.

For the first time, the story of how the Cultural Olympics came into being, is told, by one who has played a central role in the planning process over two-and-a-half years.

To begin at the beginning . . .

SCAN-FOTO/LOG Archives

Baron Pierre Coubertin always emphasised the importance of balancing sports and arts.

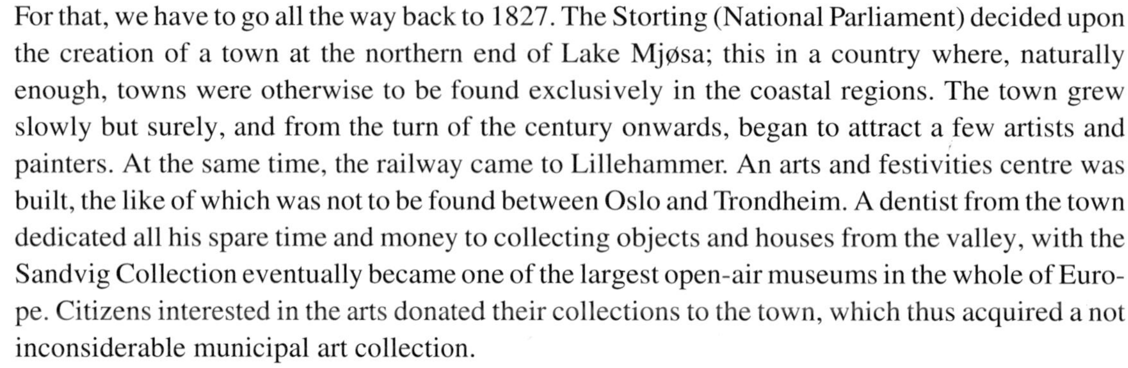

For that, we have to go all the way back to 1827. The Storting (National Parliament) decided upon the creation of a town at the northern end of Lake Mjøsa; this in a country where, naturally enough, towns were otherwise to be found exclusively in the coastal regions. The town grew slowly but surely, and from the turn of the century onwards, began to attract a few artists and painters. At the same time, the railway came to Lillehammer. An arts and festivities centre was built, the like of which was not to be found between Oslo and Trondheim. A dentist from the town dedicated all his spare time and money to collecting objects and houses from the valley, with the Sandvig Collection eventually became one of the largest open-air museums in the whole of Europe. Citizens interested in the arts donated their collections to the town, which thus acquired a not inconsiderable municipal art collection.

Some Lillehammer-folk began to talk about living in a centre for the arts, and for a while it looked as though Lillehammer might well become one. Unfortunately, the initiatives dried up. During the 1950s-60s and 70s, the phrase 'centre for the arts' rang more and more hollow, as culturally engaged people both within and without the town pointed out the gap between the claim and the reality.

Not Everyone Laughed

And then came the 1980s. A handfull of Lillehammer-folk began to fantasize about applying to host the Winter Olympics. Haha-ha, how people in the valley, and the whole country, laughed at this! Except for a few, that is, who saw the potential the Olympics would offer the town. Some of these people belonged to the arts community. What would the Olympics mean in cultural terms, people asked, whether in Oslo or Lillehammer. And thus the cultural aspect was included, at a very early stage, in the application process. The first application was defeated by the French. The second application went in, and this time the president of the IOC announced, «The decision is Lillyhammer». *(sic)* It was 15th September, 1988.

Three months later and the energetic Olympic Director, Petter Rønningen was already in place, together with the president, Ole Sjetne. This energetic pair, who had won the Olympics for Norway and Lillehammer, began to put together an administration in record time, (now thought to number some five hundred employees.) In the spring, an Artistic Director was appointed. There was a choice between two completely different personalities. One, the current director of the National Opera in Oslo, Bjørn Simensen, had revitalised one of the country's most monolithic institutions. The other was Oppland's high school director, Ivar Skelde, a highly skilled school administrator.

The latter took up the position on 1st August, at the same time as an advisory Arts Committee began its work. The Cultural Administration of the Lillehammer Olympic Organisation Committee (LOOC) and the advisory committee were given the task of developing a so-called «framework of cultural events prior to and during the 1994 Games», which was to be presented by June 1990. In reality, the task involved convincing first the Olympic leadership, then the board, then key individuals in both the Ministry of Culture and the Ministry of Finance, and finally politicians in the Government and the Storting, that the arts not only belonged in the 17th Winter Olympics, but should be given a central place in the whole arrangement.

Public Figures

What sort of people did the leaders of the Olympic organisation choose to advise them on the first Olympic Arts Festival in Norway's history? There were two main criteria; competence and experience. Her Royal Highness Crown Princess Sonja accepted the post of honourary president. The director of the Norwegian Arts Council, Halvdan Skard, a cautious but extremely skilled arts bureaucrat, was appointed chairman. Otherwise the committee included one of the Ministry of Culture's most senior officers, Helge Sønneland; the previous Minister of Culture and current Director of Culture in Oslo, Lars Roar Langslet; Storting's president, Kaci Kullman Five, who also sat on the board of the LOOC; Svein Erik Brodal, a leading figure from the theatre, at the time coming to the end of his period as artistic director for The Norwegian Theatre, in Oslo; and the multi-talented Egil Monn-Iversen, with his broad experience from the music world, the theatre, and not least, of the private arts and entertainment sector. Another multi-faceted public figure to take her place on the committee was former musician, former chairperson of the Norwegian Musician's Association, theme-park director, and – currently – Minister of Culture, Åse Kleveland. The pop musician Dag Kolsrud was also given a place. All disciplines of the arts community were represented, with the curator of the National Gallery, Tone Skedsmo, director of the Industrial Arts Museum, Anniken Thue, the artist and leader of the Norwegian Council of Artists, Jan Brænde, and sculptor Hilde Mæhlum.

But what about representatives from the local cultural community?

The leader of the board of culture in Oppland County and Labour Party politician Odmund Kristiansen was included, as was, of course, the Cultural Administrator in Lillehammer, Hanne Mari Nyhus.

Two politicians from Lillehammer with a special interest in arts policy, Olemic Thommeson from the Conservative Party, and Randi Thorsen from the Socialist Left Party, were appointed to the committee, and the superb mainstay of the local team was director of the Sandvig Collection at Maihaugen, Magne Velure.

First Criticisms

The make-up of the committee, of course, came in for criticism. There were three main aspects to this. Firstly, it was pointed out that the representation did not reflect all areas of cultural activity in the country; what about architecture, design, Lappish culture, the church, classical music, dance, literature, arts for young-people? In the event, Kjærsti Evjen was taken onto the committte as representative for the last named group, but resigned after a year, dissatified with her own work on the committee.

Secondly, it was claimed that the committee was too conservative. Which of its members would speak out on behalf of experimental art, for new visions and ideas? To this the committee answered that all areas of the artistic community would be invited to present their ideas.

The third area of criticism arose from the classic conflict between artists and bureaucrats. The 18-member committee included only four active artists. The answer to this point was that musicians, dancers, actors, writers, etc, would be extensively drawn into the committee's work. The constitution of the committee was appropriate to its task, which was not to decide the content of the final programme, but to prepare a document of sufficent political, economic and philosophic credibility to convince all the relevant decison-makers that the Arts Festival was as vital to the Lillehammer Olympics as the sports programme.

'The Wishing Well'

The committee got under way, but it soon became apparent that a smaller working group was necessary, which could meet more often and coordinate more effectively with the LOOC's cultural administration. This turned out to be a wise move; work on the document, which all knew would decide the fate of the cultural aspect of the games, proved not to be easy. The first step taken by the committee was to invite the entire artistic community to a conference in Lillehammer, in October 1989. 'Everyone' came, and 'everyone' demanded 'everything', not least for themselves. The dance around the wishing well had begun. All the resolutions and wishes so forcibly argued for at the conference were collected together in a thick pamphlet. It might be interesting one day for a researcher to compare this pamphlet with the final Olympic arts programme.

The Cultural Administration and the committee had to fill many a blank page with ideas, arguments and figures. No one believed reference to the French Baron Coubertin's views on the holy pact between culture and sport would suffice, so, naturally enough, comparisons were made between the Norwegian situation and that of previous Olympic hosts.

Calgary had arranged an enormous festival of the arts, spread over the four weeks of the 16th Winter Games. For years prior to the Games, the whole of Canada was involved in cultural events directed by the Calgary Olympic Committee. The budget for these events, including the ceremonies, was some 300 million kroner. 200,000 tickets were sold, for a total of 16 million kroner. The organisers of the Seoul Summer Games invested almost 450 million kroner in their cultural programme, whilst Barcelona was preparing to mount the largest arts arrangement of all time over the four years leading up to the 1992 Olympics, with a budget of half a billion kroner.

Another set of arguments revolved around the fact that Norway is a small country. Through our cultural programme, especially in the time prior to the actual games, it would be possible to open doors abroad which otherwise tended to stay shut.

As was claimed, quite correctly, the media focus on Norway during February 1994, had to be used as an opportunity to exhibit the country's cultural qualities to the world.

Further, it was argued that Norway is under great pressure from the rest of the world, not least culturally. Our own culture needed not merely defending, but the opporunity to develop. The arts programme leading up to, as well as that taking place during, the Olympic Games could be a great boost for the artistic life of the country.

Yet another strong argument was that inland Norway – that's to say, the Olympic region – lies at the bottom of the list of statistics of cultural activity, facilities and services. An extensive Olympic arts programme would have a huge effect on the region as it approaches the end of the century. Finally, it was, of course, pointed out that the Olympic Charter, and Norway's application to host the games, placed special emphasis on the cultural element.

A Touch of Nerves

The Arts Committee and the cultural section of the LOOC had frequent meetings with each other. Much of the work in 1989 concentrated on defining what facilities would be required, how much they would cost and what kind of budgetary framework was implied.

There were many who experienced a touch of nerves when the final calculations resulted in a figure of half a billion kroner. Was it really feasible that such a sum would prove acceptable? But the figures were most eloquent. A proper Olympic arts programme, with the necessary buildings and equipment, together with the game's opening and closing ceremonies, would cost a minimum of 500,000,000 kroner!

The next phase was to substantiate the figures, and thus work was started on «A Framework for the Ceremonies and the Arts Programme». The purpose of this document was to convince two government departments, the cabinet and parliament that such an investment was necessary and would turn out – albeit eventually – to be profitable.

At the start of 1990 the number employed in the LOOC's cultural section was increased to five, myself included, following a period helping to develop the LOOC's information network in the wake of the resignation of the director of information. No sooner had we began work, when health problems forced Artistic Director Ivar Skelde, to throw in the towel after barely six months. Under duress, the undersigned agreed to function as a caretaker in the post until it could be filled.

The Royal Contribution

The work of the committee intensified. Individual members were drawn into the work on the document, firstly through fortnightly meetings, then weekly meetings, finally, in the closing stages of the work, several meeting per week. It would be hard to exaggerate the contribution to this process made by Crown Princess Sonja, as she then was. Whilst the then Crown Prince Harald sat on the board of the LOOC, as honourary president, Crown Princess Sonja fullfilled the same role on the Arts Committee. It would not be correct to describe her efforts in detail, but her broad knowledge of, and intense interest in, Norwegian cultural life is well known. Suffice to say, even the most hard-baked republican would have ended up a wholehearted supporter of the monarchy having had the opportunity to work together with Her Royal Highness, now Her Majesty, in what is, clearly, her specialist area.

Of course, the duo of arts-bureaucrats, Halvdan Skard and Helge M. Sønneland, performed a central role in the committee's work. The skilled arts-enablers Anniken Thue and Tone Skedsmo drew upon their considerable experience. Åse Kleveland was, on all levels, a driving force. Magne Velure threw himself into the task with all his knowledge and understanding of cultural politics. Egil Monn-Iversen brilliantly cultivated support for the ideal of the ceremonies.

Tense Meetings with the Politicians

Both we employees of the LOOC and individual members of the committee engaged in extensive lobbying of important decision-makers, in the first instance Government and parliamentary politicians. I will never forget a number of tense meetings during this period. The high-point was reached in our meeting with the Storting's Church and Education Committee, during which Egil Monn-Iversen achieved the impossible, by convincing initially totally unsympathetic representatives of the Progress Party of the necessity of granting 100 million kroner for the opening and closing ceremonies of the games!

Work on the policy document continued apace. Many hundreds of people from the Norwegian arts community became involved in the process. One of the most eminent firm of consultents in the country, Holthe Prosjekt, was brought in by one their leading planners and project coordinators, Einar Amlie Karlsen. This, together with the LOOC's own demands as to how planning processes should be carried out, led to the whole process following the models used in business. It was entertaining, though also throught-provoking, to see how some leading personalities from the Norwegian arts community reacted to having to use planning procedures and tools which hundreds of thousands of Norwegian engineers and economists employ daily in their work. Phrases were introduced which few, if any, had even heard before, let alone used. «Project Breakdown Structure». «Constituent Projects of the Main Project». «Identification of Critical Timing Conditions». «Controller function». «Success criteria». «Risk analysis». Computer diagrams presenting various analyses or suggestions for subsequent action, could provoke both laughter and aggression. One such diagram moved a committee member to ask whether it wasn't the diagram from the back of his television set, informing the technician of the layout of circuitry inside!

I name this incident as an example of a general lack of, and strong resistence to, structured thinking in the arts community. For far too long, far too many artists in Norway have been allowed to get away with claiming, in all seriousness, that creativity and structure do not belong together, and living their lives in accordance with this belief. «Don't try and press me into some bloody planning system put together by engineers building oil-platforms. That sort of thing detroys my creativity!», as one committee member screamed at me, on one occassion.

The new wing of Lillehammer's art gallery, Lillehammer Bys Malerisamling, is shaped like a grand piano. The museum stands in the centre of town, facing the central square and City Hall.

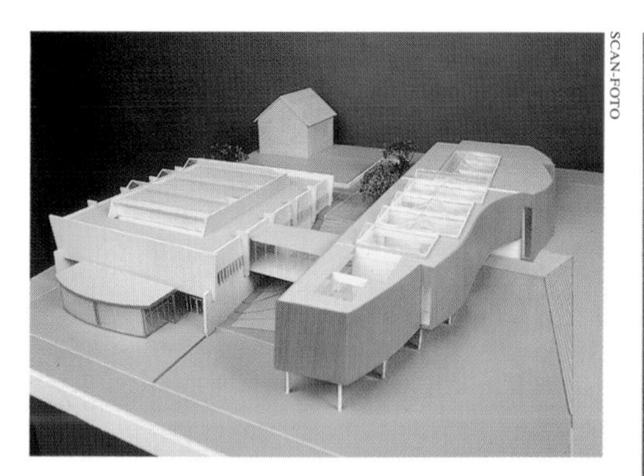

SCAN-FOTO

SCAN-FOTO/Erik Poppe

Many of this country's most prestigious artists have been engaged by the LOOC to take part in artistic arrangements both before and during the Olympic Games. Bård Breivik (above), Ole Edvard Antonsen, and Sissel Kyrkjebø are some of the artists that have been selected.

SCAN-FOTO/Knut Falch

Every discipline of the Winter Olympics has its own pictogram, inspired by ancient Norwegian cave carvings. The ones above represent ski-jumping, skating, ice-hockey, slalom and biathlon.

In 1984, the Winter Olympics were held i Sarajevo. Eight years on, civil war has ravaged what used to be Yugoslavia, and the Olympic city of Sarajevo is among the worst hit. For a long time it was shelled and the casualties were great. Lillehammer took the initiative to help Sarajevo and in particular, the many children that have been hurt. The very day the Summer Olympics in Barcelona ended, an appeal was launched to previous and coming Olympic cities. The response to the appeal was positive and in many cities, arrangements were held, under name of «Olympic Aid». Sizeable sums were collected to aid the children of Sarajevo.

The staging of historical plays is a natural part of the arrangement.

SCAN-FOTO/Jarle Kjetil Rolseth

SCAN-FOTO/Terje Andersen

The cultural arrangements range from tours on horse-drawn sledges to concerts in the newly constructed concert hall.

SCAN-FOTO/Jarle Kjetil Rolseth

The old village bank used to serve as a ballroom. Now entirely restored, the concert hall will serve an important role during the Games.

SCAN-FOTO/Knut Falch

The city of Lillehammer has a fine collection of paintings, and the art gallery has been substantially enlarged in the wake of the Olympic arrangement.

But What About Aesthetics?

The once-so-blank pieces of paper gradually filled up with systematic thoughts about why Norway needed also to invest in the cultural programme of the Olympics; what, where, when and how was the most advantageous course of action, and what would it cost?

Two areas not specifically included in the assignment but which occupied the cultural administration and the Arts Committee greatly, were architecture and design. Many, justifiably, doubted the Olympic organisation's ability or willingness to set adequate aesthetic standards. Quite another organisation than the LOOC, namely Lillehammer Olympic Construction, was responsible for the construction work, and the barriers between the two organisations quickly proved to be total. This caused us on the committee much disquiet. We successfully initiated the formation of a group of 'aesthetic watchdogs'. Professor of Architecture Thomas Thiis-Evensen, design technician Odd Thorsen, and the landscape architect Jan Feste have been particularly successful in this area, mixing themselves into most of the building work, energetically expressing their opinions, pointing out, underlining, suggesting. . .

Overall responsibility for coordinating the design of the arrangement was eventually given to Petter Mohus. He went to work, methodically and creatively. Aesthetic guidelines were drawn up for everything from Olympic clothing, signposting, television graphics and letterheads, mascots, symbols and building styles. The fact that the Olympic project has resulted in buildings which will become national monuments, and design in many areas which will provoke international interest, is very much thanks to the inclusion of aesthetic considerations very early on in the Olympic organisation's work.

On the Government's Table

In the beginning of June, the document was ready. After the various boards had approved it, it was sent on to the Ministries, the Government and the Storting. The budget demands were put at 215 million kroner for concerts, exhibitions, ceremonies, etc, and 213 million for the building of new facilities, the restoration of old ones and the decoration of all Olympic buildings. The LOOC's budget already included some twenty odd million kroner earmarked for the running of the cultural section up to the games.

The following main objective was formulated; The Cultural and Ceremonial Programme shall, together with the sports programme and other aspects of the Olympic Games, constitute a whole event which presents a positive impression of Norway and of Norwegian society to the world. It shall be accessible to a broad audience. It shall include artistic and cultural manifestations of our special Norwegian identity, quality and variety, preferably in the context of international cultural trends. It shall contribute to the widest possible social benefit in the form of new skills, lasting enterprise, new forms of cooperation and potential for developement.

New Music and Art

A number of central problems had been under discussion from the start. During the process, however, it proved possible to reach agreement on a number of decisive issues. All effort both prior to and during the Olympic Games would be concentrated under four major programmes – a preliminary arts programme in Norway; one overseas; an arts programme during the games; and the programme of ceremonies. Music and theatre, the visual arts, handicraft, and cultural history were named as the major areas of consideration, along with Lappish culture during the Olympics. In addition to exhibitions of various kinds, it was decided to undertake a comprehensive programme of decoration to enhance the aesthetic qualities of the Olympic buildings, at a cost of some 30 million kroner. A cultural programme for churches was organised under the Churches' own special Olympic Committee, and it was also decided to prioritise childrens' and youth events.

But what about all those who, for various reason, would not take advantage of the concerts, exhibitions, theatre and dance performances, etc, on offer during the Olympics? Only a small percentage of visitors to the games would be able to gain access to these. The Arts Committee and the Cultural Administration found a solution to this problem. The so-called 'everyday-life project' was established. The idea of this is to present both professional and amateur artists in surprising, but appropriate, situations in which the Olympic public happens to find itself, ie on trains, in intervals between sports events, at taxi ranks, on the streets, queueing in shops, in backyards, etc. The project also includes the organisation of a limited number of arts and entertainment events in restaurants, where Norwegian food and drink will be served and a festive atmosphere created. This will occur primarily in Lillehammer, but also in Oslo, and the other towns in the Olympic region.

Judgement!

The summer and early autumn were spent further going over the details of the budget and developing ideas about the programming. Of course, there was much anticipation amongst those of us who had worked on the policy document as to whether the Government would agree to such a high level of funding. What was clear was that the leadership of the LOOC, with Gerhard Heiberg at their head, were firmly behind the concept of an Arts Olympics, depite criticism from various fronts. The judgement came at the end of September. 238 million kroner was granted to the building programme – ie 25 million *more* than we had applied for, and 207 million for running costs and events – ie 25 million *less* than we'd applied for. (These figures were subsequently adjusted, both up and downwards, by the LOOC.)

It was time to celebrate our victory. It was no small victory, either, nor a semi-victory, but a huge, thunderous complete victory for the arts. A victory for 'the arts' against the wider definition of 'culture' (which in Norway includes more or less everything, including sport!). Not least, it was a victory over the widespread antipathy towards the arts in certain sports groups. It was also time to ask who profitted most from the victory. The answer to this was crystal clear – Lillehammer, which will now receive an unparalleled injection of arts subsidy. To take the buildings first. Lillehammer's extraordinary collection of paintings has largely been confined to cramped and inappropriate storage conditions; the 3,000 square metre museum building raised with the help of almost 40 million kroner from the Olympic budget, opened in October 1992, will be a pearl in the artistic landscape of the country. 'Banken', the turn-of-the-century banquet hall, had deteriorated so badly there had been suggestions of it being demolished. Following its re-opening in January 1992, it has become an arts centre much-used by many different groups in the town. The 750 seater concert hall-cum-theatre at Maihaugen, which will open in February 1993, will be the most modern facility of its kind in the country. In the course of the spring, the door will open on the permanent exhibition of Norwegian history at Maihaugen, also financed from the Olympic arts-budget. In addition, perhaps as much as 10 to 15 million kroner of the events-budget will be directly to Lillehammers advantage, supporting the professionalisation of the town's artistic life.

The people of Lillehammer, who have for so long insisted that they live in a 'centre for the arts', are finally seeing their town make it onto the cultural map of the country. It's a paradox, but no less true for that, that it took a sports event to refashion Lillehammer into a cultural centre!

Who Are the Losers?

And so, – we have a clear winner, but who, one may ask, are the losers?

The answer to this question is also clear as day. The other Olympic boroughs, Hamar, Gjøvik, Øyer and Ringebu had great, and in many respects justified hopes of receiving the funds to develop their own cultural facilities in the run up to the Olympics. At one point or another, Øyer wished for 4.5 million kroner, Gjøvik for 6 million, Ringebu 7 million and Hamar 8 million. As events have turned out, they might end up with as many hundred-thousands as they had wished for millions! On the other hand, the development of Lillehammer as a cultural centre will be to the advantage of the whole region of Gudbrandsdalen, Vest-Oppland and the northern parts of Hedmark, a region not previously noted for its cooperation over borough and county boundaries.

Indeed, one of the positive side-effects of the Olympic project so far is that the five boroughs and two counties have been obliged to work together on specific tasks in a totally different way than previously, also within the area of culture and the arts.

Money or Ideas?

Much of the time from September 1990 has gone to establishing close cooperative links between all sectors of the arts community, both locally, regionally, nationally, and in fact internationally, also. It has taken time to persuade the arts community that LOOC's cultural administration is not primarily interested in blindly scattering largesse, but sees as its main task the unearthing of ideas and projects which can be developed to 'Olympic' standard.

Many fundamental attitudes have had to be changed. «We have a right to our slice of the Olympic arts cake», it has been said, by writers and musicians, dancers and theatre people, Christians and Lapps, folk and rock musicians, curators of museums and video-artists.

The need to have one, strong, high-profile arts personality to lead the whole process was clear from the start. The line was cast and eventually, there was a bite. In August 1990, Åse Kleveland finally agreed to take on the job, having hesitated for a long time, for a variety of reasons. A perfect choice. She knew the Olympic Arts issue in all its detail from her work with the committee. She had strength of personality, a wide frame of reference, and commanded respect throughout the arts community. For just over three months, she commuted between the Tusenfryd Theme Park, outside Oslo, and LOOC's so-called copper castle in Lillehammer. She threw herself into the work and achieved much in a short time. The same week as she was due to begin working full time, she recieved an offer it was impossible for her to turn down. She became Minister of Culture.

And so the search for an artistic director – the fourth in a row – started anew, and in the first half of January 1991, film producer Bente Erichsen accepted the post, launching immediately into her most pressing task, namely to communicate the vision of the Arts Olympics to the relevant groups and key figures within the artistic community. She managed the difficult task of charming the somewhat self-important gathering of the IOC at their meeting in Birmingham, in May 1991, where the Arts Olympic-concept was presented to the IOC, officially, for the first time.

Apart from this, Bente Erichsen has dedicated much of her time to shaping the Arts Olympics' overseas programme.

Right Price, Right Time, Right Place

The time leading up to the Olympics will be used for negotiating contracts and ensuring that theatre productions, exhibitions, concerts, etc, will be as good as promised, not more expensive than agreed, and ready at the right time. This last point is not the least important. The Arts Olympics is an extraordinarily complicated jig-saw puzzle consisting of an unbelievable number of pieces which must fit together, minute by minute, over 16 whole days. The slightest delay will immediately create a wave of unfortunate consequences. And the Norwegian artistic community is not famous for its ability to deliver the right product for the right price, at the right time, to the right place!

The time will also be used to develop and test models, projects, buildings, etc. In February 1992, the pre-Olympic arts programme began with «Winter Plays at Lillehammer», a broad based festival, heavily supported by the LOOC's cultural administration. Cooperative models were tested, indoor and outdoor arenas were used in order to gather experiences with an eye to the Olympic programme. Various experimental projects were executed and analysed. The festival was a great success, attracting more than 30,000 visitors in a town of only 22,000 people. Similar festivals, only on a slightly smaller scale, were organised in the other Olympic towns, also. In February 1993, there will be more.

And no one can doubt any more that Lillehammer has become a centre for the arts. It even managed to become so before the Olympic Games. . .

The parts fall into place

By autumn 1992 most of the parts of the 1994 Winter Olympics cultural programme had fallen into place. Here, LOOC Cultural Director Bente Erichsen tells about the extensive plans:

The final programme will comprise concerts, dance performances and theatrical productions – along with a general entertainment category including films, seminars and conferences, presentations of literature, art projects of all types and exhibitions.

Book projects and catalogues, other culturally-related products, and productions for or in cooperation with radio and television, are also planned.

Although a number of events have already taken place in Lillehammer, the cultural programme will not begin in earnest until 1993.

It starts in February with the fine arts festival in Lillehammer and surrounding Olympic venues, and continues that summer with greater intensity – with the final kick-off of the Olympic Cultural Festival planned for January 1, 1994.

February 1993 also marks the start of the parallel international promotion of the Lillehammer Games. First on the agenda is «Winter Land», a collection of classic and contemporary paintings with winter themes selected by H.M. Queen Sonja. After opening in Atlanta, the exhibition will travel to Tokyo in April, Barcelona in September, and Munich in November. Also planned are theatrical performances, film festivals, literary and culinary presentations, and, not least, concerts by the Olympic musicians.

One of the purposes of LOOC's cultural programme is to give young artists the opportunity to gain international exposure and recognition, in the same way that the Olympics give young athletes a chance to compete internationally.

The following musicians/artists have been appointed Olympic performers:

Ole Edvard Antonsen
Leif Ove Andsnes
Bodil Arnesen
«The Three Billy Goats Gruff» (Steinar Ofsdal, Annbjørg Lien, Arve Moen Bergset)
Jon Balke
Bel Canto (Anneli M. Drecker, Nils Johansen)
Grieg Trio (Ellen Margrethe Flesjø, Sølve Sigerland, Vebjørn Antvik)
Sissel Kyrkjebø
Ole Kristian Ruud

In addition to performances abroad and at the Winter Games, the musicians will be given the opportunity to invite an internationally known artist to a so-called «master meeting» in Norway.

Four new ballets and an opera will be created in cooperation with The Norwegian Opera, and a magnificent performance based on «Draumkvedet», the dream saga from Norse mythology, will be produced in cooperation with the Norwegian Theatre. A theatrical piece revolving around the theme of ice and snow will be performed at the Olympics in cooperation with Beivvas Sami Theatre, Studio Theatre, Sampo Theatre, and Hålogaland Theatre.

The National Theatre will present works by Ibsen during the Olympics, while projects with other Norwegian theatres will be performed both prior to and during the Games.

Series of concerts – jazz, pop/rock and classical – are also planned.

Cooperation with Bokklubben, the Norwegian book club, has resulted in a series of books related to the Olympic cultural programme, while a similar project with record producers has brought about a series of recordings of Norwegian music and a «play Norwegian» offensive.

Folk life

The informal folk life programme will reach out to the public wherever they are – on the street, in the arenas, in hotel lobbies – in short, wherever people naturally congregate.

Emphasising joy and celebration, the informal programme will be filled with everything from presentations of Norwegian food and drink, to magicians, song, dance, theatre and folksy competitions where spectators can, for example, try their hand at milk-can tossing. The only ground rules are that the presentations, geared for mobile Olympic spectators, be short and entertaining.

The informal programme will take place during the Games, when the influx of visitors to the area is the greatest, but there are also plans to introduce the presentations on a smaller scale at trial competitions and pre-Olympic arrangements.

Exhibitions

A number of exhibitions will be arranged in the Olympic communities, in Oslo, and overseas from autumn 1992 to summer 1994.

The Lillehammer art gallery, Lillehammer Bys Malerisamling, will open with new works by Bård Breivik and parts of the permanent collection. Autumn 1993 will see the results of various art workshops held in the Olympic region that summer, together with an international photo exhibition dubbed «Pictures from the Real World». On display in Lillehammer during the Olympics will be H.M. the Queen's «Winter Land» exhibition, following its showing in Atlanta, Tokyo, Barcelona and Munich.

Maihaugen, the open air folk museum in Lillehammer which has been expanded in connection with the Olympics, will mount a large historical exhibition entitled «Slowly the Country Became Our Own». Other exhibitions at the museum include «Master Meeting», a collection of Norwegian and foreign traditional crafts, «Wood – the Norwegian Challenge», Norwegian home arts and crafts, and Sami huts.

The Lillehammer Olympic Information Centre will present various informational exhibitions tied to the cultural programme, such as a presentation on the aurora borealis, or northern lights. Exhibitions on other themes will also be arranged in the outlying Olympic venues both prior to and during the Olympics.

LOOC has also coordinated an exhibition programme for nearly 40 public and private exhibition localities in Hedmark and Oppland Counties, and a number of the major art institutions in the capital will take part in the exhibition programme.

Visual design

Art work and visual designs have been selected to enhance the visual quality of the Olympics, in Lillehammer as well as in the neighbouring Olympic communities.

An emphasis has been made on selecting works of art that will remain in place as a lasting memory of the event for inhabitants and visitors.

The majority of the 30–40 commissioned pieces of art and design work planned for the Games will be carried out by Norwegian artists. Some are already finished, while others are in progress – such as Carl Nesjar's work at the Olympic Hall in Hamar, and Inger Sitter's project at the Hamar Olympic amphitheatre. Other artists and commissions include: Per Inge Bjørlo, Gjøvik Fjellhall, an ice arena built inside the mountain; Bård Breivik, Lillehammer Bys Malerisamling, Lillehammers collection of paintings; Jon Gundersen, Birkebeineren Ski Stadium; Søren Ubisch, Maihaugen; Ulla Mari Brantenberg and Finn Lande Andersen, «Banken» fine arts centre; and Lillian Dahle, LOOC reception area.

In addition, competitions will be held for several design projects, such as the Olympic Flame and Olympic Torch which will be used to light the Olympic Flame.

Ceremonies

The opening and closing ceremonies will be the largest single cultural arrangements staged during the Games. They will take place in the ski-jumping arena where the landing area is especially well suited to the task. LOOC has engaged Jo Vestly of Polyvision A/S as producer of these arrangements, while choreographer Kjersti Alveberg is artistic director. Both ceremonies will be based on elements of Norwegian cultural history from its roots in Norse mythology up to the present time.

The highlight of the day at the Games will be the victory celebrations with the presentations of the medals. Apart from the skating events, these will all be awarded at a special arena for ceremonies set up at Stampesletta. The ceremonies will include cultural programmes, for which information will also be provided.

The ceremonies are to serve as a positive and unifying experience for all participants and viewers.

Torch relay

By custom, the Olympic Flame is lit in Olympia, Greece. Plans are under way for a relay through Europe to bring the Flame to Lillehammer. The carrying of the torch is intended to be the dynamic force in relation to other arrangements, cultural as well as athletic, that naturally follow in its path. In addition, work is in progress on campaigns and informational programmes in which the Olympic Movement and Ideals and the Lillehammer Games are central elements. Cities that have previously arranged Winter Olympics will be involved in these efforts.

Long-standing traditions bind Norwegian skiing, Morgedal - the birthplace of modern skiing – and the Olympic Movement. Plans are being made to light, as was done in 1952 and 1960, a second flame in Morgedal, which after a relay through Norway, will be joined with the flame from Olympia before it is carried to the opening ceremony.

Torchlight festivals based on local traditions and featuring local talent are planned at each of the 74 places in Norway where the relay will stop for the evening. As such, the torch relay in Norway will be a reflection of the depth and breadth of Norwegian culture at that time.

The Norwegian Postal Service, one of the main sponsors of the Lillehammer Games, is in charge of organising the relay.

One of the most renowned Norwegian painters, Jacob Weidemann, lives nearby Lillehammer and is actively interested in sports. He has been engaged in the cultural activities in the Olympic city, and has contributed to this book, through his illustrations.

SCAN-FOTO/Rolf M. Aagaard

HM Queen Sonja's

Winter Land

There is a special vibrance to the art of a country which for much of the year is marked by the winter's cold and snow, by the dusks of wintry skies, deepening later to endless darkness and by the shimmering light above snow-decked uplands, all underlined by the innate and unyielding vitality of the people who inhabit this rugged land.

When it was decided that prior to the Lillehammer Olympics Norway was to be presented to the world trough a travelling exhibition of art based on winter themes, it was precisely this special vibrancy that the organisers strove to find. The advisory committee appointed to help HM Queen Sonja select the works of art had a difficult task. It decided to single out a few artistic personalities from the old school, and to let contemporary art be represented by some of the artists of the last 15 to 20 years. Many important trends and prominent artists have been omitted. In contemporary art, for example, modernism, neo-expressionism and post-modernism have been intertwined, with no systematic division between them.

The selected contemporary works will show how Norwegian artists have dealt with the relationship between art and nature, or between the artist as an individual and existence as a whole. This is portrayed through pictures which depict space, light, darkness, time, the threat of annihilation and the indomitable power of life; seemingly abstract themes which nevertheless are given concrete associations in that they are linked in different ways to the Norwegian winter landscape.

In the exhibiton's older works of art, themes representing this special vibrancy also have a central place. Yet, in the art of more recent times, the more abstract elements of such themes appear to have become the actual motif of the pictures. The artistic expression has been more sharply focussed and is more intelligible as a pictorial concept because the descriptive motifs have been subordinated. The pictures are more concerned with the relationship between darkness and light than with starlight above the spruce forests, and with vitality breaking through its bonds, than with children out sledging.

The exhibition is to be shown in some of the cities which have previously hosted the Olympic Games. But it will start its tour in Atlanta, Georgia, USA, where the 1996 Summer Olympics are to be held. After this it will continue to Tokyo, Barcelona and Munich before terminating its tour in Lillehammer during the XVIIth Winter Olympics.

In Atlanta the exhibition will be housed in The Fernbank Museum of Natural History, one of the USA's leading educational institutions within the fields of natural science, physics and meteorology. At the same time, the Fernbank Museum will mount its own exhibition on the theme of the Nordic winter climate, snow crystals etc, and the museum's planetarium will be simulating the Northern Lights, winter skies and cloud formations, among other things. The exhibition will be on show from 11 February to 31 March 1993.

In Tokyo whe exhibition will run from 25 April to 30 June 1993, in The National Museum of Western Art. This is one of the most centrally situated museums in the Japanese capital, located in a large park where one of the main attractions is the cherry blossoming – an event which draws many of the city's inhabitants to the park. The Norwegian exhibition will coincide with the cherry blossoming – forming a contrast to the summery scene outside.

From Tokyo the exhibition will go on to Barcelona, where it will be on show from 5 September to 30 October. One of Spain's big savings banks, Fundacio «La Caixa», is strongly culture-orientated and has its own art galleries in Barcelona and Madrid. The Norwegian exhibition will be housed either in the bank's own museum in Barcelona or in the City Hall.

In Munich the pictures will be exhibited in the well-known Kunsthalle, from 18 November 1993 to 16 January 1994. After this, the entire exhibition will be transported to Lillehammer.

NASJONALGALLERIET/Jacque Lathion

MUSEET FOR SAMTIDSKUNST/Jaques Lathion

SCAN-FOTO/Hugo Bergsaker

A unique collection of Norwegian art has been put together by a committee under the auspices of H.M. Queen Sonja. Before the Games begin, the works will be exhibited in several of the world's largest cities, before they are returned to Lillehammer.

Two of the selected winter pictures. Above: Thorvald Erichsen's painting, «Winter» from 1908. It is exhibited at the National Gallery, Nasjonalgalleriet. Next to it, Gunnar S. Gunnersen's «Winter Sun» from 1966. The picture is owned by the Museum of Contemporary Art, Museum for Samtidskunst. H.M. Queen Sonja has a keen interest in the arts, and has put great effort into the selection of the pictures for the «Winter Land» exhibition.

An important part of the cultural scene

Historical large farms in the Olympic communities

Some of the richest agricultural communities in Norway are located near the Olympic venues, in particular those around lake Mjøsa. The area is home to many large farms dating back to the Viking Age; some are even built on land inhabited as far back as the Iron Age, 400–500 A.D. The entire area is rich in cultural treasures.

While the present owners run their farms in exemplary manner, they are also careful to preserve and uphold traditions. Farms are passed down from generation to generation, placing serious obligations on each new owner. As one farmer put it: «We know that we are only caretakers of our land.»

Given their historical significance and traditions, it is only natural that the large farms of the region have been drawn into the cultural programme of the 1994 Winter Olympics. Altogether nine farms will provide accommodations for special VIP guests during the Games. Still other guest farms will open their doors to allow visitors to the Olympic Games a chance to see what life is like today on a large farm. Not only will the hosts be able to offer delicious, traditional foods, but they will also be able to talk engagingly about life on the farm years ago, about art and culture associated with Norwegian farm communities, and about present day agricultural policy. Several of the farms have their own museums containing farm implements, kitchen utensils, and work and festive clothing dating back hundreds of years. Some places have forges in working order, and several farms have preserved the old type country kitchens with their bakery ovens and open fireplaces for cooking.

Most of the large farms had tenant farms located on their outskirts. Some of these are still intact, while most were taken over years ago by former tenant farmers, who, when they bought their properties, purchased enough land from the main farm to create a small farm. Today, many of these small holdings are well-run operations that provide a good income for their owners. Life was difficult on tenant farms where there were often six, eight, or 10 children to feed, but generally speaking most tenant families were able to keep hunger at bay, even in hard times. The tenant farmer, and members of his family worked on the main farm. Some were required to work for the farmer at all times and were in reality a sort of serf. Most had the opportunity to grow crops for their own use and many broke new land so that they could have livestock, usually a cow or two, some sheep and chickens. In the mid 1800s there were more than 65,000 tenant farms in Norway. With the start of industrialisation and massive emigration the number of tenant farmers sank dramatically. By 1929 there were only 6,000 tenant farms left, and these disappeared quickly after the Land Act of 1928, which allowed tenant farmers to buy their properties, was put into effect.

One of the guest farms, Segalstad in Gausdal, is mentioned in historical sources dating back to the 1200s. The farm has been in the same family for five generations, and the present owners, Dagny and Hans O. Seielstad, talk vivedly about everything that previously took place on the estate, which at one time boasted a store, dairy, sawmill and grain mill, potash factory and clay pipe production plant. Periodically the farm had a school and doctor's office. Flax and hemp were raised and beer and wine were produced. At one time the farm also had a stage coach station, but this was later moved to Aulestad, the home of the great Norwegian poet Bjørnstjerne Bjørnson which is located not far away. The grandfather of the present owner was a pioneer in many respects, and many of the enterprises that he started in the community are still in operation today. He set up his own electrical power plant on the farm in 1909, just after Bjørnson had one installed on Aulestad.

As many as 30 workers once sat down to the dinner table at Segalstad, and in addition the farm had nine tenant farms providing a ready source of labour. The fact that many hands were needed to keep the farm running becomes evident when one tours the farm museum located in an old stabbur, or storehouse. From the primitive farm tools of bygone days, it's easy to visualise the gruelling labour and drudgery accompanying each season on the farm. It wasn't so easy in the kitchen, either. Dagny will show how bread was baked in the old bake-ovens. On the first floor of the large storehouse the guests will be invited to pull up to solidly built tables and eat home-baked bread with brown goat cheese and black currant jam, all made with products grown on the farm. Today, the farm is still a diversified operation producing milk, meat and grain, with forestry representing another source of income. Hans Seielstad has calculated that the farm produces enough food to feed 1,730 persons for one year.

The farm is located above Segalstad bridge, scene of a fierce battle in 1940 between Norwegian and German forces. The farm lay in the line of fire, but for some inexplicable reason the house dating back to 1747 and the barn and stables built in 1750 escaped major damages.

The heir to the farm is 19-year-old Ingeborg who has studied travel and tourism at an area college. Ingeborg believes farm tourism will expand, based on her opinion that urban people have a steadily increasing need to experience both nature and farm life, be close to animals, and breathe the scent of luxuriant grass meadows and blooming gardens. She assures that she will take good care of her considerable inheritance, even though she is very much aware of how much work it is to run a farm and keep the farm house of several hundred square metres in good condition.

In the heart of the Mjøsa district's rolling farmland near Hamar, 50 kilometres from Lillehammer, lies tradition- rich Stor-Deglum farm, built on a hill overlooking the Furnesbydene. The farm's history dates back to the Iron Age. Finds from several large burial mounds bear witness of past generations' lives and times on Stor-Deglum before Christianity came to Norway. Deglum Church was built around 1300 and served as a parish church until 1708. As a meeting place and host farm for the church, Stor-Deglum was a parish centre in the Middle Ages. The ancient Royal Road traversed the farm which is referred to in chronicles many hundreds of years old. The farm was originally a church estate run by the powerful bishop of Hamar but since the 1700s has been a family farm.

The present owners and hosts, Åse-Marit and Jørgen Dobloug, operate a model farm specialising in fur and egg production, supplemented by grain-growing and forestry. The owners are fully aware of the obligations of running a such a long-established farm, and all necessary changes and additions have been carried out with pietistic regard for their surroun dings. The Doblougs have found it natural to open their estate, which also functions as a guest farm, to VIP guests who will be housed there during the Olympics. They will have a memorable stay in the old and beautiful main building, surrounded by an elegant mixture of solidly-built farm furniture and old, carefully refurbished drawing room furniture in large sitting-rooms with wide floor boards and high ceilings.

The storehouse from the 1700s houses a farm museum containing the farm's oldest tools and kitchen utensils, while the old barn houses the farm's earliest implements such as reapers, binders, and tractors. «Mimbre-bu» museum located in another building has an exhibit of clothes and kitchen utensils dating from the last 10 years of the 1800s and the early years of the 1900s. The old farm forge is also in working order, and Mimrebu has an country store offering several farm specialties, including caramels and distinctive home arts and crafts.

Simenstad, which has also opened its doors to tourists, is located at Rudshøgda, a half hour drive from either Lillehammer, Hamar or Gjøvik. The farm, named in writings as far back as 1327, has been in the present owner's family since 1771. The hosts, Brit Skurdal Braastad and Gisle Braastad serve their guest traditional, home-made food, made from the farm's own products. They have many interests and can tell their guests about the farming societies of years ago, old folklore and fairy tales, and not least, the tradition-rich Christmas celebrations on large farms in the olden days.

The 1994 Olympics will show the breadth of Norwegian culture, and by visiting these farms, Olympic visitors will come face to face with a valuable part of the Norwegian cultural mosaic.

The Ringnes farm is in Ottestad, not far from Hamar. The hostess and host are Gerd Wikan and Erik Ringnes.

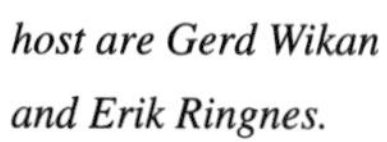

Stor-Gaalaas in Furnes is run by Marit and Thor Bøhmer and the farm has been in the family since around 1600.

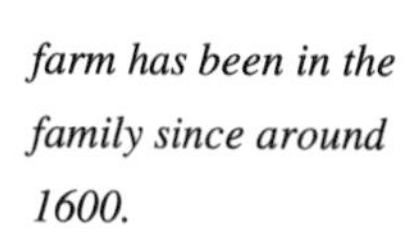

The Sperre farm is in Ringebu, not far from Kvitfjell where the alpine disciplines will be held. The hosts are Rut and Einar Høystad.

Mæhlum Nordre is situated in Brøttum, not far from Lillehammer. The farm was established in around 1575 and the owners, Ingeborg and Gunnar Mæhlum are the 15th generation running the farm. Right: The spacious farm kitchen could seat 20 to 30 around the table.

Far left: Huseby farm in Stange. Hosts are Bibbi and Jens Huseby.
Left: Simenstad in Rudshøgda is equidistant to the three Olympic towns, Lillehammer, Hamar, and Gjøvik. Hosts are Brit Skurdal Braastad and Gisle Braastad.

Nord-Håve is situated in Fåberg, only five km oustide Lillehammer. Kari and Johannes Haave run the farm.

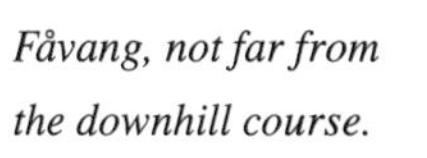

Framigard Romsås, owned by Else and Lars Romsås, is located in Fåvang, not far from the downhill course.

Alle bilder LANDBRUKETS OL-UTVALG/Jarle Kjetil Rolseth

Lundgaard Fåberg also has long-established traditions. The farm is situated 8 km from the centre of Lillehammer. Hosts are Marie and Iver Lundgaard.

In mediaeval times, Skredshol was a mountain pasture belonging to the landed noble gentry. Up until the Reformation, there was a church on the premises. The oldest parts of the main building date back to 1680. The hosts, Gislaug and Jan Moslet, work to keep the traditions of the farm alive. The farm has been independently owned and run since 1720.

Glestad farm in Brumundal has been in the same family since the 1400s. Marie and Eivind Glestad are the present owners.

Sygard Grytting in Harpefoss, 70 km north of Lillehammer. Hosts are Hilde Nustad Grytting and Stig Skurdal Grytting.

The Vesle Ulland farm, in Saksumdal, 20 km from Lillehammer. The family farm is run by Eldbjørg Brekke and Tore Svelle.

SCAN-FOTO/Jan Greve

Hosts Åse Marit and Jørgen Dobloug are conscious of their responsibility; the farm is to be kept in first class order, as their ancestors did before them.

LANDBRUKETS OL-UTVALG/Rolseth

LANDBRUKETS OL-UTVALG/Rolseth

Stor Deglum is beautifully situated close to the Furnes church. The main buildings, pure in style, are conscientiously maintained, and the large rooms are filled with old and beautiful furniture, as below, in the dining room.

SCAN-FOTO/Jan Greve

Historical festive clothing are featured in the museum.

LANDBRUKETS OL-UTVALG/Rolseth

A mediaeval church stood on the site where the farm is situated, and some of the materials from the old church were supposedly used in the construction of, amongst other things, the door of the store-house which houses the farm museum.

SCAN-FOTO/Jan Greve

SCAN-FOTO/Jan Greve

SCAN-FOTO/Jan Greve

Old items have been preserved on the farm. Picture: One of the oldest beer jugs, possibly used in the beginning of the last century when the farm was used as countryside inn. The museum also houses old and fine clothing.

LANDBRUKETS OL-UTVALG/Rolseth

The farm has its own museum where farm tools and common household furniture are exhibited. The museum is housed in the old storehouse.

The storehouse museum has a hospitality room where visitors can sample the farm's products.

Jarle Wæhler/Rune Nilsson

Jarle Wæhler/Rune Nilsson

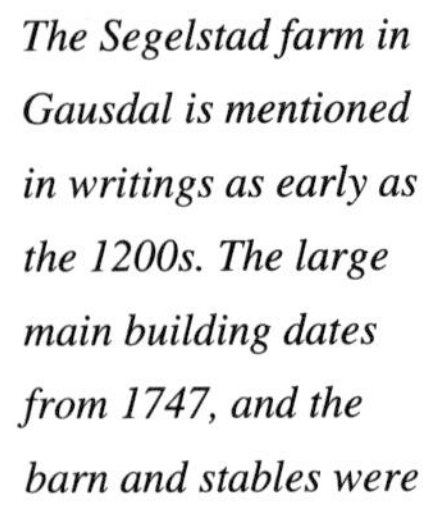

The Segelstad farm in Gausdal is mentioned in writings as early as the 1200s. The large main building dates from 1747, and the barn and stables were erected a few years later. The old storehouse has been turned into a museum and the entrance (over) dates back several centuries.

Jarle Wæhler/Rune Nilsson

Jarle Wæhler/Rune Nilsson

Jarle Wæhler/Rune Nilsson

LANDBRUKETS OL-UTVALG/Jarle Kjetil Rolseth

Dagny and Hans O. Seielstad are 5th generation owners of the farm.

LANDBRUKETS OL-UTVALG/Rolseth

The mistress of the house keeps the kitchen in spotless condition. In the old days, up to 30 people could gather round the table.

LANDBRUKETS OL-UTVALG/Rolseth

LANDBRUKETS OL-UTVALG/Rolseth

Hans O. Seielstad has to maintain 22 buildings in all, including the pasture resort sheds. There used to be nine tenant cottages on the farm.

Gerhard Heiberg

SCAN-FOTO/Jan Greve

Bjørg Jønsson (b. 1940), M.A. in literature, is director of the publishing house, J. M. Stenersens Forlag. An experienced journalist, she started her career as a literary critic for amongst others, the daily VG, and built herself a name writing for the weekly magazine, Farmand, using the pseudonym Femina. She has also worked as commentator and reporter for Aftenposten. She is the author of several books of fiction.

Interviewed by Bjørg Jønsson

The taste and ingenuity with which Gerhard Heiberg has decorated his office at Aker Brygge in Oslo is astounding. It is the beautiful setting for the unfolding of a play. The light from the fjord outside the office building enhances his role. It is a glittering stage set, and adds strength and meaning to the perception that he in fact is *the* mastermind behind the Olympic Winter Games in Lillehammer. Deadline: 12th February 1994.

SCAN-FOTO/Tor Richardsen

Gerhard Heiberg goes about his job with an air of professionalism. So much so, that even in the early stages of the process toward Lillehammer, the prospects looked bright. Most of us are incurred to hold a certain degree of admiration for such a talent – when success is sensed even the persistent sceptics tend to stay attentively quiet in the background.

The world of Gerhard Heiberg, however, is not all politicking to the setting of suave offices. His job involves mastering all aspects of the Olympic arrangement. It demands a strict master plan. The rarity of such professionalism in Norway makes one want to explore the philosophical foundations of his task.

SCAN-FOTO/Knut Falch

– We have been given a unique opportunity to develop our sense of solidarity with the rest of the world.

This exploration will be at the centre of this interview.

Mr Heiberg has a boyish appeal, his background to be found in an established lawyer's home in Oslo, and, through the media, he emerges as a superman. So, he is a public and successful winner, but what does the mask of prophetic symbolism unveil?

At the age of 21 he went to Copenhagen, taking on business studies. That completed, he spent a couple of years in the USA. After that he went to Paris, and then to Vienna, where he stayed on for six years.

At his return to Norway in 1972 he became the executive director of Norcem and Aker and, in 1989, the chairman of the board of that company. At which time he had reached the age of 49. The diversity of his background has made Gerhard Heiberg an ***internationalist,*** *his soul belonging to Europe, his roots to be found in Norway. People pay lip service to the notion of internationalisation, but few seem to grasp its true meaning. To Heiberg the notion is rooted in* ***communication,*** *across the boundaries of nations, cultures and social backgrounds. The Olympic Winter Games represent a thorough lesson in cross-cultural communication.*

– What ideal attributes would you regard as essential to co-existence with the outside world, Mr Heiberg?

– *Openness and humility.* Those are preconditions. It's about absorbing and understanding other realities. Consider the times we're in, the opening of the 21th century; it is not a time of vanishing boundaries, but the opening of global frontiers. Think of the challenge this constitutes, if we are prepared to act on it. It has not to do with EFTA or the EC, a Yes or a No. World society is already in the midst of something new, and we should be able to play an important part in that. Think of the upcoming generation. – We have to help them understand the issues at stake. It is truly fantastic to be a part of what is currently happening, not least in Europe. Boundaries disappear, ideologies are being rejected, society is faced with a new set of demands. Just think of how extraordinary a challenge it is to be a part of the shaping of tomorrow's everyday life.

SCAN-FOTO/Dag Bæverfjord

– My task may prove to be impossible, but I still have faith in it.

– Yes, certainly, but aren't you really saying that a new spirit must be cast, that a change of mentality is at the dawn, so to say. And doesn't this amount to pumping new life into an old body, in the name of faith?

– The task may prove to be impossible, but I still have faith in it. The main issue would have to be – quality of life, I suppose; the pleasure of giving, the joy of experiencing. The prepareness to interact demands at least a degree of openness. But what you are suggesting about our mentality is right, only a minority believed Norway would actually come to host the Olympic Games, we've got a highly developed social conscience in this country and after all, we had hospitals, old peoples' homes and schools to take care of. And all four million Norwegians had an opinion on Olympic Games '94 and wanted a say in the decision-making process. It was all black or white, nothing in between, and all that came out of it, was chaos. And envy and pettiness flourished.

– Isn't this in fact a description of the very opposite of the ideal attitudes when communicating with the outside world?

– It may seem that way, yes. Please allow me a quotation at this stage: «Norwegians perceive themselves as being able to succeed in all things, so long as there are enough obstacles put in their way.» We are not easily open to enthusiasm, and scepticism is more readily arosed. It is easier to express second thoughts than joyful expectations. But as Gudmund Hernes said during an address in Lillehammer in 1989: «We have been given a mandate the ramifications of which cannot be recalled, an arrangement the dimensions of which cannot be denied. This is not a question of whether we actually can do it, but of what we are able to do with it. In other words, the entire nation must take part in the effort. We are facing a world exposition on Norwegian soil, and mostly with Norwegian presentators. It is coming at a time of great pessimism, and unemployment is worse than at time since World War Two. Seen in those perspectives, the challenge of arranging the Olympic Games comes at an ideal point in time. There exists no better, nor any cheaper opportunity to set in motion huge sections of Norwegian society, and it is entirely up to us to make something out of this unique opportunity, at Lillehammer.

– In other words you are saying that the Olympic Games to be held in Lillehammer in 1994, represent a means of implementing social policies, rather than being a goal in its own right.

– That is one way of putting it. Our goal is not to produce merely a glittering prospectus of 16 days in February 1994, but, at a time of great hardship, to define ourselves as a nation. On the one hand we are going to produce the greatest olympic arrangement ever, but on the other hand, what is built and done in Lillehammer must also be felt ten-fifteen years on. What is seen in the Lillehammer area is quite spectacular, it is a question not only of rehabilitation, but about an improvement in standards, resulting from the investment in hospitals, roadworks, railways, education etc. Thus this part of Norway faces new and rare opportunities. It is important that the people of the Lillehammer region realise this, and recognise the responsibilities it entails, and prepare to get on with their lives *after* 27th February 1994. When the Games are over, we mustn't content ourselves with looking back at the Olympic arrangement with pride and joy, but retain and further develop the

SCAN-FOTO/Knut Falch

LOOC President Gerhard Heiberg with IOC President Juan Antonio Samaranch.

new levels and standards of performance. And in addition to this we will have to have become better at cooperating and coexisting among ourselves.

– And change our mentality, in other words, as we mentioned earlier. And you are saying that this, the population of Lillehammer must grasp the meaning. You are changing the appearance of an entire region, all of it, which no-one asked for. The local population is getting a facelift whether they like it or not. Thus you are running the risk of altering the facial expression of an entire population. If this is of no concern to politicians, it might at least draw the attention of psychologists, sociologists and anthropologists.

– Yes, and this constitutes a tremendously interesting set of problems. But I have to remind you that ours is a time of great unemployment. Hopefully we'll be able to create employment in various sectors of the industry, in connection with the Olympic arrangement. Such as the textile, confectionary, furniture, and wooden industries. Moelven, for instance, is situated in the area, and the Norwegian engineering we're witnessing in connection with the mountain hall at Gjøvik is nothing short of fantastic, as is the use of concrete in the construction of the bobsleigh-tracks. In these areas huge sections of the Norwegian business community have the opportunity to forge new alliances for the period following the Olympic Games in '94.

– But surely there must be a purposive element to communication, beyond that of the entrepreneurial logic. Trade alone doesn't make you an internationalist. It seems to me that our conversation is about to lose sight of the Olympic spirit and the homo ludens.

– The spirit encroached in the Olympic idea is that of pushing a performance to the limits of the possible, to bring forward the outmost of our creative powers. One should not forget that the reason behind our application to host the games was a wish to offer a chance for development to a part of Norway that was hit by recession. The aim of our effort is therefore to bring forward the best we can offer in various fields, without losing sight of costs. We are going to produce an olympic arrangement which is economically viable – but also one that puts to the forefrunt the best of Norwegian quality.

SCAN-FOTO/Tor Richardsen

The Olympic Games should unite people, particularly as ideologies are disappearing and old mentalities are facing a new world.

– What amounts of money are we taking about?

– The Olympic budget was as of 1991 NOK 7 billion. One must add to that 2 billion in direct public investment in infrastructure. But do note that this is not all a question of spending; we also have independent sources of income!

– You are a part of what one may call an «entrepreneurial culture». It is evident why the business community is involved and what their goals are. But you are also acting on behalf of an arrangement of innumerable vested interests. When you became the president of the LOOC, you were appointed director of a multitude of actors, with various backgrounds and establishments. Who are these people, and what values do they represent?

– As you say, they are drawn from different backgrounds and interest groups. But the values they represent are the traditional values of our society, those of equality, participation and common decision-making. Besides, the level of education in this country is generally high, and constitute what the Minister of Education calls «the quality of equality». We all agree that these are the values that we shall build on, and create the opportunity at an important point in time, to bring Norway back on the world map, to expose Norwegian industry and business, as we will with the arts and our culture in general. We are trying to make Norwegians open up a little, and give a little of themselves to others. This is a badly needed opportunity to set in motion the process of internationalisation that we need, no matter what formal forms our relations with the outside world may take. I see it as a great demonstration of honour to have been chosen to lead this work. But the period leading up to my decision to acccept the job was agonising.

– What constituted your agonising dilemmas?

– The budgetary sides to things forced me to examine my own moral positure. The question that came up was, can I defend the use of these means, or were they right, the critics who claimed the money would be better spent on schools, hospitals and old peoples' homes. I had to justify to myself that the task we had taken upon ourselves would result in more than just hard money: A greater belief in ourselves in this country, the belief that we can actually succeed at something when we are set on it, and, within the realms of Norwegian sports, art, architecture, the environment, and in society as a whole, joy and pride with what we can produce with common efforts. You were enquiring about the ideal requirements for the process of communication with the outside world. Whether we like it or not, we are a part of that outside world, and we are dependent upon it for the life we are accustomed to. We cannot manage alone. We are very good at expressing concern with problems outside Norway, be it racism or poverty. In doing so, we should at least do better than bringing forward our prejudices whenever a few immigrants arrive in this country. Look at the world of today: Ideologies are disappearing, we're in search of a map to fit our mental terrain. We don't know what to expect of the future, but we need something we can gather around, both in the world and in Norway. The Olympic Games is a thing to gather around. It is about peaceful competition, people coming together with the best of intentions. We've got a unique chance of doing something good, and not just for Norwegians. I am fully convinced of the importance of the 1994 arrangement of the Olympic Games, I believe in and try to uphold the ideals we have talked about. There are enough of those who want to belittle the arrangement, the narrow-minded, who say: 'We could have said «no»'. I don't believe we could. Inside all Norwegians, there's a feeling that states: In that case the Swedes would have gotten the arrangement! And *that* would have been an intolerable defeat for most Norwegians.

SCAN-FOTO/Tor Richardsen

The colourful 17th of May children's parade in Oslo is proudly presented by LOOC President Gerhard Heiberg to IOC Vice-president Marc Hodler, president of the international skiing committee.

The pictures in this book are provided by the very best suppliers of illustrations and photographers in Norway. In addition, illustrations reflecting the history of Norway from the earliest times, have been collected from the Norsk Folkemuseum, Universitetsbiblioteket, and other museums and collections.

Other sources which must be mentioned include «Norge i 1905», published by Aschehoug Forlag, «Norske Portretter», «Hanna Winsnes – mer enn en matmor», both published by Gyldendal Forlag, «SNORRI – The Sagas of the Viking Kings of Norway», and the libraries at the Nasjonalgalleriet (the National Gallery) and Museet for Samtidskunst (the Museum of Contemporary Art).

All illustrations in this book carry the name of the photographer/ agency in the top right corner – as far as this has been possible with the information available.

Of the major suppliers, particular acknowledgment should be paid to HUSMO-FOTO and photographers Arnulf Husmo and Kristian Hilsen; KNUDSENS FOTOSENTER, in particular Arne Knudsen; SAMFOTO's various photographers, Ola Røe in Tromsø, Jarle Kjetil Rolseth, and Jarle Wæhler in Lillehammer, in addition to Bengt Wilson and his foodpictures; The Schibsted Group's photographic agency, SCAN-FOTO, representing the photographers of the daily newspapers VG and Aftenposten, several licensees, and photographers. SCAN-FOTO has also produced original illustrations for this book, through photographs taken in some museums, and of the entire stamp collection shown in the chapter by Schreuder.

The editors have received valuable help from the junior editor Asgeir Sektnan, of SCAN-FOTO. The lay-out has been carried out by Enzo Finger design, by Enzo himself and his colleague Johanna Figur a.o.